Selling the American Way

Selling the American Way

U.S. Propaganda and the Cold War

Laura A. Belmonte

PENN

UNIVERSITY OF PENNSYLVANIA PRESS

PHILADELPHIA

Published by
University of Pennsylvania Press
Philadelphia, Pennsylvania 19104-4112

Printed in the United States of America on acid-free paper
10   9   8   7   6   5   4   3   2   1

Library of Congress Cataloging-in-Publication Data
ISBN-13: 978-0-8122-4082-5
ISBN-10: 0-8122-4082-0

For my family

CONTENTS

ABBREVIATIONS

ADA   Americans for Democratic Action
AFL   American Federation of Labor
AIF   Americans for Intellectual Freedom
ALA   American Library Association
AP   Associated Press
ASNE   American Society of Newspaper Editors
BBC   British Broadcasting Company
CBS   Columbia Broadcasting System
CCF   Congress for Cultural Freedom
CIA   Central Intelligence Agency
CIO   Congress of Industrial Organizations
CPI   Committee on Public Information
DDEL   Dwight D. Eisenhower Presidential Library
ECA   Economic Cooperation Administration
EDC   European Defense Community
ERP   European Recovery Plan/European Recovery Program
FBI   Federal Bureau of Investigation
FRUS   *Foreign Relations of the United States*
GDR   German Democratic Republic
GUFAC   Georgetown University Foreign Affairs Oral History Collection
HSTL   Harry S. Truman Presidential Library
HUAC   House Committee on Un-American Activities
IBS   International Broadcasting Service
IIA   International Information Administration
IIIS   Interim International Information Service
IMP   International Motion Picture Division
IOP   Information Office of Policy
JCS   Joint Chiefs of Staff

NA2	National Archives II
NAACP	National Association for the Advancement of Colored People
NBC	National Broadcasting Corporation
NCFE	National Committee for a Free Europe
NSC	National Security Council
OCB	Operating Coordinating Board
OEX	Office of Educational Exchange
OIAA	Office of Inter-American Affairs
OIC	Office of Information and Cultural Affairs
OIE	Office of Information and Educational Exchange
OII	Office of International Information
OPC	Office of Policy Coordination
OSS	Office of Strategic Services
OWI	Office of War Information
PCA	Progressive Citizens Alliance
PSB	Psychological Strategy Board
RCA	Radio Corporation of America
RFE	Radio Free Europe
RG	Record Group
RIAS	Radio in the American Sector
RL	Radio Liberation/Liberty
UNESCO	United Nations Educational, Scientific, and Cultural Organization
UP	United Press
USIA	United States Information Agency
USIAA	United States Information Agency Archives
USIE	United States Information and Educational Exchange Program
USIS	United States Information Service
VOA	Voice of America
WNRC	Washington National Records Center

CHRONOLOGY

August 1945	President Harry S Truman abolishes Office of War Information (OWI), appoints William B. Benton assistant secretary of state for public affairs
December 1945	Office of International Information and Cultural Affairs (OIC) formed (referred to as United States Information Service, USIS, abroad)
February 1946	George F. Kennan's "Long Telegram"
March 1946	Winston Churchill's "Iron Curtain" speech
November 1946	Republicans win control of both houses of Congress
January 1947	George Marshall succeeds James Byrnes as secretary of state
February 1947	Voice of America (VOA) begins Russian language broadcasts
March 1947	Truman Doctrine speech
June 1947	Secretary of State George Marshall proposes European Recovery Plan
Summer 1947	OIC reorganized and renamed Office of Information and Educational Exchange (OIE)
October 1947	Soviets announce creation of Cominform
January 1948	Smith-Mundt Act signed into law
February 1948	George V. Allen succeeds William B. Benton as assistant secretary of state for public affairs
February 1948	Communist coup in Czechoslovakia
April 1948	State Department abolishes OIE and creates Office of International Information (OII) and Office of Educational Exchange (OEX)
May 1948	Soviets launch "Peace Offensive"
November 1948	Truman reelected

January 1949	Dean Acheson succeeds George Marshall as secretary of state
April 1949	Soviets begin jamming VOA Russia
April 1949	North Atlantic Treaty signed
October 1949	Mao Zedong proclaims People's Republic of China
January 1950	Edward W. Barrett succeeds George V. Allen as assistant secretary of state for public affairs
February 1950	Senator Joseph R. McCarthy alleges communist infiltration of State Department
April 1950	NSC-68 advocates expansion of U.S. information activities worldwide; U.S. begins "Campaign of Truth"
April 1950	Communist Chinese government outlaws listening to VOA; Czech authorities demand closure of USIS facilities
June 1950	Korean War begins
November 1950	Communist Chinese enter Korean War
April 1951	Truman establishes Psychological Strategy Board (PSB)
January 1952	State Department reorganizes information operations again; creates United States International Information Administration (IIA); Dr. Wilson Compton named IIA director
July 1952	State Department suspends publication of *Amerika*
November 1952	Dwight D. Eisenhower elected president
December 1952	Eisenhower appoints C. D. Jackson special assistant for psychological warfare
February 1953	Senator Joseph McCarthy begins official investigations of VOA; Secretary of State John Foster Dulles fires chief VOA engineer George Herrick and accepts Compton's resignation
February 1953	Dulles issues Information Guide 272 banning IIA use of "materials by any Communists, fellow-travelers, et cetera"
February 1953	Eisenhower and Dulles separate IIA from State Department, appoint Dr. Robert L. Johnson director
March 1953	Dulles rescinds Information Guide 272
March 1953	Joseph Stalin dies; Vyacheslav Molotov, Lavrentii Beria, and Georgii Malenkov form coalition

March 1953	McCarthy aides Roy Cohn and David Schine investigate USIS libraries and information centers in Europe
June 1953	United States Information Agency (USIA) created; Theodore C. Streibert appointed director
June 1953	Riots in East Germany crushed by communist authorities
July 1953	Korean War ends
Summer 1953	Eisenhower abolishes PSB, establishes Operations Coordinating Board (OCB)
August 1953	Soviets test hydrogen bomb
December 1953	Eisenhower gives "Atoms for Peace" address at United Nations
August 1954	Congress grants Eisenhower $5 million discretionary fund for expanding U.S. participation in trade fairs and supporting U.S. cultural and artistic endeavors abroad
December 1954	Senate censures McCarthy
May 1955	West Germany joins NATO; Soviets announce Warsaw Pact
July 1955	British, American, French, and Soviet leaders meet in Geneva
February 1956	Nikita Khrushchev denounces Stalinism in "secret speech" before 20th Communist Party Congress in Moscow
February 1956	USIA debuts "People's Capitalism" exhibit
October 1956	USIA resumes distribution of *Amerika* in USSR
October 1956	Protests in Poland and Hungary
November 1956	Hungarian Revolution brutally suppressed; Suez Canal Crisis
January 1957	Arthur Larson succeeds Theodore Streibert as director of USIA
February 1957	VOA begins English language broadcasts to Africa
March 1957	Congress authorizes expanded financial and military aid to fight communism in Middle East
September 1957	Eisenhower sends troops to Little Rock, Arkansas, to ensure integration of Central High School
October 1957	Soviets launch *Sputnik*
October 1957	Eisenhower appoints George V. Allen to replace Arthur Larsen

January 1958	U.S.-Soviet Cultural Exchange Agreement signed
May 1958	Anti-American protests in Middle East and Latin America
July 1958	14,000 Marines deployed to Lebanon
Summer 1959	American National Exhibition in Moscow
September 1959	Nikita Khrushchev visits United States

Introduction

The vast majority of Americans are confident that the system of values which animates our society—the principles of freedom, tolerance, the importance of the individual, and the supremacy of reason over will— are valid and more vital than the ideology which is the fuel of Soviet dynamism. Translated into terms relevant to the lives of other peoples— our system of values can become perhaps a powerful appeal to millions who now seek or find in authoritarianism a refuge from anxieties, bafflement, and insecurity.
    —NSC-68: United States Objectives and Programs
        for National Security, April 14, 1950

The great struggles of the twentieth century between liberty and totalitarianism ended with a decisive victory for the forces of freedom— and a single sustainable model for national success: freedom, democracy, and free enterprise. . . . These values of freedom are right and true for every person, in every society—and the duty of protecting these values against their enemies is the common calling of freedom-loving people across the globe and across the ages.
    —National Security Strategy of the United States of America,
        September 2002

IN THE IMMEDIATE aftermath of the 9/11 attacks, millions joined vigils held worldwide in response to what Pope John Paul II called the "unspeakable horror." *Le Monde* proclaimed, "We are all Americans." During a changing of the guard at Buckingham Palace, a band played "The Star-Spangled Banner." In Tehran, a million people marched in sympathy for the 2,800 victims. This singular display of harmony bequeathed the United States a priceless opportunity to transform its foreign policy and end years of vacillation following the collapse of the Soviet Union. The Bush administration seized the moment and implemented a sweeping strategy combining global military hegemony, preemptive war, unilateralism, and efforts to spread democracy.[1] In explaining this fusion of neoconservatism and liberal internationalism, President George W. Bush denied having imperial aspirations.[2] "America," he told the 2002 class of West Point, "has no empire to extend or utopia to establish. We wish for others only what we wish for ourselves—safety from violence, the rewards of liberty, and the hope for a better life."[3]

In framing the "war on terror," Bush and others invoke an "America" that is, paradoxically, exceptional *and* universal. They cite America's "victory" in the Cold War as proof that democracy and free markets will ensure justice, prosperity, and stability in the post-9/11 era.[4] On August 19, 2004, seventeen months after U.S. and British troops commenced a preemptive war in Iraq, National Security Advisor Condoleezza Rice argued, "The victory of freedom in the Cold War was won only when the West remembered that values and security cannot be separated. The values of freedom and democracy—as much, if not more, than economic power and military might—won the Cold War. And those same values will lead us to victory in the war on terror."[5]

Such claims raise questions about how the United States explains its values and notions of freedom to the world. How and why does the U.S. government sell "America" to foreign audiences? What role do symbolic representations of the "American way of life" play in the defense of U.S. political, strategic, and economic interests abroad? What do these official narratives suggest about American political culture, public diplomacy, and foreign policy?[6] In tracing the Cold War origins of U.S. information programs, this book examines these issues.

The 9/11 attacks and their reverberations have undoubtedly highlighted continuities and discontinuities between American projections of national identity and international perceptions of the United States and its citizens. These problems are not new—nor are the federal government's efforts to address anti-Americanism overseas. Foreign citizens have long expressed resentment of U.S. policies coupled with admiration of American democracy, technology, and culture. Since their inception during World War I, public diplomacy programs have been reorganized several times—and have always received a mere fraction of the funds devoted to defense spending. Where their political forefathers mistrusted propaganda and Wilsonianism, today's neoconservatives extol public diplomacy and "exporting democracy." But while the structure and advocates of America's propaganda efforts are fluid, a shared belief in the universality of American freedom, democracy, and free enterprise links U.S. information experts from the era of Harry S. Truman to that of George W. Bush. As the United States attempts to sell itself to a post-9/11 world, the initial U.S. response to the Cold War is highly instructive.

In 1955, the United States Information Agency (USIA) printed 12,400 copies of a lavishly illustrated booklet called *My America*. Written by Arthur Goodfriend, a former State Department official, the pamphlet featured forty-one celebrated Americans struggling to define their nation and its people. Brought together for "The American Round Table," sponsored by the Advertising Council, participants spent a week exploring several topics including "the basic elements of a free dynamic society," "the moral and religious basis of the American society," and "our concepts of political and civil liberties."[7] The roster of conference participants was impressive. Frederick Lewis Allen, W. H. Auden, Henry Steele Commager, Allen Nevins, Paul Hoffman, and Peter Drucker were among the luminaries from American culture, business, journalism, theology, and academia.

Goodfriend interwove quotes from the Round Table sessions with autobiographical information. Recalling the neighborhood where he lived as a boy, he wrote, "I played with Nick, whose parents came from Italy. Hans, whose father was German. Phil, whose folks had fled a Russian pogrom. Jimmy Kee, the Chinese laundryman's boy. Bob, whose great-grandfather had come from Africa, a slave."[8] After attending City College, Goodfriend and his childhood friends attained professional success, raised happy families, and enjoyed spiritual fulfillment.

Cultural diversity, political freedom, and social mobility were the most common themes in *My America*. In this "classless society," mass production and good wages enabled most people to purchase "so-called luxury goods." Voters voiced their opinions without fear of reprisal. Audiences flocked not only to baseball games and Hollywood movies but also to operas and art exhibits. Communities helped the less fortunate and worked for the common good. Because Americans valued individualism and equality, any child could realize his or her potential. *My America* describes a country in which racism, sexism, and poverty are conspicuously absent or easily defeated. The array of beautiful photographs and inspirational quotations does not include McCarthyism, the arms race, or the Cold War.

There are hundreds of pamphlets like *My America* now gathering dust in archives. They are anachronistic, hyperbolic, and even silly. Yet they also provide cogent illustrations of efforts to define American national identity. Hundreds of U.S. propagandists in the State Department and the USIA echoed the views espoused by Goodfriend and the American Round Table participants. They traveled the same corridors of power. They shared the hope that materials like *My America* could persuade foreigners of the virtues of democratic capitalism. While their promotion of classically liberal principles such as individual rights, private property, and free markets is not surprising, their celebration of modern liberal values like guaranteed annual wages, social welfare program, and multiculturalism is quite striking. Whatever their partisan affiliations, they forged a remarkably consistent collective defense of "the American way of life" in the uncertain world of Cold War rivalries.

Facing threats of communism and anti-Americanism, U.S. information officials embarked on America's first peacetime propaganda offensive in 1945.[9] Former members of the postwar information establishment have offered narratives providing little insight into the motives for the U.S. international information program. They rarely address the connections between information programs and foreign policy, the presentation of the American way of life, or the effects of cultural diplomacy.[10] Scholars examining the development of the information division of the State Department and the USIA give useful material on the structure and operations of these organizations without analyzing how cultural diplomats defined the values of America and what they hoped to achieve by disseminating such messages.[11]

Such constructions of national identity inform several fine studies on the intersections of U.S. foreign policy and culture. Drawing heavily on discourse analysis, Christina Klein and Melani McAlister investigate how private and public cultural representations of foreign peoples shaped and echoed international projections of American military, economic, and political power.[12] Richard Kuisel, Reinhold Wagnleitner, Richard Pells, Jessica Gienow-Hecht, and others delve into the ways that American culture has been defined, deployed, contested, and reinterpreted at home and abroad. In evaluating the impact of American products, values, and culture upon a variety of foreign audiences, these critics differ widely in their appraisals of American "cultural imperialism."[13] Through this literature, we are gaining valuable insights about transnational exchanges among tourists, international businesspeople, soldiers, journalists, missionaries, public health workers, intellectuals, performers, and artists.[14]

A closely related body of work focuses on the U.S. government's efforts to export American culture and ideas as part of a broader Cold War foreign policy. Walter Hixson, Scott Lucas, and Gregory Mitrovich have produced excellent studies on the strategic objectives and tactics of U.S. policymakers targeting audiences behind the Iron Curtain. Shifting the geographic prism to "the Free World," Kenneth Osgood's magisterial volume situates the U.S. propaganda offensive within the larger context of the mass communications revolution of the 1950s. Turning toward domestic politics, David Krugler demonstrates how debates over Voice of America broadcasts, the largest component of American overt propaganda operations, reflected conservative and liberal differences on statism, the balance between executive and legislative power, and the proper direction of U.S. foreign policy.[15]

Others have emphasized specific cultural programs in America's ideological offensive against communism. Naima Prevots, Michael Krenn, Damion Thomas, David Caute, Yale Richmond, and Penny Von Eschen illuminate how dance, art, sports, film, literature, and music became critical elements of the cultural Cold War. While U.S. officials primarily viewed these programs as tools with which to diffuse Soviet allegations of American racism, cultural vapidity, and parochialism, performers and athletes often used their status as cultural ambassadors to make trenchant critiques of U.S. political culture. Differing interpretations of the appropriate scope and content of U.S. cultural diplomacy initiatives triggered vociferous disagreements among government bureaucrats, politicians, and program participants. At the core of these debates lay passionate beliefs about freedom, nationhood, and globalism.[16]

In highlighting U.S. propaganda campaigns designed to export democratic capitalism, this study synthesizes and amplifies this scholarship. While scholars have touched on this theme, they have not adequately explored how visions of family and gender, notions of work and worship, and conceptions of freedom and free enterprise infused America's ideological response to communism.[17] In explicating the creation and international dissemination of American political culture, I hope to inject some precision into how "cultural diplomacy" is used in Cold War scholarship. While it is hardly groundbreaking to assert that culture is innately political (rooted in, and reflective of, power), culture harnessed specifically for the purpose of exercising and expanding U.S. military, economic, and political power takes on forms distinct from other cultural transmissions and receptions.

U.S. information officials viewed themselves as frontline warriors defending a way of life they considered sacred if imperfect. In illuminating why culture formed a key element of their efforts to explain Americans and U.S. policies to foreign peoples, USIA leaders asserted:

> American culture is far more than the aggregate of achievements in the humanities. The arts are a tangible expression of the non-utilitarian values which give dimension to a society and so have an important place in this program. Beyond them, however, are the social and spiritual dynamics, the thought, principles, behavior which are characteristic of America. Within the scope of the cultural program comes the whole of America's national life as portrayed by all media, at all levels of sophistication, in all its maturity.[18]

While the symbolic "America" put forward by the propagandists was consciously and excessively self-congratulatory (what variety of propaganda is not?), cynical readers should not dismiss the deeply held beliefs informing their narratives about the United States.

U.S. information experts were also quite good at gauging what aspects of American life and culture resonated most with foreign audiences. They carefully tailored their methods and tactics to appeal to different countries and meticulously described aspects of American political, cultural, social, and economic life. America's ideological offensive was not a ham-handed, one-size-fits-all model, but a sophisticated endeavor utilizing the most advanced communications methodologies of the era.

Nonetheless, these techniques did not make it easy to explain the complicated realities of modern America. To U.S. information officials, life under democratic capitalism meant far more than escaping communist oppression. It signified a world of spiritual, material, social, political, and cultural benefits of which communists could only dream. But exposing the harshness of life under communism was considerably less challenging than producing compelling and consistent international messages about American life. Frequently divided over the question of precisely what "an American" *was*, U.S. policymakers focused instead on what "an American" *was not*. Unified in their belief in the superiority of democratic capitalism, information experts depicted communists as atheistic, militaristic, anti-family, violent, unfree, undemocratic, uncultured, and unquestionably un-American.

Exploring the images of America offered by U.S. propagandists provides a way to assess the state's construction of national identity as a means of defining and protecting national security. Contrary to interpretations found in much foreign policy historiography, U.S. policymakers did not define the national interest exclusively in concrete political, economic, and military terms. Nor were they blind to the ways in which America's pluralistic society could complicate—or facilitate—the pursuit of global power. Instead, American officials fused the material and immaterial into a discourse justifying American predominance in international affairs. Through radio shows, films, and publications, U.S. policymakers propagated a carefully constructed narrative of progress, freedom, and happiness. With mixed results, they presented their vision to the world in hopes of persuading foreign peoples to reject communism and to adopt democratic capitalism. They faced difficult choices in reconciling their symbolic "America" with the complex political, economic, and strategic realities of the early Cold War.

Throughout this text, I refer to "propaganda" and "information." Like U.S. policymakers of the era, I use these terms interchangeably. But while these officials privately acknowledged the manipulative nature of "propaganda," "psychological warfare," "political warfare," and "psychological strategy," they publicly described these activities as "information." "Information," they claimed, connoted an impartial recounting of facts, not precisely calibrated communication that shaped popular attitudes. Readers should approach this distinction with a healthy level of skepticism. While I focus here on certain types of propaganda, I think the concept is best explained as "any organized attempt by an individual, group, or government verbally, visually, or symbolically to persuade a population to adopt its views and repudiate the views of an opposing group."[19]

Given the breadth of this definition and the extent of Cold War propaganda operations, I have adopted specific parameters here. Because it is extremely difficult to verify the extent of covert American information activities, my analysis focuses mainly on materials prepared for international dissemination by the State Department and the USIA and openly identified as American.[20] Because other scholars have already addressed the administrative and tactical development of Cold War propaganda, this is not my primary aim.[21] Conceding the impossibility of isolating the effect of propaganda materials from that of other influences, I explore the nuanced ways international audiences responded to government attempts to shape their opinions of the

United States and its people. I am, however, most interested in the ways propaganda texts represent the U.S. government's efforts to explain American national identity to itself and others. In an age where the actions and images of the United States receive relentless scrutiny and can quickly provoke violence, understanding these initiatives is more vital than ever.

CHAPTER ONE

The Truman Years

As WORLD WAR II ended, U.S. policymakers relished their nation's new predominant status. They expected to build a world order based upon the financial, military, and political superiority of the United States and resolved to protect the "American way of life" from the vicissitudes and dangers of the postwar world.[1] Their challenge was to design a security apparatus that protected the nation without making America a garrison state or destroying the country's unique political culture.[2]

Reconciling these material and ideological goals proved exceedingly difficult. For years, fascist propagandists had claimed that Americans were weak, lazy, immoral, greedy, and uncultured. Despite U.S. attempts to correct such misinformation, many foreigners remained wary of the United States.[3] At home, many U.S. citizens associated propaganda with lies, manipulation, and violations of their civil liberties.[4] As American-Soviet relations deteriorated, U.S. information officials began describing their program as a defense against communism and thereby gained the fiscal and political support of congressional conservatives. But as the Cold War escalated, information experts, politicians, and private citizens fought bitterly over which values, symbols, and people best exemplified "America." Before assessing more fully the visions of the nation present in U.S. propaganda, we must first examine how U.S. officials shaped America's international image, and why propaganda became an important if highly controversial element of U.S. foreign policy during the Truman and Eisenhower eras.

The Postwar Information Program Begins

On August 31, 1945, President Harry S. Truman designated "information activities abroad as an integral part of the conduct of our foreign affairs." He
abolished the Office of War Information (OWI) and placed all information
activities of the Office of Strategic Services (OSS) and the Office of Inter-
American Affairs (OIAA), under the jurisdiction of the Interim International
Information Service (IIIS) in the State Department. The information program, Truman declared, sought to present "a fair and full picture of American
life and of the aims and policies of the United States government."[5]

William B. Benton, newly appointed assistant secretary of state for public
affairs, began implementing these two objectives. Benton made a fortune creating radio advertisements for Maxwell House coffee and Pepsodent toothpaste.
To the detriment of elevators everywhere, he also founded the Muzak Corporation. After leaving the advertising industry, he served as vice-president of the
University of Chicago and chairman of the board of *Encyclopedia Britannica*.
Like most of his cohorts in the government information programs, Benton
understood the power of communications and supported an internationalist
foreign policy.[6] Benton, however, lacked experience in the State Department
and faced several pressing challenges. Truman's consolidation order required
cutting the staffs of the IIIS and former OWI from more than 11,000 to
approximately 3,000 by July 1946. While supervising American "re-education"
programs in Germany and Japan as well as U.S. involvement in the United
Nations Educational, Scientific, and Cultural Organization (UNESCO), he
tried to preserve government relations with private executives in radio, the
press, and the film industry. But Benton's most difficult battle proved to be
persuading Congress to support the information program.[7]

On October 16, 1945, Benton testified before the House Foreign Affairs
Committee in behalf of legislation authorizing international information and
cultural activities.[8] Benton explained that the emergence of the United States
as a superpower necessitated a postwar information program. "Our military
and economic power is so great," he declared, "that it is bound to lead many
people and groups throughout the world to distrust us or fear us or even hate
us." Although Benton conceded that an information program could not entirely prevent others from misperceiving America, he claimed that U.S. officials could try to minimize "the unfair or untruthful impressions of this
country" and to ensure that "accurate knowledge counteracts the growth of

suspicion and prejudice." Without mentioning America's emerging rivalry with the Soviet Union, Benton declared cultural relations a crucial element of U.S. foreign policy.

Benton envisioned an alliance of public and private officials working together to safeguard American commercial and security interests. Cognizant that several politicians believed that federal bureaucracy impinged on free enterprise, Benton insisted that government information policies would not interfere with private industry. "The State Department," he asserted, "should not attempt to undertake what private press, radio, and motion picture organizations do better, or what our tourists, the salesmen of our commercial companies, our advertisers, our technicians, our book publishers and play producers, and our universities do regularly and well." Benton celebrated the potential benefits to be accrued by disseminating information about American technology, medicine, and education. Stimulating international interest in U.S. industry, Benton argued, would foster peace by creating global prosperity.[9]

Other policymakers joined Benton in emphasizing the importance of maintaining information activities. Throughout the fall of 1945, W. Averell Harriman, U.S. ambassador to the Soviet Union, suggested topics for propaganda programs and pushed successfully for the continued publication of *Amerika*, the State Department's Russian language magazine.[10] One of the postwar U.S. information program's earliest successes, *Amerika* made an enduring impression on Soviet audiences. Modeled on *Life*, *Amerika* contained no advertisements or editorials and was packed with lavish photographs. Soviet readers eagerly (and anxiously) consumed the magazines and passed them on until they disintegrated. U.S. officials estimated that between five and fifty Russians read each copy.[11] Typical of the publication's format, the October 1945 issue featured soaring skyscrapers, gleaming suburban homes, attractive women's clothes, cargo ships, penicillin, cattle ranches, George Washington Carver, and Arturo Toscanini.[12] Although sales revenues did not cover the costs associated with printing and distributing 10,000 monthly copies, George F. Kennan, U.S. chargé d'affaires in the Soviet Union, deemed *Amerika* a sound investment for U.S. taxpayers. "A picture spread of an average American school, a small town, or even an average American kitchen dramatizes to Soviet readers . . . that we have . . . a superior standard of living and culture."[13] *Amerika*'s blend of inspirational biographies, technological and scientific prowess, and consumerism became hallmarks of U.S. propaganda during the Cold War (Figure 1).

Figure 1. In publications like *Amerika*, U.S. information officers carefully selected photographs that highlighted the comforts and achievements of American life. National Archives.

Convinced of the global appeal of the American way of life, U.S. information leaders worked hard to secure backing for their programs. During a December 1945 radio forum on NBC's *University of the Air*, Benton, William T. Stone, director of the new Office of International Information and Cultural Affairs (OIC), and Loy Henderson, the director of the Office of Near Eastern and African Affairs, sought public support for the Bloom bill, the legislation creating a permanent international information service. Sol Bloom (D-N.Y.), chairman of the House Foreign Affairs Committee, had introduced a bill to allow the State Department to "carry out its responsibilities in the foreign field" through "public dissemination abroad of information about the United States, its people, and its policies" in addition to existing cultural and educational exchange programs.[14]

Benton, Stone, and Henderson possessed a clear vision of the role of propaganda as a tool of foreign policy. Arguing that international information programs provided a relatively inexpensive way to defuse fears of American military power, Benton proclaimed, "A good many people in other countries think of us as the nation with the atom bomb, the B-29 planes, the huge navy and air forces. This impression is liable to give rise to misunderstanding, fear, and hatred if we don't make our aims clear, and convince people that ours is a peaceful way of life." Although a propaganda program would not entirely prevent international suspicions and hostilities, Benton asserted, "it one of the cheapest ways I know to guard against friction with other nations."[15]

Henderson added that U.S. information activities would correct foreigners' stereotypes of American society and culture. He maintained that other nations "knew more about the American gangsters of the 1920s than they knew about the American educational system of the 1940s. They thought we were all very wealthy, and that we got divorces every year or two. Thanks largely to the Axis propagandists, too many of them still think we are a rich, tawdry, gun-toting, jazz-loving, unscrupulous lot." Despite the pervasiveness of such false impressions, the three officials stressed that American information experts would not resort to lies or distortion in explaining the United States to foreign audiences. "The best propaganda in the world is truth," Benton asserted.[16]

Sterling Fisher, the commentator for the radio program, pushed the trio to define more precisely their conception of "the truth." When he asked how the State Department would report labor unrest, Stone replied, "We will report major strikes. But we won't play them up sensationally. We'll try to tell the whole story—the issues in the strike, what it means to the industry and to the workers." Moving to a more difficult question, Fisher then inquired whether the information officials would tell the world about a race riot in the United States. "It would be pretty hard for some of our friends—China and the Soviet Union and the Latin Americans—to understand," Fisher declared. Stone and Benton assured Fisher that the State Department would address "the race problem" forthrightly. Stone claimed, "We won't hide the fact that we have social problems. But we'll try to present them in perspective." Benton interjected, "At the same time, we can describe the progress we are making toward removing the causes of racial conflict. And we can make it very clear that we don't consider ourselves a master race."[17]

Benton and his colleagues believed that it was unnecessary to hide the unpleasant elements of American society. Throughout the early Cold War, U.S. officials drew a stark distinction between totalitarian "propaganda" characterized by falsehoods and democratic "information" marked by honesty.[18] This tactic enabled American policymakers to present the United States as the world's exemplar of pluralism, freedom, and truth. While finessing their depiction of some unpleasant "truths" about America, they crafted a national narrative of progress, prosperity, and peace.

But forming a permanent information service in a democratic society presented special problems. State Department officials and their successors at the U.S. Information Agency (USIA) continually found the content and objectives of their programs questioned by Congress, the media, and public interest groups. Many politicians had despised the OWI. While alleging that communist subversives controlled the OWI, conservative members of Congress attacked U.S. propagandists for promoting New Deal statism and liberal internationalism. By 1944, the House Appropriations Committee had reduced funding for OWI's domestic branch by 40 percent to $5,500,000.[19]

In the postwar era, bipartisan conservatives continued to assail information activities as elitist, leftist, and fiscally unsound.[20] On February 14, 1946, after ridiculing the State Department as "the lousiest outfit in town" and "a hotbed of reds," Eugene E. Cox (D-Ga.) and Clarence J. Brown (R-Oh.) led a successful drive in the House Rules Committee against immediate approval of Benton's programs. "The people of the country are getting a little fed up on this cultural relations stuff," Brown asserted.[21] Benton began privately lobbying representatives, especially the powerful Cox, to rescue the legislation authorizing the OIC.[22]

While Benton tangled with legislators, the U.S.-Soviet alliance crumbled. Communist propagandists publicized the labor unrest convulsing the United States. At the Council of Foreign Ministers and the United Nations, negotiations on atomic energy, Eastern Europe, and Germany deadlocked. Soviet troops threatened Iranian oil reserves.[23] On January 20, 1946, Harriman appraised the deteriorating situation. He claimed that the average Soviet citizen wanted to understand Americans, but Communist leaders "have consistently sought to present . . . a distorted and unfavorable picture of the USA." The state-controlled Soviet press and radio, Harriman warned, excluded mention of positive events in America and focused on "strikes, unemployment and industrial strife, racial discrimination and crime." He proclaimed, "It is obviously in our national interest to attempt to correct this grotesque and slightly

sinister conception of the USA presented to [the] Soviet people by their leaders." The "only practicable alternative at this stage," Harriman concluded, "is
a vigorous and intelligent American information program designed to bring
somewhat into balance [the] picture of [the] USA available to [the] Soviet
public."[24]

Because radio broadcasts provided the only means of reaching people isolated by illiteracy, geography, or political censorship, Harriman wanted Voice
of America (VOA) to begin direct broadcasts to the Soviet Union. Soviet authorities, he stressed, would not welcome such broadcasts, but could not prevent them. "The USSR could not win a radio war with the USA." The Soviet
government would not jam VOA broadcasts to Russia, because jamming
"would be an admission to [the Soviet] people that it feared outside ideas and
[would] intensify public curiosity over American broadcasts." Though Harriman did not provide detailed recommendations on the nature of newscasts to
the USSR, he cautioned VOA not to criticize the "Soviet system, government, or personalities" for fear of arousing Soviet patriotism.[25]

George F. Kennan recommended more aggressive measures to fight communism. On February 22, prompted by an election speech in which Stalin
proclaimed the fundamental incompatibility of capitalism and communism,
Kennan sent his famous "Long Telegram." He explained that Soviet leaders
condemned bourgeois nations in order to bolster their claims of "capitalist
encirclement." Because of what he viewed as the "instinctive Russian sense of
insecurity," he considered the Soviets a weak adversary. Rather than attempt
to placate the USSR, Kennan concluded, the United States should challenge
and contain communist expansionism.[26]

Kennan viewed propaganda and information activities as vital tools in
combating communism. He warned that the Soviet government would try to
limit cultural interactions with Americans to "arid channels of closely shep-
herded official visits and functions, with superabundance of vodka and
speeches and dearth of permanent effects," but stressed the importance of
explaining the United States to foreign audiences. Certain that U.S. policymakers could easily counter "negative and destructive" Soviet propaganda,
Kennan proclaimed,

> We must formulate and put forward for other nations a much more
> positive and constructive picture of the sort of world we would like
> to see than we have put forth in the past. It is not enough to urge
> people to develop political processes similar to our own. Many

foreign peoples, in Europe, at least, are tired and frightened by experiences of the past, and are less interested in abstract freedom
than in security. They are seeking guidance rather than responsibilities. We should be better able than the Russians to give them this.
And unless we do, Russians certainly will.

Ready to brand the Soviets an enemy, the Truman administration enthusiastically welcomed Kennan's remarks.[27] In March, Winston Churchill's "Iron Curtain" speech and the Iranian crisis intensified anticommunist sentiment.[28]

The positive response to Kennan's telegram energized Benton. On February 28, Benton appeared before the House Appropriations Committee
and confidently declared the information program "essential" in maintaining
world peace. Arguing that his program provided a relatively inexpensive
means of countering the confusion, ignorance, and suspicion that often led to
war, he pointed out that his funding request amounted "to about one-fifth of
one percent of the budget proposed by the Army and Navy for achieving
peace through force of arms and the threat of force of arms."[29] The proposed
$19-million information program included "no elements of psychological
warfare, no so-called black [covert, not openly linked to the country of ori-
gin] propaganda, and no secrecy. It deals only in facts. Its purpose is to gain
understanding for America, as America actually is, and not even as we hope
America may sometime be."[30]

Some members of the House greeted Benton's claims with skepticism.
House Appropriations Committee chairman Louis C. Rabaut (D-Mich.) expressed concern that propaganda activities might increase the national debt.
Dean M. Gillespie (R-Colo.) pressed Benton for details on the role of the
American Library Association (ALA) in choosing selections for U.S. libraries
overseas. ALA leaders believed that overseas libraries should foster the free exchange of ideas, and that no author should be censored because of his or her
personal beliefs.[31] Suspicious of such expansive standards, Gillespie alleged
that some ALA members thought "leftist ideas are the stuff that make America." Gillespie disagreed and stated his preference for the works of Ralph
Waldo Emerson and Benjamin Franklin's *Poor Richard's Almanac*. "Let us find
out what we are feeding these people and let us give them the stuff that America was built up on instead of the stuff that is carrying America down," he
implored. Making no comment on Gillespie's choice of literature, Benton
promised to produce a list of the books held by U.S. government libraries
abroad.[32]

The complaints about the costs and content of the information program were ominous. But Benton continued undeterred, publicizing how the Axis Powers had distorted the truth about America during World War II. In an address delivered in Los Angeles on March 6, Benton explained that authoritarian propaganda had convinced the world that "the American system is degenerate and debilitated, that democracy is hypocrisy and so-called freedom a joke. They were told that our leaders were scoundrels; that our culture was semi-barbaric; our ideals tainted; our morals base. And they believed all of this and more." Nations emerging from totalitarianism found the complexity of the American democratic system "bewildering." Because of U.S. dominance of industry, trade, and science, it was imperative that foreign peoples have accurate information about the United States. "*How* we live, *what* we do affects everyone," Benton declared. "A hurricane in Florida, a strike in New York Harbor, a bumper wheat crop in Nebraska, the color of the bread we eat—all have a direct impact on the economy and living conditions of other peoples." [33]

To bolster his argument, Benton provided several examples of widespread misinformation about America. He cited a Rumanian report describing endemic crime in the United States. The document quoted J. Edgar Hoover, director of the Federal Bureau of Investigation (FBI), saying that six million American criminals had been arrested in the aftermath of World War II. In reality, Benton explained, Hoover had stated that the U.S. government had collected six million sets of fingerprints in the previous twenty-two years. Benton then mentioned a Rome newspaper that connected Truman to the Ku Klux Klan, described as "the most powerful latent organization in the United States today." Without information programs, Benton concluded, the U.S. government could not effectively correct such damaging lies. [34]

Despite their growing antipathy toward the Soviet Union, Benton's efforts failed to impress Congress. In May 1946, the House Appropriations Committee cut his request by 48 percent, from $19,284,778 to $10,000,000. Although the Senate eventually allotted $25,636,357 for information and cultural activities, the figure was a significant reduction from the 1946 appropriation of $36,000,000. To make matters worse, Senator Robert A. Taft (R-Oh.), a renowned isolationist, led a successful movement to kill the Bloom bill establishing a postwar information program. Consequently, when the 79th Congress adjourned, the OIC continued to lack legislative authority. [35]

While battling Congress, the OIC established key U.S. information objectives for specific countries. For example, a November 1946 regional guide described the Czechs as "realistic, technical-minded, fond of folkish tradition, extremely musical, and very devoted to the arts." To reach them, the OIC recommended promoting U.S. achievements in art, music, architecture, literature, and education. Cautioning against the use of sarcasm, the OIC asserted "it is far more important to achieve the impression that America is serious than to make our audience laugh." To counteract communist stereotypes of U.S. capitalism as a system where monopolists ruthlessly exploited hapless workers, OIC policymakers directed their field officers to stress U.S. civil liberties and anti-trust regulations. They listed political organizations, trade unions, youth groups, farmers' associations, sports clubs, and cultural and scientific societies as the most important target audiences.[36] Through such elaborate strategies and "country plans," information officials promoted global themes about the American way of life while acknowledging different national political cultures.

At the same time, OIC leaders remained carefully attuned to the vicissitudes of American politics. In November 1946, after winning majorities in both houses of Congress, conservative Republicans stood poised to slash taxes and reduce government expenditures. Although GOP legislators voiced anti-communist sentiments and worried about Soviet aggression, they resisted the foreign entanglements desired by the Truman administration. Cognizant of conservative animosity toward cultural and information activities, Benton expected the new congressional leaders to attack his program.[37]

International Art and Domestic Political Controversy

He did not have to wait long. In the fall of 1946, Benton announced the opening at the Metropolitan Museum of Art of seventy-nine oil paintings selected by the State Department for a worldwide tour.[38] Because foreign critics frequently dismissed American art as a tame imitation of French Impressionism, several U.S. embassy officials in Europe had requested a collection highlighting experimental U.S. styles and demonstrating the vitality of American culture. After closing in New York, the collection was divided into two exhibitions, one sent to Paris and Prague, the other to Latin America. The exhibit, "Advancing American Art," received wide acclaim from the arts community. *Art News* selected the collection as the "most significant modern exhibition" of 1946.[39] Noting the popularity of the exhibit, the Soviet Union quickly assembled a collection of "socialist realist" paintings for display in Prague.[40]

Despite the success of "Advancing American Art," many traditional artists and conservative politicians assailed modern art as communist-inspired and inherently un-American.[41] Claiming "more than 20 of the 45 artists were definitely New Deal in various shades of communism," Representative Fred Buseby (R-Ill.) protested the inclusion of paintings by Milton Avery, Stuart Davis, Philip Evergood, and Ben Shahn in "Advancing American Art."[42] Others denounced the collection as a waste of money. *Look* magazine printed an acerbic profile of the exhibition called "Your Money Bought These Pictures." On February 7, 1947, Fulton Lewis, Jr., a Mutual Broadcasting Network radio show host, urged listeners to buy the magazine, "turn to pages 80 and 81, and you will find seven colored pictures that will make you very, very mad indeed." "The idea of spending money collected from the American taxpayer," Lewis continued, "to buy a lot of paintings to send around to American embassies all over the world for a few individuals to look at as a means of combating antagonistic propaganda ought to sound idiotic enough to make your blood boil."[43]

Although the State Department publicly stressed the artistic merit and critical acclaim of the exhibition, information officials privately worried that the purchase of the paintings could inflict "irreparable damage" on the OIC. None of the three top administrators of the division—Benton, Charlie Hulten, and William T. Stone—even knew the pictures existed before the *Look* story appeared.[44] Singed by congressional hostility toward the OIC, Benton admitted, "I would not have bought such pictures."[45]

Nonetheless, in March 1947, Benton found himself explaining the paintings to the House Appropriations Committee.[46] During the hearing, Karl Stefan (R-Neb.), chairman of the subcommittee on the State Department, held photographs of the paintings in front of Benton and pointedly asked, "Do you know what that is?" No modern art expert, Benton replied, "It does have a resemblance to many things that are not fit to mention before this committee."[47] But he also defended the purchase of the collection. Because "Americans are accused throughout the world of being a materialistic, money-mad race without interest in art and without appreciation of artists or music," Benton explained, the State Department wanted to highlight America's culture. He contended that modern art "is a better illustration of our current artistic interests . . . than the more orthodox or traditional forms of art." But Benton's explanations did not persuade critics of "Advancing American Art." He soon recalled the collection from Prague and Port-au-Prince, enraging several artists, museum officials, dealers, and art writers. Secretary of State

George Marshall announced that no additional tax dollars would be spent on modern art.[48]

The controversy reflected long-standing debates on the connections between American politics and culture. During the 1930s, many conservatives opposed public funding of "subversive" artists in New Deal programs. These traditionalists, historian Jane De Hart Mathews argues, "attempted to link ideology and art in the person of the artist irrespective of the content of specific works." Accordingly, "iconoclasm in art was assumed to extend to the broader realms of the cultural and social order, threatening ultimately all established norms and values."[49] In the eyes of conservatives, "American" art was representational, technically proficient, and easily understood by the masses. "American" artists glorified the nation and its people. Conservatives viewed modern art as abstract, technically flawed, and elitist—in a word, un-American. Only subversives could produce such unpatriotic work. If the American government sponsored modern art and radical artists, it betrayed not only the nation's cultural heritage but also democracy itself.[50] The state, therefore, should only fund art that reflected the values of the masses.

The similarity between this position and Nazi and Soviet attacks on "degenerate" art obviously eluded the critics of "Advancing American Art." So did an understanding of trends in contemporary art. Although artists like Ben Shahn and Yasuo Kuniyoshi used their art to make personal political statements, other artists were adopting the consciously *apolitical* methods of the abstract expressionists. Not willing to bend their artistic vision to partisan standards, abstract expressionists like Robert Motherwell, Jackson Pollock, and Mark Rothko produced ambiguous work filled with personal symbolism. Although abstract expressionism did not contain overtly political content, it demonstrated the freedom of expression only open societies allowed to flourish. Unable to grasp that such creativity and individualism embodied democratic values, conservatives perceived modern art as communist-inspired.[51] This anti-intellectualism and anti-modernism combined with anti-statist and nativist views accounted for much of the conservatives' continuing hostility to information and cultural activities throughout the Cold War.

Facing such obstacles, it is hardly surprising that Benton grew frustrated. Frequently out of the country, Secretary of State James F. Byrnes provided little assistance in gaining political support for propaganda activities.[52] Although Byrnes's successor, George C. Marshall, was a committed advocate of the OIC, Benton's battles with Congress continued. When the 80th Congress convened in January 1947, conservatives intensified their allegations of communist infiltration of the State Department.[53] On January 27, Benton warned Undersecretary of State Dean Acheson, "Members of Congress . . . have repeatedly told me that this is the single issue on which they must be completely satisfied if they are to support the appropriations . . . for the information program."[54] Four days later, Benton encouraged Marshall to review department personnel policies.[55]

Reaching the Russians

Amid this political controversy, U.S. policymakers had to deal with an increasingly ominous international situation. During the frigid winter of 1946–47, shortages of food and fuel engulfed an already suffering Europe and exacerbated global political and economic instability. Local Communist parties in France and Italy were exploiting this distress. In Southeast Asia, the French, British, and Dutch fought revolutionary nationalists. Noting a marked increase in anti-Americanism in several countries, State Department researchers warned that "practically all of the anti-American slogans and concepts which are found in the Soviet press and radio are also observed in countries under direct Soviet control or influence, namely Yugoslavia, Albania, Poland, Romania, Bulgaria, Czechoslovakia, Finland, Hungary, Communist North China, and North Korea."[56] Seeking to protect American economic, political, and strategic interests, the Truman administration began pursuing a more active foreign policy.[57]

The strategic shift prompted U.S. information strategists to appeal directly to the Soviet populace. In December 1946, the State Department warned OIC officers that no country was more significant in U.S. foreign policy than the Soviet Union. "It is not an exaggeration to say that the fate of the world rests on relations between [the] USA and [the] USSR." Conceding the impossibility of "influencing the Russian masses at this time," the State Department ordered OIC officers to reach the "five or ten thousand people" who shaped Soviet national policy. In addition to providing a "realistic picture of the United States as a powerful but friendly industrial nation," information officers were to explain how "despite great organizational and ideological differences, there can be peace and friendship between the USSR and USA." To facilitate these objectives, the State Department increased the circulation of *Amerika* magazine from 10,000 to 50,000, augmented the OIC libraries in the Soviet Union, and developed plans for Soviet-American academic and technical exchanges.[58]

Since none of these tactics would reach as many communists as the Voice of America, State Department leaders also pushed for expansion of U.S. broadcasting in the Soviet Union. In the fall of 1946, they discovered that Charles Thayer, a veteran diplomat and former OSS officer, was studying Soviet propaganda at the National War College. A Russian and German expert, Thayer had served in Afghanistan, Iran, Yugoslavia, Italy, and Austria, and witnessed the awesome power of fascist and communist propaganda. Thayer's study emphasized the pervasiveness of Soviet propaganda and outlined a strategy for countering it. Impressed with the diplomat's analytical and linguistic abilities, Benton appointed Thayer the first chief of the VOA desk for the Soviet Union.[59]

Thayer found VOA operations in disarray. In consolidating the wartime information agencies, Benton discharged more than 50 percent of VOA personnel. VOA operatives rarely received guidance from the State Department on foreign policy and instead depended on the American media. In November 1946, Thayer began redressing this situation by seeking qualified editors, writers, and announcers. He found his options limited by a congressional mandate that VOA hire U.S. citizens, thereby precluding the use of recent Russian immigrants and war refugees. Thayer selected Nicholas Nabokov, a composer and Soviet émigré who had come to the United States as a music student in 1933 and then served as cultural advisor for the U.S. embassy in Germany, as his editor-in-chief. Thayer and Nabokov gave potential staff rigorous interviews and rejected those with poor Russian language skills, tepid personalities, or limited knowledge about the Soviet Union and the United States. Significantly, Thayer and Nabokov also refused to hire applicants who were "too anti-Soviet." Hampered by a lack of radio experience, a budget of $150,000, and a staff of only twelve, Thayer and Nabokov doggedly recruited volunteers, including Averell Harriman's daughter Kathleen, to assist the VOA Russian unit.[60]

The State Department spent weeks preparing guidelines for broadcasting to the Soviet Union. It insisted that VOA Russian programming avoid "polemics, invective, [or] argumentation" which could "inspire active opposition to" or "instigate the replacement or modification of" the Soviet regime. Any attempt to incite a popular uprising, the State Department warned, "would jeopardize the entire broadcasting project." Thayer's staff received instructions about tailoring programming to the "sensibilities, taboos, tastes, and interests" of Soviet audiences. Because of "nationalist sensitivity and xenophobia," broadcasters were to avoid any criticism of the Russian nation, the Russian people, and the Soviet government. The State Department urged radio announcers to respect the dignity and morality of Soviet audiences, adding, "The Soviet regime has gone far in developing a Puritanism or prudishness scarcely outdone by the Pilgrim fathers." Although their greatest programming priority was reporting important developments in U.S. foreign and domestic policy, U.S. officials also hoped to attract people bored by Soviet propaganda aired by Radio Moscow. VOA broadcasters were directed to "to play upon the Russian's passion for tragedy, comedy, and pathos." Suggested features included "the fables of Johnny Appleseed, the short stories of O. Henry, and dramatizations of [John] Dos Passos's reportage style."[61]

On February 1, 1947, the State Department announced that it would begin sending direct newscasts to the Soviet Union. After the Soviet government refused to print this press release, officials at the U.S. embassy in Moscow personally passed the news of the upcoming broadcasts to Soviet friends. On February 17, the first Russian language broadcast included a news summary, an explanation of American federalism, and musical interludes.

The following day, Lt. Gen. Walter Bedell Smith, Harriman's successor as U.S. ambassador to the USSR, reported that some members of the Soviet audience gathered at the U.S. embassy described the broadcasts as "just fair." They complained of "too much talk" and poor reception. The Soviets were, Smith told Benton, "rather bored with long-winded discussions of political conditions, which to them mean very little." Furthermore, an Aaron Copland piece sounded "like a bagpipe solo" because of technical problems. But, when Cole Porter's "Night and Day" began playing, Smith reported, "about half the audience sat up and said, 'This is what we have been waiting 45 minutes for.'" Smith concluded, "The Russian people are starved for humor, bright music, folk songs and any form of entertainment which offers an escape from [the] grim reality of daily existence." Accordingly, VOA executives soon livened up the show with more American jazz songs and news items.[62]

The Truman Doctrine

While VOA improved its output, the Truman administration adopted a tougher posture toward Soviet expansionism. On February 21, 1947, after British leaders informed American officials that financial difficulties necessitated termination of British military assistance to Greece and Turkey, U.S. policymakers decided that the United States must defend the Eastern

Mediterranean from possible communist aggression. Rather than retreat into political isolationism and economic nationalism, America would champion democratic capitalism abroad.[63]

On March 12, the Truman Doctrine speech heralded this change. In a special joint session of Congress, the president appealed for $400 million in aid to Greece and Turkey and enunciated an implicit contrast between democracy and communism. "Nearly every nation," Truman proclaimed, "must choose between alternative ways of life":

> One way of life is based upon the will of the majority, and is distin-
> guished by free institutions, representative government, free elec-
> tions, guarantees of individual liberty, freedom of speech and
> religion, and freedom from political oppression. The second way of
> life is based upon the minority forcibly imposed upon the majority.
> It relies upon terror and oppression, a controlled press and radio,
> fixed elections, and the suppression of personal freedoms.[64]

Without mentioning the Soviet Union, Truman eloquently articulated the benefits of free enterprise. His juxtaposition of democracy and communism would infuse American propaganda throughout the Cold War. On March 21, he further demonstrated his commitment to national security by instituting a loyalty program for federal civil servants.[65] He did not, however, ask Congress to support the international information program.

This omission did not escape Benton's attention. The day after Truman's speech, Benton asked Henry R. Luce, president of Time-Life, Incorporated, "Does it make sense to put $400,000,000 into Greece and Turkey without setting up an adequate program of explaining to the Greeks and Turks and others why we are doing so?" Of the $31 million in his 1948 budget projec-tions, Benton earmarked little more than $300,000 for Greece and Turkey. But "even these figures are in jeopardy," Benton told Luce, because he ex-pected opposition from the House Appropriations Committee.[66]

Literature and Conservative Opposition

Benton's pessimism was justified. On March 20, prior to attacking "Advancing American Art," Karl Stefan (R-Neb.) portrayed the OIC as wasteful and inef-ficient. Like many congressional conservatives, Stefan believed that national security was best ensured through balanced budgets, limited government, and a hemispheric system of defense. Accordingly, he grilled Benton about the expenditures, management, and activities of the OIC. Stefan claimed that a productive American economy, not U.S. propaganda activities, would most effectively stem the spread of communism in Europe. Put on the defensive, Benton insisted that the international information program had "proved itself to be an effective and, indeed, an indispensable instrument of United States foreign policy." He defended the radio broadcasts of Voice of America, the publication of *Amerika* magazine, and the salaries and selection of employees in his division. Most of his words, however, fell on deaf ears as Stefan, though a friend of Benton's, seemed intent on embarrassing the State Department.[67]

At one point during the hearings, Stefan asked the ladies in the hearing room to leave. He then read a rather racy excerpt from Edmund Wilson's *The Memoirs of Hecate County*. After he finished, he asked Kenneth Holland, OIC assistant director for cultural affairs, "Do you approve of a book like that being sent out?" Holland replied, "No sir; I do not." Stefan retorted, "It may cost the taxpayers of the United States at least $31,000,000 to undo the damage if such literature is allowed to be circulated in the name of the United States government." Benton countered that State Department librarians chose books "about America." "It so happens," he continued, "that obscenity can be about America; this book is one of the top sellers in the United States." But Benton also promised to investigate why such a book was chosen. Unfortunately, neither Benton nor Holland knew that the Department's library committee had removed Wilson's book from the list of those slated for distribution abroad.[68]

Like the assault on "Advancing American Art," the criticism of Edmund Wilson reflected anti-leftist and anti-intellectual views. After years of blending communist politics with modernist literary criticism, Wilson had rejected Stalinism in the late 1930s and then opposed World War II. Written in 1946, *The Memoirs of Hecate County* marked Wilson's rejection of ideological approaches to culture and politics. But the political content of the novel—as well as Wilson's renunciation of his revolutionary socialist past—continued to elude many conservatives. In 1952, Senator Joseph R. McCarthy (R-Wis.) denounced *The Memoirs of Hecate County* as "pornographic and pro-Communist."[69] In a political atmosphere with narrowing views of what constituted "American" culture and who was an "American" artist, the fact that the anticommunist Wilson could write an "obscene" book was irrelevant. Drawing distinctions between nontraditional cultural expression and political subversion became virtually impossible.

Karl Mundt Becomes an Unlikely Champion

In May, the OIC received more bad news when the House Appropriations Committee denied the entire $31 million requested for information programs. With the current appropriation for the OIC set to expire on June 30, Secretary of State Marshall urged chairman John Taber (R-N.Y.) to change his mind. But, citing the lack of authorizing legislation for the program, Taber stood firm. He also derided VOA's decision to broadcast a favorable review of a book about Henry Wallace, and the posting in the New York office of the OIC of a notice denouncing Truman's federal employee loyalty program.[70] Privately, Benton complained bitterly about conservatives using such minor episodes to justify attacking a program they had long viewed as elitist, statist, and liberal.[71]

But the information program soon found an unlikely savior in Karl Mundt, a Republican from South Dakota. A former social studies teacher and college speech professor, Mundt was a strong believer in the power of education to diffuse international tensions. Citizens with firsthand exposure to foreign countries, he reasoned, were much less likely to permit their elected representatives to wage war. Such views aligned Mundt with liberal organizations like the American Council of Learned Societies and the American Library Association, not his conservative Republican colleagues. But while Mundt wanted to promote peace and understanding in the postwar world, he was equally determined to thwart the spread of communism at home and abroad.[72]

This weave of liberal and conservative principles was evident throughout Mundt's congressional career. Elected to the U.S. House of Representatives in 1938, he eventually obtained seats on the House Foreign Affairs Committee and the House Committee on Un-American Activities (HUAC). In May 1945, Mundt introduced legislation creating an International Office of Education within the Department of State. The House passed the bill unanimously. That fall, an extensive tour of Europe and the Middle East persuaded Mundt of the necessity to repel Soviet gains in Eastern Europe and to expand U.S. efforts to interact with foreigners. In March 1947, he broke with his party's right wing and supported Truman's aid package for Greece and Turkey.[73]

Mundt's vehement anticommunism and advocacy of international exchanges made him an ideal candidate for assuaging conservative concerns about the OIC. Benton spent months convincing Mundt that the State Department had instituted proper security procedures and would not impinge on private media before Mundt agreed to sponsor HR 3342, a bill authorizing the State Department to continue its overseas information and cultural activities. While calling for the promotion of "mutual understanding between the people of the United States and other countries," the legislation also required FBI security clearances for all OIC employees and perspective employees. In order to prevent the government from compromising free enterprise, the resolution mandated that the government allow private individuals and agencies to conduct information activities abroad. Finally, in a nod toward fiscal conservatism, the bill stipulated that the State Department use existing facilities whenever possible. On May 13, the Information Subcommittee of the House Foreign Affairs Committee began hearings on HR 3342. Dean Acheson, undersecretary of state, and Averell Harriman, new secretary of commerce, encouraged the House to support the OIC. Both officials strongly endorsed the continuation of Voice of America broadcasts, *Amerika* magazine, and educational exchanges. In following days, Walter Bedell Smith, Benton, Marshall, and Army chief of staff Dwight D. Eisenhower also testified in support of Mundt's legislation.[74]

The hearings and Mundt's efforts in the House sparked a bipartisan effort to save the OIC. Acknowledging the reservations some of his colleagues voiced about the alleged leftist leanings of State Department personnel, Mundt highlighted the section of his bill that permitted federal investigation of information employees. "That provision," Mundt explained, "should permit us to consider the program on its merit without fear that it will be sabotaged by disloyal or apologetic Americans." He stressed the objectivity and nonpartisan nature of U.S. information programming. He claimed that his bill would prevent programming "mistakes" such as the Wallace broadcast and the inclusion of Kuniyoshi's *Circus Girl Resting* in the "Advancing American Art" exhibit.[75]

Mundt's bill began to gather congressional backing. On May 17, Taber announced his support for limited VOA broadcasts. Nonetheless, he remained critical of State Department employees and the content of some information programs. Articulating the widely held suspicion of foreign nationals employed by the State Department, Taber insisted, "If we are going to interpret America abroad, it should be done by Americans." Furthermore,

Taber added, this interpretation "should advertise our delinquencies as little as possible."[76] Like Taber, members of subcommittee considering the Mundt legislation put aside their reservations about the OIC and unanimously recommended the continuation of its activities abroad.[77]

On June 6, an intense debate ensued on the House floor. Eugene Cox (D-Ga.), who just months earlier had claimed the OIC was "chockfull of reds," now lauded Benton for his administrative and leadership abilities. Cox then quoted several members of the Truman administration who claimed countering Communist propaganda about the United States was "essential as a part of the foreign program of the State Department." Unimpressed by Cox's remarks, John Chenoweth (R-Colo.), the chairman of a subcommittee on expenditures in the State Department, retorted, "I doubt if any foreign country is going to sever relations with us if this bill fails to pass. This is not quite as serious as some would have you believe."[78]

Mundt disagreed. Only the day before, he reminded his colleagues, the House had passed a $5.28 billion budget for the War Department in response to "the chaotic, uncertain, and disturbing conditions prevailing in the world today." "This afternoon," Mundt continued, he appealed for the "comparatively paltry sum" of $31 million and congressional authorization of the information program "so that the Congress at long last can do something constructive to win the peace, to prepare for peace, to give the peace department of this government a little money and a little authority and a little equipment for once as we so rightfully give it to the War Department." Mundt then emphasized that the United States had already authorized $12 billion for foreign assistance to achieve the security objectives and to maintain world peace.[79] In Mundt's view, funds spent on information and cultural programs were an investment in America's future.

But other House members feared "selling" or "advertising" the American way of life would jeopardize its very existence. They invoked the xenophobic specter of hordes of subversive academics using the exchange program to infiltrate America. Some argued that funds for information programs would be better spent on rebuilding areas devastated by World War II. If these humanitarian efforts failed to convey the values of America, Walter Brehm (R-Oh.) argued, then "the rest of the world . . . is just too stupid to ever understand our ideals regardless of any type of program which the State Department may institute."[80] Overt attempts by the federal government to manipulate international opinions of the United States, the conservatives argued, risked damaging America's reputation as a bastion of freedom.

Opponents of the information program made these allegations only a day after Marshall called for the establishment of the European Recovery Plan (ERP). In addition to stemming the spread of communism, a long-term U.S. commitment to the economic reconstruction of Europe promised to serve American financial and political interests. By offering aid to any European nation, the plan that became synonymous with Marshall challenged Stalin's tightening grip on Eastern Europe. Having already solidified their hold on Poland, Bulgaria, and Romania, Soviet authorities had just forced the resignation and exile of Hungarian Premier Ferenc Nagy, a non-communist.[81] On June 10, Marshall followed up his famous speech at Harvard with an appeal to the Senate Appropriations Committee for restoration of funds for the OIC. In an international environment fraught with tension and danger, Marshall asked the Congress to consider the sagacity of cutting funding for the information program. He assured them that the OIC would be "very carefully administered."[82]

Meanwhile, the House debate on the Mundt bill continued. Supporters of the legislation cited the 25,000 letters a month being received by the Voice of America as evidence of a global audience looking toward the United States as "a stabilizing influence in the aftermath of the most destructive war in history."[83] Everett M. Dirksen (R-Ill.) and Harold Cooley (D-N.C.) mentioned recent trips to Europe that exposed them to virulent anti-American propaganda abroad. By mid-1947, approximately half the members of Congress had made similar journeys, augmenting support for the information program. On June 24, HR 3342 passed by a decisive 273–97 margin.[84]

The Senate proved more difficult to persuade. Although the Appropriations Committee restored $12.4 million to the OIC with $6,387,250 allotted for VOA broadcasts, the figure was a 50 percent reduction of the previous year's funding.[85] But at the suggestion of H. Alexander Smith (R-N.J.), the Information Subcommittee of the Foreign Relations Committee held hearings on the Mundt bill and the OIC.[86] On July 2, Benton told Smith's subcommittee that $12.4 million "will certainly not enable the Department to carry on the information activities which our Embassies abroad consider to be essential." Delays on the Senate vote on the Mundt bill, Benton argued, created "serious personnel problems growing out of the insecurity of this program." With its funds limited and its political future in flux, the OIC was hardly an attractive employer.[87]

Hoping to dispel congressional allegations of communist infiltration of his department, Marshall discharged ten employees suspected of disloyalty.[88]

Such measures, however, failed to persuade the Senate to pass the Mundt bill before the summer recess. Instead, the Foreign Relations Committee endorsed the continuation of peacetime information activities but elected not to vote on the Mundt legislation until a joint panel of ten congressional investigators assessed the efficacy of propaganda operations abroad. In deference to H. Alexander Smith's contributions, the Mundt bill was soon renamed the Smith-Mundt bill.[89] Over the next several weeks, interim reports and private messages from the examiners convinced Benton that the legislation would easily pass when Congress reconvened.[90]

In the meantime, Benton announced plans to reorganize the OIC "to achieve maximum results under its reduced appropriations." Adopting the language of the Mundt bill, Benton jettisoned the controversial word "cultural" from OIC and renamed his domestic section the Office of Information and Educational Exchange (OIE). To avoid confusion abroad, foreign operations remained the U.S. Information Service (USIS). Benton also consolidated divisions and cut staff. Although he conceded these changes represented "a sharp curtailment of our activities," Benton expressed confidence in the eventual passage of legislation recognizing the necessity of information strategy.[91] Exhausted by his two-year battle with Congress and convinced that the information program now had a secure foundation, Benton submitted his resignation and declared his intention to return to *Encyclopedia Britannica*.[92]

The Cold War Intensifies

Throughout 1947, the ideological conflict between the U.S. and the USSR continued to sharpen. In July, unwilling to permit Western intrusion into his sphere of influence, Stalin ensured that the Czech, Polish, and Yugoslav governments did not pursue aid under the ERP.[93] On October 5, the Soviet Union announced the creation of the Cominform (the Information Bureau of Communist Parties) to combat the American "dollar imperialism" of the Marshall Plan. Seeking to align foreign communists firmly with the Soviet Union, the Cominform declaration heralded the consolidation of Soviet power in Eastern Europe.[94]

U.S. officials in the USSR found these developments ominous. On November 15, Ambassador Walter Bedell Smith warned Marshall that the totalitarian Soviet propaganda machine could destroy American plans for the economic rehabilitation of the postwar world. Unless the United States refuted communist claims of political and economic superiority, Smith asserted, Europeans would continue to misunderstand democratic capitalism.[95]

Accordingly, Smith recommended that the OIE begin stressing the inconsistencies between Soviet words and deeds. He suggested that the United States publicize Soviet subjugation of Eastern European; the impotence of Soviet labor unions; and the drudgery inflicted on women and children in the USSR. In addition to exposing Soviet lies, Smith urged U.S. propaganda strategists to demonstrate the advantages American capitalism accorded the average worker. "Above everything else, and by all possible means," Smith pleaded, "counteract the terrible and developing fear of imminent war which is overpowering Europe and which the Soviet Union is fostering by 'warmonger' propaganda in order to retard economic recovery." This fear, he concluded, loomed as the biggest obstacle to the implementation of the Marshall Plan.[96]

Already considering more stringent measures to combat Soviet propaganda, State Department leaders welcomed Smith's remarks. On December 1, 1947, no longer willing to ignore "the unscrupulous measures and techniques currently employed against us by elements seeking to discredit the U.S.," OIE leaders released new guidelines to counter anti-Americanism. Calling for a continuation of "factual, truthful and forceful presentation of U.S. foreign policy and American ways of living," they focused the American information campaign on "impressing the peoples of the world with the reliability, consistency and seriousness of the U.S. and its policies." OIE strategists sought to counter Soviet accusations by affirming American policies, rather than denouncing communist ones. "The U.S.," they declared, "should not give the impression that it is on the defensive, or vulnerable to hostile charges, but rather that Soviet policy, where it conflicts with ours, works to the detriment of the particular country, while U.S. policy consistently supports the principles of freedom, prosperity, and independence implicit in the Charter of the United Nations."[97]

Earlier in the fall of 1947, while investigating twenty-two USIS operations in Western and Eastern Europe, the Smith-Mundt congressional group saw firsthand evidence of the ideological struggle enveloping Europe. During visits to Romania, Bulgaria, and Poland, the politicians witnessed the "successive nightmares" left in the wake of Soviet repression. They were appalled by the expulsion of leaders who opposed communism. Describing contemporary Europe as "a vast battlefield of ideologies in which words have to a large extent replaced armaments as the active elements of attack and defense," the committee concluded that the efforts of U.S. embassies abroad were "woefully inadequate" in combating the "misrepresentation, falsification, division, chaos, compromise, despair and ultimate absorption" fostered by Communist propaganda. U.S. propaganda efforts, they claimed, lagged behind those of Russia and Britain. Distressed at the low number and quality of several USIS facilities, they suggested construction improvements and increased appropriations for the information program. "The Soviets and the Communists are today," the committee wrote, "conducting aggressive psychological warfare against us in order thoroughly to discredit us and drive us out of Europe. In order to prevent this, to safeguard our national security, to promote world peace and implement our own foreign policy, based primarily on economic reconstruction and political freedom, a strong and effective information and educational exchange program is essential." OIE officials could not have asked for a more ringing endorsement.[98]

Passage of the Smith-Mundt Act

Congressional support for American propaganda continued to grow even while negotiations on the European Recovery Program and plans to reinvigorate Germany reached a temporary impasse. In January 1948, having amended the original HR 3342 more than 100 times, the House hammered out final compromises that ensured passage of the Smith-Mundt bill. In deference to those wary of government bureaucracy, the law directed the State Department "to utilize, to the maximum extent practicable, the services and facilities of private agencies, including existing American press, publishing, radio, motion picture, and other agencies." To appease those who feared communist infiltration, the Smith-Mundt bill required all information officials to undergo FBI loyalty investigations. It also mandated the deportation of exchange participants found to be engaging in subversive political activities. Finally, to ensure that no individual, party, or agency used government propaganda to influence the American people, the Smith-Mundt legislation prohibited the dissemination of U.S. information materials to the general public. While representatives of the press and members of Congress could request transcripts of government programming, private U.S. citizens could not.[99]

On January 16, 1948, satisfied with these compromises and recognizing the imperative need to explain American foreign policy and political culture to the rest of the world, the Senate unanimously passed the Smith-Mundt bill. Designed "to promote a better understanding of the United States in other countries," the measure established an information service and an educational exchange division. Separate advisory committees supervised each and were required to report to Congress twice a year on expenditures, activities, and effectiveness. Eleven days later, Truman signed the bill into law. He appointed George V. Allen, a career diplomat currently serving as U.S. Ambassador to Iran, as Benton's successor as assistant secretary of state for public affairs.[100] In April 1948, the State Department, responding to the Smith-Mundt Act, abolished the OIE and created the Office of International Information (OII) and the Office of Educational Exchange (OEX).[101]

"Know North America" Sparks Another Clash with Congress

Passage of the Smith-Mundt Act did nothing to shield the leaders of State Department's information programs from yet another public dispute with Congress. In February 1948, transcripts of the weekly Voice of America series "Know North America" drew the ire of several representatives. Beamed to Latin America every Monday, the program described the "intellectual adventures of two travelers who are discovering the multiple surprises of present-day life in the United States." Unfortunately, some of these descriptions were rather imprudent. For example, the two voyagers stated, "New England was founded on hypocrisy and Texas by sin." The duo claimed "feathered and naked Indian girls" walked the streets of Cheyenne, Wyoming. Outraged, John Taber (R-N.Y.) summoned Assistant Secretary of State for Public Affairs Allen and VOA Director Thayer to a closed session of the House Appropriations Committee. Taber grilled Thayer on supervisory procedures and programming content at VOA.[102]

On May 26, 1948, after Senator Homer Capehart (R-Ind.), a VOA critic, publicly read excerpts of "Know North America," a bipartisan group of senators angrily defended their states against the "damnable lies," "downright falsehoods," and "drivel" in the broadcasts. H. Alexander Smith pointed out that "Know North America" had been prepared by the National Broadcasting Company (NBC) because the Smith-Mundt Act required the State Department to use private radio facilities whenever possible. Capehart retorted that the State Department bore ultimate responsibility for broadcasts that did "this country more harm than good." Homer Ferguson (R-Mich.) suggested that funding for Voice of America be withdrawn until "every word is supervised"[103] (Figure 2).

Figure 2. The largest component of America's postwar information programs, Voice of America enabled U.S. officials to reach audiences isolated by political barriers, geography, or illiteracy. Although the backgrounds of VOA employees and content of VOA programs remained flashpoints with Congress, the network played a critical role in the U.S. ideological offensive and enjoyed great popularity overseas. Here, a team of VOA announcers addresses audiences in Southeast Asia. National Archives.

Although NBC immediately fired the writer responsible for the series, Truman and both houses of Congress hurriedly formed committees to investigate VOA. Within days, a subcommittee of the House Executive Expenditures Committee interrogated René Borgia, author of "Know North America." Borgia readily conceded that the scripts were poor and claimed he had repeatedly protested his superiors' orders to write the programs in a sarcastic style. During his testimony, Thayer emphasized that budget constraints and congressional mandates forced VOA executives to rely on private contractors for

approximately 70 percent of VOA broadcasts—a situation he had been attempting to change.[104] A month later, Allen announced that the State Department would assume sole responsibility for all radio broadcasts effective
October 1, 1948. Although conservative legislators excoriated VOA leaders for
inadequate program supervision, the "Know North America" incident resulted in the bureaucracy they had long opposed. The State Department
would now prepare all news and commentary broadcast by VOA.[105]

The Soviets Raise the Stakes

Unimpeded by such political disputes, Soviet propagandists escalated the information war throughout early 1948. In February, shortly after a communist
coup in Czechoslovakia, the USSR built transmitters designed to block VOA
broadcasts to Russia. In mid-May, Soviet radio stations unexpectedly broadcast confidential notes exchanged by Soviet Foreign Minister Vyacheslav
Molotov and U.S. Ambassador Walter Bedell Smith. The incident received
wide attention in the American and European media and marked the beginning of the Kremlin's "peace offensive." VOA stations, caught without a copy
of Smith's text, were forced to rely for several hours on the Soviet version of
his remarks.[106] A week later, Secretary of State Marshall publicly denounced
"cynical" attempts by the Soviets to use peace negotiations as propaganda.[107]

Privately, Marshall released new guidelines on preparing materials designed to challenge anti-American propaganda. In a July 20 memorandum,
Marshall stressed the continued importance of reporting only "the truth
about United States life, policies, and actions." "We should bear in mind,"
Marshall declared, "that the people of third countries do not react with shock,
anger, or indignation to the charges made in anti-American propaganda as do
some Americans." Marshall added that foreign peoples cared about "the
righteousness of United States aims or the sincerity of the United States motives" only when doing so served their direct interests.[108]

This ambivalence, Marshall argued, made it necessary to correct "the false
or distorted stereotypes concerning the United States." Marshall explained that
Soviet propaganda had instilled perverse notions that Americans possessed unlimited wealth and that "monopoly capitalists" dominated the imperialistic
U.S. government. Foreigners believed "Americans are wholly materialistic, have
no culture worthy of mention, and judge everything by its value in dollars."
They also perceived U.S. citizens as libertines with little regard for family life.

Furthermore, Marshall concluded, "American democratic principles are loudly proclaimed as a cloak for undemocratic practices and for the purpose of concealing widespread racial and economic discriminations and extensive concentration of the political and economic power in the hands of the few."[109] Unwilling to allow the Soviets to continue denigrating the United States, U.S. information officials more aggressively publicized American virtues and values.

Voice of America played a vital role in this new strategy. On July 10, several American newspapers published a statement in which Allen berated the Hungarian government for arresting people who listened to VOA broadcasts. Although Hungarian officials denied Allen's charges, they reluctantly acknowledged the popularity of VOA.[110] On August 12, after Mrs. Oksana Kasenkina defected by jumping out the window of the Soviet consulate in New York, VOA beamed the news worldwide. "This is what we have been waiting for in our war of words," one VOA official declared, "This is something that can be easily understood by people all over the world."[111]

But the communists also scored victories in the escalating Cold War. On April 24, 1949, the Soviets began jamming VOA broadcasts to the USSR.[112] Foy D. Kohler, newly appointed chief of the State Department's international broadcasting division and current chargé d'affaires of the U.S. embassy in Moscow, urged his superiors to prepare for a long fight against Soviet jamming. "To do less," he asserted, "would be to abandon any real hope of reaching Soviet peoples, of impeding their complete perversion and delaying or preventing [the] catastrophe to which their despotic rulers would lead them. . . . [The] drive for air mastery is [a] vital part of [the] drive for world mastery."[113] By year's end, the Soviets' detonation of an atomic bomb and Mao Zedong's defeat of the Nationalist Chinese forces of Jiang Jieshi forced a major overhaul of the U.S. containment policy.[114]

The McCarthy Era Begins

The communist gains did not escape the attention of the Republicans. Following the unexpected loss of Thomas E. Dewey in the 1948 presidential election, the bipartisanship displayed in passage of Greek and Turkish aid, the European Recovery Program, and the North Atlantic Treaty Organization (NATO) began to unravel. As followers of Senator Taft gained ascendancy over the supporters of Senator Arthur H. Vandenberg (R-Mich.), the ailing chairman of the Foreign Relations Committee, they denounced Truman's labor policies and plan for national health insurance. In January 1950, Taft led a fiery discussion on American foreign policy in the Far East and called for the United States to defend the Nationalist Chinese stronghold Formosa (Taiwan). On January 22, after the perjury conviction of former State Department aide Alger Hiss, the debate became even more vitriolic. Republicans noted that Acheson, like Hiss, exemplified the internationalist elite synonymous with discredited New Deal liberalism. Following Taft's lead, they began demanding the resignation of the secretary of state.[115]

On January 1, 1950, Truman appointed Edward W. Barrett to lead the information program. Barrett, a former editorial director at *Newsweek*, had supervised the overseas branch of OWI.[116] Just three days later, the second annual report of the United States Advisory Commission on Information criticized both Congress and the executive branch for the financial shortages handicapping VOA.[117] Cognizant of these limitations, State Department leaders reevaluated the information program. In January 1950, a report by the OII cited recent references to VOA by the Soviet government. It estimated that VOA had received 66,746 audience letters from May 1 to December 15, 1949. In November 1949, after months of denials by communist officials, Soviet foreign minister Andrei Vishinsky acknowledged that the Soviet Union had been intentionally jamming VOA broadcasts. Cominform speakers repeatedly dismissed VOA as "The Voice of Goebbels" and "The Voice of Wall Street." Boris Lavrinov's new play, *The Voice of America* played before packed houses in Moscow. Designed to highlight the "true voice" of America, the play praised American communists, disparaged actual VOA scripts, and denigrated VOA commentator Alexander Nazaroff.[118]

OII officials viewed these responses as evidence of VOA's efficacy. They were especially encouraged by the extent of Soviet jamming, characterized by one analyst as "the most eloquent proof that the Soviet government is afraid of the voice of a free world getting through to the Russian people in their language and giving them truthful information about America."[119] On January 31, VOA director Kohler, conveyed these findings to the House Appropriations Committee. He asserted that, despite the success of Soviet jamming, increased production of radios in the USSR boded well for a larger VOA audience in the future. Kohler claimed that most Soviet citizens were willing to spend approximately $125 for a radio because few other luxury items were available. Furthermore, the Soviet government encouraged radio purchases as a means to propagate its own messages throughout the vast nation.[120]

While Kohler defended VOA, OII authorities formulated new guidelines for the creation of anti-Soviet materials. They drew tactical distinctions. Now willing to attack the Soviets more forcibly, the State Department approved the use of "grey" propaganda that extolled American life. Unlike the openly identified "white" propaganda, "grey" materials might or might not be directly attributed to the U.S. government. Although information officials continued to prohibit the use of covert "black" propaganda that used "innuendo" and "exaggeration" in pursuit of psychological warfare objectives, they directed U.S. diplomats to modify propaganda materials to meet local needs. To counter the revolutionary nationalism spreading throughout Southeast Asia, aides began revising pamphlets such as *Soviet Imperialism, Russia the Reactionary,* and *The Fate of the Intellectual in the Soviet Union.*[121] Although the Soviets did not yet jam VOA broadcasts to Eastern Europe, U.S. information leaders derided the Czech government's refusal to distribute *Amerika* and harassment of visitors to USIS libraries in Czechoslovakia.[122]

The challenges facing U.S. propagandists soon converged with rancorous partisan disputes about America's international role. On December 23, 1949, as conservative Republicans lambasted the Truman administration's China policies, the State Department ordered U.S. information officers to counter the "false impression" that Taiwan held strategic value to the United States. The memo stressed the futility of defending the Nationalist Chinese; 350 copies were circulated throughout VOA and USIS operations. Not surprisingly, subordinates of General Douglas MacArthur, commander of the U.S. occupation of Japan and a formidable critic of the Truman administration's Far East policies, leaked the directive to the Tokyo press, and the United Press (UP) wire service picked up the story. Enraged by the perceived betrayal of the Nationalists, Republicans alleged that subversives had infiltrated the State Department's China desk. Acheson's subsequent efforts to defend U.S. policies on Taiwan and the Far East faltered badly.[123]

These events inspired Senator Joseph McCarthy to attack the State Department and the U.S. information program. In a February 9, 1950 speech in Wheeling, West Virginia, McCarthy accused the State Department of harboring 205 communists. In the wake of the Hiss conviction and the arrest of British scientist Klaus Fuchs for passing atomic secrets to the Soviets, McCarthy's charges resonated with the American public. Although the numbers varied from 205 to 57 in subsequent speeches, McCarthy's allegations remained the same. On February 20, he brought his claims to the Senate floor and read the case files of 81 anonymous State Department employees whose loyalty he found suspect. Within hours, the senator drew national attention.[124]

McCarthy closely scrutinized the information program. Thirty employees of the OIE were among those he accused, and he characterized VOA as a "prime target" of the Soviet conspiracy to invade the U.S. government. The "typical Voice of America" employee, he declared, "is affiliated with Communist-front organizations and has communistic sympathies." He denounced a top VOA consultant as one of the three most "dangerous and active" communists in public service.[125] Although Truman and State Department spokesmen denied McCarthy's charges, Democratic leaders in the Senate directed Millard E. Tydings (D-Md.) to investigate his allegations.[126]

The Campaign of Truth

Partisan attacks and foreign policy setbacks inspired the Truman administration to launch its biggest propaganda offensive yet. On March 1, at the suggestion of Radio Corporation of America (RCA) chairman David Sarnoff, Truman instructed Acheson "to look into the problem of improving the Voice of America." The president's directive soon evolved into a government-wide exploration of all possible techniques for penetrating the Iron Curtain with American ideas.[127] On March 9, Truman approved NSC 59/1, a document calling for a dramatic expansion of the information program and VOA.[128]

William Benton, newly appointed Democratic senator from Connecticut, championed the new strategies being adopted by his former colleagues.[129] On March 22, Benton proposed that Congress approve "a Marshall Plan of ideas." Defending Acheson and the State Department against McCarthy's charges, Benton argued that the real threat to the United States resided in Soviet assaults on the American economy, political system, and character. He introduced a Senate resolution proposing dramatic increases in international broadcasting, film programs, and educational exchanges. He urged the State Department to cooperate with private American organizations in letter writing campaigns, donations, and speaking tours designed to counter communist propaganda. By making the "international propagation of the democratic creed . . . an instrument of supreme national policy," Benton concluded, the United States could win this "struggle for the minds and loyalties of mankind."[130]

In April, the United States Objectives and Programs for National Security, commonly referred to as NSC-68, gave the U.S. information program a huge boost. Prepared by Paul Nitze, head of the State Department's Policy Planning Staff, NSC-68 painted a stark contrast between the slavery imbued in the Soviet system and the freedom inherent in democracy. Nitze described "a basic conflict between the idea of freedom under a government of laws, and the idea of slavery under the grim oligarchy of the Kremlin." In an impassioned defense of democracy, he praised "the marvelous diversity, the deep tolerance, [and] the lawfulness of the free society." Unless the United States protected these values, Nitze warned, communists would destroy freedom throughout the world. He recommended exponential increases in defense spending and the American nuclear arsenal.[131]

Although Truman feared that the enormous defense budget Nitze advocated would jeopardize social programs, the president immediately adopted the rhetoric of NSC-68.[132] On April 20, in an address before the American Society of Newspaper Editors (ASNE), Truman called for the United States to mount a "Campaign of Truth" designed to expose "deceit, distortion, and lies" used by the Soviets. "All too often," he continued,

> the people who are subject to Communist propaganda do not know Americans, or citizens of the other free nations, as we really are.
> They do not know us as farmers or as workers. They do not know us as people having hopes and problems like their own. Our way of life is something strange to them. They do not even know what we mean when we say democracy.

Echoing calls for an improved information program, Truman proclaimed, America must "promote the cause of freedom against the propaganda of slavery."[133]

But U.S. information strategists faced enormous challenges in disseminating Truman's inspiring message. On April 15, the Communist Chinese government had outlawed listening to "reactionary" VOA broadcasts. On April 19, the Czech Foreign Ministry had publicly accused USIS officials of espionage and other anti-state activities. The Czech authorities then demanded the immediate closure of the USIS libraries in Prague and Bratislava and the removal of Joseph C. Kolarek, American press attaché for USIS affairs in Czechoslovakia. The following day, after USIS published an announcement offering free American books, magazines, and phonograph records,

5,000 Czechs packed the USIS library in Prague. Although State Department leaders denied that Kolarek and other USIS officials had engaged in improper activities, they agreed to close the libraries and remove Kolarek, but also demanded that the Czechs shut their consulate office in Chicago. In late April, U.S. diplomats in the Soviet Union complained of continuing Soviet restrictions on the distribution of *Amerika*.[134]

This volatile political climate inspired many anticommunist liberals to join the U.S. government's fight against communism. Arthur M. Schlesinger, Jr., Sidney Hook, Nicholas Nabokov, and many others played critical roles in "private" groups like the National Committee for a Free Europe (NCFE) and the Congress for Cultural Freedom (CCF). Subsidized by the Central Intelligence Agency (CIA), such organizations stemmed from close relationships among noncommunist liberals working at the highest echelons of American industry and government. Encompassing public officials, businesspeople, journalists, labor leaders, and others, this "state-private network" was instrumental in the U.S. information war against communism.[135]

There are several examples of the fluidity of this network. Nicholas Nabokov served on the VOA Russia desk and later became secretary general of CCF. After heading NCFE's Crusade for Freedom, Abbott Washburn was appointed deputy director of the USIA. C. D. Jackson, managing director of Time-Life Inc. and president of NCFE's Radio Free Europe, was Dwight Eisenhower's special advisor on psychological warfare.[136] Such connections help to explain the thematic similarities of U.S. propaganda throughout the Truman and Eisenhower eras.

The CIA placed support of the noncommunist left at the core of its political operations. For the next two decades, the CIA covertly subsidized dozens of counter-protests at international communist gatherings and organized festivals and conferences throughout the world. Wittingly or unwittingly, hundreds of noncommunist leftists aided the CIA's strategy for winning the cultural Cold War.[137]

As the CIA, NCFE, and CCF secretly collaborated, State Department officials sought additional allies in America's propaganda activities. In May 1950, Assistant Secretary of State Barrett went to Europe in order to discuss cooperation in information activities with British, French, and Italian policymakers. Barrett also pushed USIS officials to work more closely with labor groups and the information staffs at NATO and ECA.[138] Through these measures, American officials aimed to demonstrate the permanent U.S. interest in the eventual freedom of people living behind the Iron Curtain.[139]

VOA staff members offered differing opinions on the proper tone of American broadcasts to Eastern Europe. The head of the Russian desk, Alexander Barmine, who had served as a general in Soviet military intelligence until defecting in 1937, advocated an aggressive approach that stressed the liberation of the satellite nations. Barrett and Raymond Swing, the chief VOA English commentator, argued against encouraging revolution. They believed the vehemently anticommunist tone of VOA rhetoric was alienating some listeners. They thought that VOA should inspire nationalism as well as resistance to collectivization and production quotas.[140]

But even this cautious strategy gave some Eastern Europeans false hopes. On May 29, officials at the International Refugee Organization claimed approximately 7,000 people a month fled Iron Curtain nations. Directly inspired by the promises of freedom and opportunity broadcast by VOA, many refugees arrived expecting American assistance. After discovering that the United States helped only a few communist refugees, the relief workers reported, "hundreds of disillusioned and bitter persons" drifted back to the communist countries.[141]

Despite such reports, NCFE launched Radio Free Europe (RFE), a "private" radio network featuring Eastern European refugees and émigrés who advocated popular resistance to communist rule. Frank Altschul, chair of NCFE's radio and press division characterized RFE as "a channel over which American citizens, not subject to the restrictions which hamper a government agency, could say things . . . which Voice of America, as an agency of government, was not in the position to say." In July 1950, RFE used a tiny 7.5-kilowatt transmitter in Lampertheim, West Germany, to broadcast its first program. By 1953, the network aired 218 hours of daily programming and employed more than 1,700 people. A chain of powerful transmitters based in Portugal and West Germany carried output from RFE's Munich headquarters to Czechoslovakia, Poland, Hungary, Bulgaria, and Romania.[142]

To maintain the illusion of RFE's independent status, NCFE organized the Crusade for Freedom, a series of rallies and fundraisers held across the United States beginning in September 1950. Chaired by General Lucius Clay, former commissioner of the U.S. occupation of Germany, the Crusade urged Americans to donate "Truth dollars" for RFE. Spectators listened to a Freedom Bell and signed Freedom Scrolls. Within two years, the Crusade had collected $3.5 million and 25 million names from supporters of "the fight against communism." In reality, the donations did not even cover the costs of the Crusade and the U.S. government covertly financed RFE. Trying to circumvent congressional constraints on their programming and the use of émigrés, VOA officials secretly collaborated with RFE.[143] The vicissitudes of domestic politics and the potential ramifications of undermining Kremlin control of Eastern Europe necessitated delicate compromises in the ideological battle against communism.

The Korean War and U.S. Propaganda

On June 25, 1950, North Korea's invasion of South Korea raised the stakes in the propaganda war. Two days later, the United Nations Security Council voted to "repel the armed attack and to restore international peace and security to the area." Throughout the summer, as an American-led UN force struggled to hold onto the Korean peninsula, the Soviet media released a torrent of vicious propaganda accusing the United States of starting the war and advocating biological warfare in Asia. Radio Moscow targeted different nations simultaneously, producing a total of 502 hours a week of programming. With only 203 hours of comparable weekly output, VOA broadcasters strained to challenge outrageous Soviet charges.[144]

The outbreak of war in Asia generated unprecedented levels of support for the U.S. information program. In early July, Benton, Secretary of Defense George C. Marshall, NATO Commander Dwight D. Eisenhower, Acheson, Barrett and other prominent political figures pressed the Senate Foreign Relations Committee to increase funding for the U.S. information program. The fighting in Korea, Benton insisted, demonstrated the tragic failure of the United States "to project the idea of democracy to the world." Not even the half billion dollars spent on postwar economic aid to Korea had counteracted insidious communist propaganda. The 50,000-watt radio station in Pyongyang enabled the North Koreans to drown broadcasts heralding American generosity with accusations of "Yankee imperialism" and warmongering. A successful American propaganda strategy, Benton asserted, would highlight the "moral force" of democratic capitalism, not its material advantages.[145]

Walter White, executive secretary of the National Association for the Advancement of Colored People (NAACP), offered a more cautious endorsement of the information program. Recent trips to Europe had convinced White of the "tragic lack of information regarding the functioning of American democracy and an even more tragic distortion of the truth about the United States." Despite the phenomenal success of U.S. exports, White continued, attempts

to promote "the most valuable product of America—a free society and a democratic way of life" were faltering internationally. When they read about "the
color line in the Nation's capital, filibustering in the United States Senate, race
riots and lynchings, job and educational discrimination against dark-skinned
Americans," the world's people of color doubted the sincerity of American
promises of freedom. Without simultaneous congressional approval of civil
rights legislation, White concluded, American information experts would continue to sell an inherently flawed product.[146] Although they ignored White's
criticisms of some glaring weaknesses in the U.S. propaganda offensive, Congress approved a $79.1 million appropriation for information activities, a sum
more than twice the previous year's amount.[147]

This augmented budget had an immediate impact on U.S. information
activities. By the early 1950s, the United States Information and Educational
Exchange Program (USIE) targeted ninety-three countries, distributed more
than 60 million pamphlets, and orchestrated VOA broadcasts in forty-five
languages.[148] Extolling film's unique ability to inform, USIE's International
Motion Picture Division (IMP) selected, acquired, produced, and distributed
films shown in eighty-five nations. Often collaborating with foreign governments and private organizations, IMP tailored films for specific countries and
translated them into local languages. IMP also supplied projection equipment, mobile units, and informational materials. By 1951, USIE claimed that
400 million people annually watched its films. These motion pictures featured
"Americans at home, at work, and at play" and demonstrated "the story of
democracy in action, the perils of communism, and the genuine concern of
the citizens of the United States for the freedom and welfare of others."
Through highlighting American standards of living and U.S. achievements in
science, technology, and industry, IMP aimed to convince foreigners of their
"own potentialities as individuals and nations."[149] Such claims of the universality of the American experience and the malleability of other countries became key themes in U.S. propaganda during the 1950s.[150]

The Gloves Come Off

The Korean War inspired major changes in U.S. security policy. In mid-
September, Truman approved a bold plan to send UN troops across the
38th parallel into North Korea. He also instructed his cabinet to implement
NSC-68. With a fourfold increase in defense expenditures, atomic capabilities,

and military aid, the United States launched a full-scale, global assault on communism.[151]

Eager to refute Soviet allegations of U.S. imperialism and warmongering, USIE immediately adopted a more stridently anticommunist tone.[152] While professing American support for Soviet populace, USIE harshly condemned Stalinism. Cognizant of mass discontent in the USSR, U.S. propagandists focused on the Soviet citizens most likely to abhor communism including intellectuals, industrial workers, demobilized soldiers, and agricultural laborers. USIS materials directed at Soviet youth capitalized on their interest in American consumer products and culture.[153]

In late November, after 300,000 Communist Chinese troops crossed into North Korea and thwarted the UN advance toward the Yalu River, fears of a global war skyrocketed. On December 12, Walworth Barbour, U.S. chargé in the Soviet Union, warned that the average Soviet citizen was increasingly afraid of military conflict, but did not know whom to blame for the deteriorating international situation. Barbour urged U.S. information experts to emphasize that "the West does not want war" and that events in Korea were "the direct and inevitable result of Kremlin expansionist policy."[154]

U.S. information leaders relished the opportunity to engage in psychological warfare. "At last the gloves are off," Barrett proclaimed on December 19, "we are engaged in a propaganda fight against an implacable foe—international communism and its instigators."[155] Barrett wanted the information campaign to expose the contradictions between Soviet society and ideology. In assessing the "principal psychological vulnerabilities" of the Soviet government, U.S. information experts sought to capitalize on the coercion and inequity imbued in the communist system. Travel restrictions, forced labor, collectivization, and police intimidation were evidence of communism's failure to improve the lives of the Soviet people. Because Soviet women toiled in back-breaking, unhealthy jobs, U.S. information strategists could dismiss Soviet claims of gender equality. Aware that low wages and high prices compelled most Soviet women to work, State Department analysts recommended against "suggesting that the woman's place is in the home." Instead, they advised USIE officials to assail the communist regime for exploiting Soviet women.[156]

While USIE intensified its rhetorical attacks on communism, the Truman administration became increasingly dismayed by the lack of coordination among U.S. propagandists. In addition to the State Department, the CIA, the Pentagon, the Economic Cooperation Administration, and the Technical Cooperation Administration were also conducting information activities abroad.

Turf wars, muddied lines of authority, and repetition undermined their efforts. On April 4, 1951, in an attempt to impose order on this chaos, Truman established the Psychological Strategy Board (PSB), an autonomous body charged with coordinating all government-affiliated psychological operations worldwide. Directed by Gordon Gray, president of the University of North Carolina and a former secretary of the army, the PSB was comprised of representatives from the State Department, Defense Department, and CIA.[157] Stalwart believers in the power of psychological warfare to win the Cold War, the PSB pledged to roll back Soviet power, inspire revolutions behind the Iron Curtain, and generate global support for U.S. policies. Over the next two years, though the PSB produced an avalanche of studies, it clashed frequently with U.S. foreign policy experts and ultimately achieved few of its grandiose goals.[158]

Another Reorganization

While the PSB foundered, the State Department reorganized its information activities yet again. In January 1952, in response to congressional complaints about the management of the USIE, the State Department established a semi-autonomous propaganda agency under the direction of one person. Extolling the "increased importance" of political warfare, Acheson announced the creation of the United States International Information Administration (IIA). Headed by Dr. Wilson Compton, former president of Washington State College, the IIA possessed authority over all U.S. radio, press, film, and exchange programs abroad. Required to report only to the secretary of state, Compton gained full responsibility for all information and cultural activities. Under the new arrangement, Assistant Secretary of State for Public Affairs Barrett concentrated on explaining U.S. foreign policy to the American public.[159] On February 4, Barrett warned of the dilemma posed by increased congressional and media scrutiny of IIA activities. To an increasing extent, USIE leaders were using materials that were not officially linked to the U.S. government. But the use of unidentified propaganda complicated the appropriations process. Barrett explained that

> Chowderheads continually come back from abroad and announce
> that our program is ineffective because they have not seen USIE
> clearly identified with some of the most effective free-world propa-
> ganda in the areas they visited. Some of them have even contrasted

our open efforts unfavorably with local-group efforts which we actually inspired and engineered.

To solve this problem without negating the propaganda value of semicovert activities, Barrett suggested telling Congress about the 400 indigenous groups cooperating with USIS without specifically identifying the local organizations.[160]

The maneuver seemed to appease conservatives. On June 1, Senator Pat McCarran (D-Neb.), the fiercely anticommunist chairman of the Senate Subcommittee on Appropriations, praised U.S. information tactics and strategy. In McCarran's detailed report, IIA officials explained their publications, films, radio broadcasts, information centers, and educational exchanges. They also detailed their efforts to reach international workers and audiences in India, Iran, Vietnam, and the Philippines.[161]

The "Hate America" Campaign

In the same period, U.S. information experts grappled with the Soviet "Hate America" campaign. With negotiations for an armistice in Korea at a standstill, communist propagandists accused the United States of using biological warfare and of torturing prisoners of war. On March 20, *Pravda* reported that U.S. "billionaires and millionaires" were using "sixteen types of bacteriological weapons" as a demonstration of "the American way of life and its ideals."[162]

Although the violent tone of Soviet attacks disturbed members of the Truman administration, they responded cautiously. On June 27, George F. Kennan, the U.S. Ambassador in Moscow, recommended against making a formal complaint to the Soviet government. Instead, Kennan advocated an indirect strategy using VOA and official statements to

ridicule Soviet charges by citing and highlighting their obvious absurdities and exaggerations, such as that we have buried alive 100,000 people in Korea, murdered 300,000 women and children, that 2,000,000 children in the United States sleep on the subway gratings, that the United States has 14,000,000 unemployed, etc.[163]

Acheson also advised against a direct confrontation with the Soviet regime. Instead, he suggested that American diplomats tell communist intellectuals about the "purposeful and brutally efficient" techniques that communist propagandists used to "warp" mental attitudes.[164]

Throughout the "Hate America" campaign, Soviet efforts to ban IIA materials escalated. On July 15, after two years of distribution difficulties, the State Department suspended publication of *Amerika*. The Soviets had progressively restricted access to the magazine until its dwindling readership no longer justified printing expenses. In retaliation, the U.S. demanded the suspension of Soviet embassy publications in America. Blaming the State Department's actions on "bankruptcy," the Soviet media denied that *Amerika* ever enjoyed wide popularity and that second-hand copies of the magazine flooded the black market.[165]

With fewer means of reaching the Soviet audience available, the State Department searched for the most effective propaganda messages. In early 1952, the IIA sent questionnaires to the 157 U.S. posts abroad asking the diplomats to evaluate "key words in American and Free World Propaganda." When the results were compiled in September 1952, the survey revealed that while no propaganda terms held universal appeal, "independence, freedom, education, prosperity, security, and national culture" resonated in most countries. On the other hand, the concepts of "mutual assistance, world friendship, neighborliness, brotherhood, democratic unity, and harmony" had limited propaganda value. The survey listed the concepts of slavery and communist imperialism as the most valuable phrases for discrediting the Soviet Union.[166]

The fact that U.S. officials were still searching for the proper words seven years after World War II speaks volumes about the information program in the Truman era. Unified in their belief in American exceptionalism and antipathy toward communism, Democrats and Republicans realized the vital role that propaganda could play in fostering democratic capitalism abroad. But they also had profound differences on the role of the state and the meaning of "American" political culture. In order to gain legislative and financial backing, supporters of U.S. information activities made difficult choices about *who* was qualified to speak for America and *what* they were allowed to say. Besieged by a vocal anti-modernist and anti-intellectual minority, U.S. information leaders jettisoned materials and personnel associated with the radical left. As Truman left office in 1952, the information program remained beset by bureaucratic infighting, congressional skepticism, and a lack of coherence.

Nonetheless, psychological warfare had emerged as a legitimate and important element of U.S. foreign policy. Truman and his advisors recognized that military and financial assistance provided to men and women who misunderstood the United States could not ensure world peace or create support for liberal capitalism. To counter the allure of communism, the United States put forth a vision of democratic freedoms.

Ironically, the crusade to extol democracy resorted to undemocratic means. The nativist restrictions on information personnel contradicted America's heritage of welcoming immigrants. The collaboration between the public and private sectors in creating and promoting information materials eventually limited freedom of expression by journalists, professors, and researchers receiving funding from the federal government. Artists found their creative endeavors subject to censorship before the State Department would permit foreign audiences to view, read, or hear them. Those with leftist political beliefs soon discovered that American "democracy" did not accord them freedom of association or speech.

Although President Eisenhower inherited an information program in disarray, he and Secretary of State John Foster Dulles considered propaganda an indispensable element of U.S. diplomacy. Through the creation of the USIA, the Eisenhower administration granted information activities new levels of prestige and visibility. As the ideological battle between communism and capitalism filtered into the developing world, U.S. policymakers intensified their efforts to explain why the United States was a nation worthy of defense, emulation, and victory in the Cold War.

CHAPTER TWO

The Eisenhower Years

DURING THE 1950S, President Dwight D. Eisenhower and his secretary of state John Foster Dulles raised the stakes in the Cold War. Marshaling their considerable foreign policy expertise, they implemented a "New Look" in which the United States dramatically expanded its nuclear arsenal, confronted revolutionary nationalism in the developing world, and entered new alliances with noncommunist nations. Although eager to exploit the political uncertainty behind the Iron Curtain following the death of Joseph Stalin, Eisenhower and his aides realized that "liberating" Eastern Europe could trigger a nuclear strike, exacerbate refugee crises, or antagonize Western allies.

Determined to defeat communism without provoking a third world war, U.S. officials used international information campaigns, trade fairs, and cultural exchanges as safer and less expensive means of challenging the Soviets and preserving America's international prestige.[1] At home and abroad, they defined the United States as a nation of affluence, progress, and personal fulfillment.[2] But the administration's strong support for propaganda activities did not stop the political machinations, fiscal uncertainties, and bureaucratic impediments that often undermined U.S. information programs. Officials at the U.S. Information Agency (USIA) balanced the desire to shape international attitudes toward the United States and the imperative of responding to Soviet actions and intense anti-Americanism. While the 1959 American National Exhibition in Moscow marked a stunning triumph for U.S. information experts, the overall legacy of the postwar propaganda programs was decidedly mixed.

Eisenhower and Psychological Warfare

An advocate of psychological warfare throughout his military career, Eisenhower believed that effective propaganda could help ensure world peace and promote democracy. He accorded information activities—both overt and covert—the same stature as military, economic, and diplomatic operations. He became the only president ever to appoint a propaganda advisor to his cabinet.[3]

Charles Douglas ("C. D.") Jackson was the perfect designee. A protégé of Henry Luce at Time-Life, Inc., Jackson had served as deputy director of psychological warfare for the Allied forces in the Mediterranean during World War II. Throughout the war, he convinced Eisenhower of the value of propaganda. Following V-E Day, Jackson returned to *Time*, but grew exasperated by what he saw as a decrepit American response to Soviet aggression. In 1951, he left the magazine to become president of the CIA-funded National Committee for a Free Europe. In this capacity, he worked closely with CIA leaders operating Radio Free Europe.[4]

In December 1952, Jackson jumped at the chance to become Eisenhower's special assistant for psychological warfare. Jackson decried the lack of coordination among information experts at the Psychological Strategy Board (PSB), the CIA, the State Department, the Army, and the Air Force. "This fratricidal warfare," Jackson explained to Eisenhower, stemmed from "the realization that the Government of the U.S. has neither policy nor plan for conducting the Cold War." In January 1953, Jackson easily persuaded the president to create the Committee on International Information Activities. Chaired by investment banker William H. Jackson, the committee began an exhaustive study of the U.S. propaganda apparatus and its relation to larger foreign policy goals.[5]

McCarthy Attacks VOA

Acting in his new capacity as chairman of the Senate Committee on Government Operations, Senator Joseph McCarthy (R-Wis.) was also scrutinizing the U.S. information establishment. Throughout February and March 1953, McCarthy and his aides, Roy M. Cohn and David Schine, took aim at VOA's staff of 10,000 and $88 million budget. Relying almost exclusively on the testimony of disgruntled employees and informants, they accused VOA leaders of mismanagement and subversion.[6]

McCarthy's inquiry focused on a series of costly engineering errors. Initially, testimony centered on the Baker East and Baker West transmitters in North Carolina and Washington state. Lewis J. McKesson, a former radio VOA engineer, estimated that VOA had wasted approximately $18 million dollars on the projects. Despite the warnings of several engineers, McKesson contended, VOA leaders had placed the transmitters in the path of magnetic interference. With McCarthy's prodding, McKesson hinted that the mistake stemmed from communist-inspired sabotage.[7]

Determined to calm public fears about subversion and unwilling to alienate the GOP's right wing, the Eisenhower administration assisted the senator's inquisition.[8] On February 17, Dulles suspended the Baker projects. He fired chief VOA engineer George Herrick and accepted the resignation of International Information Administration (IIA) director Dr. Wilson Compton. Many VOA officials alleged that Dulles instigated the dismissals in order to purge the State Department of Democrats. Dulles even considered disbanding VOA. But C. D. Jackson convinced Dulles of the "tremendous and almost entirely unfavorable" repercussions of doing so.[9] Nonetheless, on February 19, Dulles ordered undersecretary of state for administration and operation Donald B. Lourie "to find a basis of cooperation with McCarthy" in order to avoid being blamed for "the sloppiness and inefficiency" of the Truman era.[10]

Meanwhile, McCarthy enjoyed the attention the hearings were generating and continued his inquiry. On February 18, he called leftist writer Howard Fast to testify. After disclosing that the Office of War Information had paid Fast for 4,000 copies of his *Citizen Tom Paine*, Cohn repeatedly asked Fast if he was a Communist. Fast invoked the Fifth Amendment each time. After Fast admitted that he did not know if IIA libraries carried his books, Karl Mundt (R-S.D.) introduced recent State Department guidelines for selecting authors. Stressing the utility of a writer's work, not his or her political affiliation, the policy read:

> The reputation of an author affects the active utility of the material.
> If he is widely and favorably known abroad as a champion of democratic causes, his credibility and utility may be enhanced. Similarly,
> if—like Howard Fast—he is known as a Soviet-endorsed author,
> materials favorable to the United States in some of his works may
> thereby be given a special credibility among selected key audiences.

Incited by the description of Fast as "a Soviet-endorsed author," the senators seized on the directive as evidence of communist bias in the State Department.[11]

Dulles immediately responded to the furor. On February 19, he ordered his subordinates to cooperate with McCarthy's investigation of their security files. More important, he rescinded the controversial authors directive, proclaiming, "No materials by any Communists, fellow-travelers, et cetera will be used under any circumstances by IIA media or missions." Information Guide 272, derisively called the "et cetera" policy, prohibited even direct quotations of Soviet officials. When United States Information Service (USIS) officials discovered that no comprehensive list of prohibited authors existed, they frantically contacted the FBI, CIA, and House Un-American Activities Committee for names. A few panicked USIS officials burned books.[12] After VOA chief Alfred H. Morton claimed the ban on communist sources would undermine anti-Soviet propaganda, Dulles rewarded him with a day-long suspension and a reprimand for poor judgment.[13]

McCarthy received more direct assistance from a group of VOA employees. Calling themselves the "Pro-American Underground" or "Loyal Underground," members of the group accused their colleagues and fed information to the investigators. The situation shattered staff morale. Edwin J. Kretzmann, then the VOA Policy Advisor, later recalled:

> Within the Voice, factions formed, secret meetings were held and
> everyone looked upon everyone else with suspicion and distrust.
> Any off-the-cuff remark or innocent wisecrack could be transmitted
> to the ubiquitous and diligent [Roy] Cohn whose mind was quite
> capable of twisting the context to make . . . something verging on
> subversion out of any casual comment.[14]

Desperate to avoid being misquoted, some VOA employees brought tape recorders to meetings. Others flocked to the McCarthy team hoping to advance their anticommunist views, to gain promotions, or to avenge personal slights.[15]

McCarthy relished exposing division in the VOA ranks. On February 20, he called Virgil H. Fulling, the chief of the VOA Latin American news service. Fulling accused his superiors of "watering down" the anticommunist tone of propaganda materials prepared for South America. Later that day, Harold Berman, Donald Taylor, and Robert B. Goldman inveighed against Fulling's "fantastic" allegations and emphasized their long record of fighting communism.[16]

The "et cetera policy" drew the ire of virtually every USIS post world-wide. On February 24, Kretzmann received dozens of telegrams listing the programs and materials that the new guidelines would destroy or enfeeble. John M. Vebber, the chief of VOA commentaries and features, explained that the directive would eviscerate U.S. propaganda on Soviet labor, economics, trade, culture, agriculture, and religion. "Has anyone thought what a program of 100 percent Americana of irreproachable nature would sound like?" he asked. German language expert John Albert warned of the order's ramifications upon listeners in the Soviet bloc. The United States, Albert contended, would no longer be able to advocate the American way of life or "to keep up the courage and spirit of the captive people." North European branch chief Harry W. Idelnors added, "Not even the Holy Writ himself has found a way to combat the Devil without referring to him."[17]

Throughout the VOA hearings, Eisenhower and Dulles searched for ways to counter the formidable communist propaganda apparatus.[18] The Soviets were spending approximately $1.5 billion for propaganda efforts versus the IIA budget of $88 million. Even after subtracting the $17 million a year the Soviets spent on jamming VOA broadcasts, State Department analysts called the disparate figures "staggering."[19] Unwilling to expand the information budget exponentially and dismayed by the limitations of the Psychological Strategy Board, Dulles and Eisenhower decided to separate the IIA from the State Department. A federal agency devoted to propaganda, they believed, could produce the most effective propaganda program in the world. On February 23, they appointed Dr. Robert L. Johnson, the president of Temple University and co-founder of Time-Life, Inc., to shepherd the IIA through the reorganization.[20]

As Johnson took office in early March, Dulles suddenly rescinded the "et cetera policy." Unable to define precisely what denoted communist or fellow traveler status and downright baffled by the "et cetera" restriction, USIS librarians welcomed Dulles's move. But, in the absence of new guidelines, no one really knew which books remained inappropriate.[21]

McCarthy was furious. On March 3, he tore into Reed Harris, the deputy administrator of the IIA. During hours of televised testimony, Mc-Carthy grilled Harris about his activities at Columbia University twenty years earlier. Harris admitted that he had received a suspension for protesting the dismissal of a Marxist professor. He acknowledged writing *King Football*, a 1932 book attacking college sports, marriage, and conformity. But Harris fought back. Angered at the implication that one could not mature beyond youthful opinions, Harris stressed his long record of public service and his clearance by six different government security boards.[22]

McCarthy was relentless. Pointing to Harris's closure of the VOA Hebrew language desk, McCarthy accused Harris of abetting Soviet anti-Semitism. Harris cited Israeli audience surveys revealing a preference for English broadcasts. News about Soviet attacks on Jews, he contended, was reaching Israel "very, very effectively." Harris then attacked McCarthy for allowing Gerald F. P. Dooher and Dr. Sidney Glazer to testify in the first place. The VOA Hebrew desk, Harris explained, had been "their baby." McCarthy's "one-sided" inquiry, Harris railed, mocked VOA in front of the entire world.[23]

Exploiting the Death of Stalin

But the world's attention was focused on the Soviet Union. As news of Joseph Stalin's declining health filtered out of the USSR, Eisenhower and his security advisors contemplated the future of the Soviet bloc and Communist politics. They recognized a unique opportunity to advance peace and freedom. But, ever mindful of the raging Cold War, they also hoped that a succession crisis would propel the Soviet state into disarray. If the fragile coalition of Vyacheslav Molotov, Lavrentii Beria, and Georgii Malenkov collapsed, the United States could exploit the ensuing instability behind the Iron Curtain.[24]

C. D. Jackson could barely contain his excitement. Writing to NSC Director Robert Culter on March 4, he celebrated "the first really great propaganda opportunity" presented to the new administration and underscored the importance of a prompt American response. Discounting the possibility of such tactics sparking World War III, Jackson advocated a strategy to "advance the real disintegration of the Soviet Empire."[25]

Dulles recommended a more cautious strategy. After Stalin's death on March 5, Dulles ordered his subordinates to "sow doubt, confusion, [and] uncertainty about [the] new regime." But, cognizant that American attempts to foster dissension in the satellite nations could precipitate a general war, Dulles ordered U.S. officials "to restrain and moderate any excessive hopes of immediate Soviet collapse and liberation."[26] Prohibited from inciting unrest in the Soviet bloc, VOA commentators carefully crafted their broadcasts. They publicized Eisenhower's mild expression of sympathy for the Soviet people, but also derided Stalin as "an archtyrant" who presided over the murder and enslavement of millions. They warned that the selection of Malenkov as Stalin's successor might occasion political chaos.[27]

USIS Libraries Investigated

Linguistic gymnastics were also evident in Dulles's continued attempts to satisfy McCarthy. On March 17, he approved new guidelines for the selection of authors. Acknowledging the utility of exposing communist fallacies, he allowed general reference to Marxist doctrines. Wishing to avoid "building up Soviet personalities," Dulles proscribed identification of specific communists in most situations. He also ordered an outright prohibition of the work of communist authors in USIS libraries and information centers.[28] Dulles's revised instructions dropped the "et cetera" clause, but retained the spirit of the original directive. The order required USIS librarians to enforce a vague blacklist of authors. Throughout the VOA hearings, neither Dulles nor IIA administrator Robert Johnson defended those employees accused of subversion.[29]

But McCarthy now had his sights on alleged communist infiltration of the 150 USIS libraries and information centers. Building his case on the accusations of ex-communist informants Louis Budenz, Freda Utley, and Harvey Matusow, McCarthy claimed the USIS promoted the works of seventy-five communists. He subpoenaed several noted American writers including Langston Hughes, Dashiell Hammett, Philip Foner, and Herbert Aptheker. Although many professed communist sympathies, none of the writers knew why the USIS carried his or her books in overseas libraries. On March 27, Utley claimed that the bookshelves of the USIS libraries in Germany were "loaded up with what you might call anti-anti-Communist material." Recognizing an opportunity to salvage his waning crusade, McCarthy dispatched Cohn and Schine to investigate USIS information centers in Europe.[30]

Once again, the Eisenhower administration aided the senator. Dulles, like McCarthy, believed communist writings had no place in libraries designed to highlight "American objectives, values, [and] the nature of American institutions and life."[31] On April 2, Dulles instructed officials at the U.S. embassy in France to provide Cohn and Schine any documents they desired with the exception of personnel security files.[32] Twelve days later, in a meeting with IIA leaders Robert Johnson and Martin Merson, C. D. Jackson refused to ask the president to defend the information program. No matter how strongly Ike advocated psychological warfare or disliked McCarthy, Jackson explained, Eisenhower would not "offend anyone in Congress."[33]

Imbued with none of the president's reticence, Cohn and Schine managed to offend almost everyone they encountered. Despite discovering fewer than one hundred communist or subversive works among the six million volumes, Cohn and Schine hit Europe like a tornado. In Munich, Cohn requested two separate hotel rooms, tactlessly adding, "We don't work for the State Department." In Paris, after condemning wasteful government spending, the pair indulged in a shopping spree and skipped out on their hotel bill. Although mortified officials at the U.S. embassy paid the tab, the European press flayed the reckless duo. When asked to assess the visit, General Lauris Norstad, the new NATO commander, complained, "It was so bad it can't possibly be exaggerated."[34]

The Birth of the USIA

In June 1953, a sweeping reorganization offered U.S. information experts a much-needed opportunity to recover from McCarthy's assaults and to reevaluate their programs. On June 1, Eisenhower created the United States Information Agency (USIA) as an independent propaganda organization. The plan consolidated all information operations from the State Department, the Technical Cooperation Administration, the U.S. occupation forces, and the Mutual Security Agency. Somehow spared McCarthy's wrath, the Fulbright exchange program remained in the State Department. Information experts immediately noted the limitations of USIA. The secretary of state retained "exclusive responsibility . . . for the control of the content . . . of United States official positions on important issues and current developments." Such constraints did not bode well for ending the bureaucratic infighting that had plagued U.S. propaganda programs.[35]

Inducing someone to lead the USIA was not easy. Eisenhower first approached General Electric chairman Philip Reed, who told C. D. Jackson, "No one in his right mind would take the job." D'Arcy Brophey of the Heritage Foundation also rejected the offer. Finally, the president appointed Theodore C. Streibert, one of the founders of the Mutual Broadcasting Service and a former VOA consultant.[36]

Like the formation of the USIA, the June 30 report of the Jackson Committee (formally known as the President's Committee on International

Information Activities) greatly affected U.S. propaganda strategy. Convened in January 1953, the group gathered testimony from more than 250 witnesses and examined all aspects of covert and overt information policy. Stressing the vital role of propaganda in the Cold War, the committee asserted that "psychological activity is not a field of endeavor separable from the main body of diplomatic, economic, and military measures by which the United States seeks to achieve its national objectives."[37]

The committee stressed America's distinct advantages in the ideological Cold War. Americans shared beliefs and basic values including religious faith, individual and national freedom, peace, and the right to property ownership. The United States reinforced these commonalties with its military strength, economic system, technology, and productive capacity. But, the committee argued, the information program "should speak of the deeper spiritual values uniting this nation with the rest of the world."[38] A private memo from the committee's executive secretary, Abbott Washburn (who soon became deputy director of USIA) explicitly defined these ideals as

> Belief in God.
> Belief in the right to ownership of property and better living for each individual.
> Belief that the family is sacred.
> Belief in a better chance for our children (food, health, schooling, work of their choice).
> Belief in a peaceful world—in the common humanity of all men, negotiating and compromising their differences in the United Nations.

If U.S. propagandists presented these values as "basically American," Washburn averred, "We will begin to register a far more favorable image abroad and eventually substitute a very different picture for the present American stereotype of the vulgar Babbitt without culture or deep feeling"[39] (Figure 3).

A Rocky Start

But the USIA faced an uphill battle in achieving these lofty goals. Following a 36 percent reduction in operating funds from fiscal 1953, the USIA staff fell from 12,877 to 9,281. USIS posts declined from 255 in eighty-five countries to

Figure 3. Although dogged by fluctuating budgets, allegations of subversion, and bureaucratic obstacles, officials at the United States Information Agency remained dedicated to their mission of informing foreign peoples about U.S. policies and American society. National Archives.

217 in seventy-six countries.[40] Although Streibert dedicated himself to cooperating with other government agencies, he initially received a second-class administrative status. On the recommendation of the Jackson committee, Eisenhower abolished the Psychological Strategy Board (PSB), created an Operations Coordinating Board (OCB) to organize security affairs, and left covert operations under the jurisdiction of the CIA. USIA did not obtain membership in either the NSC or OCB until 1955, and Eisenhower did not include the USIA director in cabinet meetings until 1956.[41]

    With the initial status of USIA unclear, Agency staffers experienced great frustration in their efforts to work within the federal bureaucracy. In a 1987 interview, Henry Loomis, who held several high-ranking posts within USIA including director of the Office of Intelligence and Research, director of

Voice of America, and deputy director of USIA, vividly describes his reaction to discovering that the agency had no access to NSC documents:

> I asked Bobby Cutler [Eisenhower's national security advisor] "What the hell goes on here? How can you possibly expect the Information Agency to know what your policy is if it can't get the papers?" Cutler said, "Oh, they're a bunch of commies, you can't trust them." I said, "The hell they are, and if they are, go ahead and fire them, but at least put somebody in there that will do it. And besides, they're not commies."[42]

Loomis and Cutler made a deal in which Loomis personally, not the agency, received NSC papers. "I had to have a whole special safe and a special secretary," Loomis recalls, "and people had to come there to read them." After three or four months, Loomis persuaded Cutler to turn the documents over to the USIA Policy Office, "where it belonged."[43]

While USIA leaders navigated interagency turf wars, Eisenhower finally broke his silence about McCarthy. The president's equivocation had drawn wide criticism. Major journalists including Richard Rovere and Walter Lippmann demanded that the president confront the senator. On May 9, writing on behalf of several of Ike's supporters, Harry A. Bullis warned, "It is a fallacy to assume that McCarthy will kill himself." On June 14, while delivering the Dartmouth College commencement address, Eisenhower enjoined the students not to "join the book burners." Privately, he told Dulles his remarks were a general defense of freedom of thought, not a repudiation of McCarthy's attack on the IIA. He then ordered Dulles to retain the USIS prohibition on books "persuasive of communism."[44]

On June 22, Robert Johnson protested the president's action. In a memo to Dulles, Johnson decried "the mounting loss of the hard-won prestige and credibility of the Information Centers, known as the exemplification of American democracy on foreign soil." Censorship had alienated "the literate, highly cultured and influential minority in most foreign countries." In Johnson's opinion, only those books highlighting communist propaganda, pornography, or sensationalism should be banned.[45] On July 8, Dulles allowed Johnson to clarify IIA book guidelines. After a powerful denunciation of book burning, Johnson announced that the works of eight communists and the so-called "Fifth-Amendment" communists would be returned to the USIS library shelves.[46]

The Ambiguities of Liberation

At the same time, the Soviet leadership faced grave problems. In early June, enraged by new monetary reforms, Czechs began protesting. Then, on June 16, riots erupted among workers in East Berlin. By June 21, more than 500,000 East Germans had joined protests in more than 560 towns and cities. Through a combination of brutal suppression, mass arrests, and the imposition of martial law in 167 out of 217 districts, Soviet troops and communist officials quashed the uprisings.[47] Shortly thereafter, Beria's attempt to seize control of the Kremlin ended in his arrest and dismissal. The instability persuaded the warring factions in Korea to sign a peace agreement on July 26.[48]

While these dramatic events unfolded, the Eisenhower administration undertook a sweeping review of U.S. security policies. On September 30, after weeks of deliberation, the NSC Planning Board adopted a policy of "peaceful coexistence," moving away from attempts to force the disintegration of the Soviet empire. Although the East German uprisings indicated strong resistance to communist rule, the panel ruled unanimously that the "detachment of any major European satellite from the Soviet bloc does not now appear feasible except by Soviet acquiescence or by war." Following the first Soviet test of a hydrogen bomb on August 12, the potential catastrophe of a direct military confrontation was obvious even to the most hawkish advisor.[49]

Nonetheless, the question of what roles propaganda could play in moderating Soviet behavior remained unresolved. On October 22, the NSC carefully phrased the USIA mission statement. The agency would explain and interpret U.S. policies and culture to foreign nations. Dulles, however, warned against offering unqualified American support "of all the aspirations of peoples everywhere for freedom and independence." Eisenhower agreed. The revised statement championed only "legitimate aspirations for freedom, progress, and peace."[50] On November 10, in order to prove that the USIA differed from its predecessors, Eisenhower addressed the agency's staff. U.S. information experts, Ike declared, knew "what Americanism really is" and demonstrated that the United States stood for "those things which enrich human life." Attempting to bolster the USIA's sagging morale, the president promised, "No one who serves in this organization with what his chiefs or associates say is decency and the best of his ability is going to suffer if I can help it." The staff responded with a standing ovation.[51]

The applause obscured the continued contradictions in the president's liberation policy. On December 23, NSC 174, the administration's new directive on Eastern Europe, claimed that popular opposition to communism stemmed from "loss of personal freedom and a reduced standard of living, as well as by outraged religious and national feelings." Although NSC 174 called for "determined resistance to dominant Soviet influence," it warned against the United States encouraging "premature" revolts that could spark Soviet reprisals and violence. While recommending that U.S. propagandists build ties with religious, cultural, and social groups who "are natural allies in the struggle against Soviet imperialism," the NSC tried to distance itself from the popular uprisings that such bonds could inspire. It stressed the "continuous and careful attention" that must be paid to "the fine line, which is not stationary, between exhortations to keep up morale and to maintain passive resistance, and invitations to suicide."[52] When revolutions flared in Poland and Hungary two years later, the ambiguities of this policy would be glaringly apparent. In the interim, no one explained how the United States could encourage the "captive peoples" of Eastern Europe while simultaneously persuading the Soviets to capitulate in multinational negotiations.

"Atoms for Peace"

U.S. calls for nuclear disarmament offered a different strategy for putting the Soviets on the defensive. On December 8, 1953, Eisenhower gave the rousing "Atoms for Peace" address before 3,500 delegates at the United Nations. Rather than reveal specific numbers, he gave general descriptions of the destructive capacity of America's atomic arsenal. But instead of dwelling on the horrors of a nuclear war, Eisenhower challenged the British and the Soviets to divert some of their uranium supplies to an international atomic energy agency under UN auspices. The new organization would use nuclear energy for peaceful pursuits including agriculture, medicine, and electricity. Having already received British approval of his plan, the president placed responsibility for disarmament directly on the Soviets. Privately, the USIA ordered U.S. diplomats to publicize the sincerity of Eisenhower's proposal without creating false optimism about an immediate disarmament agreement.[53]

C. D. Jackson orchestrated international and domestic media coverage of Atoms for Peace. Voice of America and Radio Free Europe repeatedly broadcasted the address. The OCB created a working group that conducted a massive public relations effort. Its members included representatives from the Federal Civil Defense Administration, the Atomic Energy Commission, USIA, CIA, and the departments of State and Defense. In the following months, they coordinated traveling Atoms for Peace exhibits, placement of news items, publication of millions of leaflets, booklets, and posters, and screenings of films and newsreels. In order to circumvent provisions of the 1948 Smith-Mundt Act barring domestic dissemination of U.S. propaganda materials, the committee made sure that "Atoms for Peace" materials intended for U.S. audiences did not resemble those distributed abroad by USIA. The OCB group also relied heavily on "private" individuals and organizations in publicizing the initiative. In reality, though, the lines between the domestic and foreign campaigns—and between official and private communications—were porous.[54]

USIA Gains Ground

At the same time, the status of U.S. information programs rose significantly. The OCB was a vast improvement over its predecessor, the PSB. Placed in the executive branch, the OCB worked closely with the NSC and avoided the rivalries with the State Department that had plagued the PSB. By March 1954, OCB had forty-eight permanent staff members and a $450 million budget. Twenty-three OCB working groups coordinated a variety of U.S. propaganda efforts.[55]

The efficacy of the OCB may have contributed to increased support for USIA. In January 1954, the United States Advisory Commission on Information praised the USIA as an inexpensive means of maintaining world peace.[56] "The greater the success of this Agency in reducing the threat of war by psychological means," the Commission argued, "the less we shall need to tax ourselves for military security." It demanded a reprieve from the congressional investigations that destroyed employee morale and forced personnel to become anxious, prosaic, and inefficient.[57]

The report denigrated the bureaucratic and fiscal constraints impeding the information program. The system was so complicated that even simple requests, such as programming for a particular national holiday, failed to receive approval for weeks. Personnel transfers defied logic. The panel explained:

> We have seen instances in which . . . a man has been suddenly jerked
> out of an information post and given a new tour of duty, without

the slightest regard for the disastrous effect which such unheralded
transfer might have on the program from which he is taken, and
without provision for a new man being sent in his place. We have
seen occasions on which new men, finally sent after lapses of
months of time, have been entirely unprepared for the task; who
have found it necessary to get acquainted all over again with the
language, the people, the customs, the habits, and the religions of
the people.

The USIA budget was so limited that officers used their own money for embassy entertaining. How, the commissioners asked, could anyone conduct
"public relations" under such circumstances?[58]

Streibert was undaunted by such limitations. On February 19, he announced that the USIA was concentrating on explaining U.S. foreign policy
to people overseas and on combating hostile communist propaganda. The
new information agency, Streibert explained, would focus intensely on a few
key themes. Currently, it was emphasizing U.S. support for the unity of the
free world and the peaceful uses of atomic energy. Because radio provided the
only means of reaching people living in communist-controlled nations, Voice
of America directed 77 percent of its output to those areas. Meanwhile, the
overseas libraries were rebounding from Cohn and Schine's tour and served
54 million people during the previous year.[59]

Streibert formulated long-range strategic plans for the USIA. He warned
his subordinates not to present versions of U.S. objectives "so colored by regional adaptation or diversities in emphasis that the integrity of our policies and
their global consistency is called into question." Rejecting an all-encompassing
portrait of the United States, he proclaimed:

> The important aspects of American life we present are selected for
> a specific prescribed purpose. We are not required to present all
> facets of American life, nor is it our aim to create and foster an or-
> thodox official version of America, a fixed detailed stereotype, al-
> though effective propaganda will require that we deliberately foster
> certain general assumptions about the U.S. and preserve an overall
> consistency.

USIA officers, Streibert continued, should highlight U.S. military strength,
economic opportunities, technological prowess, and quality of life in order to

demonstrate America's capacity "to resist aggression and to give powerful assistance in the creation of a peaceful world order."[60]

Streibert also hoped to gain the support of U.S. citizens. Promoting the USIA in several domestic publications, Streibert described his agency's objectives and activities.[61] His efforts impressed the president. On March 27, Eisenhower gave the USIA director the authority to hear charges brought against its foreign service personnel. The USIA was rapidly gaining power.[62]

In the following months, the USIA encountered few difficulties. In mid-May, film producer Eugene W. Castle told a Senate appropriations subcommittee that USIA films were "a stupid and wasteful" duplication of Hollywood's efforts. Castle also demanded abolition of USIA posts in England, Turkey, Greece, Spain, Denmark, and Belgium. The legislators listened intently— and then ignored Castle's recommendations. In July 1954, they approved a $77,114,000 budget for the USIA.[63] Led by Ralph E. Flanders (R-Vt.), the senators began calling for the censure of the information program's biggest foe, Joseph McCarthy.[64]

An American Cultural Offensive

Encouraged by the increasing political and fiscal support his agency was receiving, Streibert turned his attention toward the content of U.S. information campaigns. He considered the best strategies for conveying the advantages of the American way of life. He pondered what aspects of U.S. society would resonate with foreign audiences. With a victory in the Cold War at stake, Streibert and his subordinates disseminated a carefully crafted vision of the United States. To inspire hope for a better life among peoples suffering behind the Iron Curtain, they stressed the happiness and high standard of living enjoyed by U.S. families. To foster international support for democracy, they emphasized the freedom, tolerance, and individuality protected by the American political system.[65]

In July 1954, Streibert announced a campaign stressing the vitality of American culture. For years, the Soviets had depicted the United States as a nation of semibarbarian materialists ill-suited for political leadership. The Russians spent vast sums of money sending sponsoring dancers, actors, and artists abroad.[66] Streibert was ready to challenge the Soviet "cultural offensive." On July 4, the USIA embarked on a new series of overseas lectures, exhibits, concerts, films, and radio and television programs. Streibert welcomed closer association with foundations, universities, and museums and appointed Dr. Jacob Canter as the agency's cultural affairs advisor. "Greater understanding abroad of the long and worthy cultural heritage of the American people," Streibert proclaimed, "is essential to our efforts to gain support in the unremitting fight against international communism."[67]

Streibert hoped to capitalize on foreign interest in American mass culture. Moving away from controversial "high culture" exhibits like "Advancing American Art," the USIA began sending popular jazz musicians like Dizzy Gillespie and Louis Armstrong on international tours.[68] On July 6, he ordered his staff to portray the "culture of the people of the United States—not the culture of an elite or an intelligentsia." He called for a sweeping program encompassing "not only scholarly and artistic fields but all significant manifestations and aspirations of the spirit of America, from athletics to political oratory."[69]

Eisenhower supported Streibert's efforts and ordered aides to suggest appropriate propaganda activities. In a July 23 letter to Dulles, Henry Cabot Lodge, Jr., U.S. ambassador to the United Nations, proposed demonstrations of industrial products and scientific achievements. Although Lodge advocated sending artists and musicians abroad, he offered specific guidelines for exhibits:

All must be skillfully keyed to the taste of the country in which shown. There must be no vulgarity—no matter how funny or clever or interesting the program which contains such vulgarity may be. I would even avoid jazz music, acrobats, and the Fred Waring type of thing at first and later work it in only as a part of a fairly high-brow program.

Whatever his reservations, Lodge recommended immediate implementation of U.S. cultural overtures.[70] Eisenhower agreed. On July 27, he requested a $5 million discretionary fund for expanded U.S. participation in international trade fairs and to support U.S. cultural and artistic endeavors abroad. On August 18, after Congress approved the appropriation, Ike appointed a special cabinet committee to ensure the effective and expedient use of the money.[71]

But finding people qualified to lead these new initiatives was incredibly difficult. Budget cuts and McCarthyism had dissuaded many people from applying for jobs at the USIA. Although the agency was authorized to hire 964 American propaganda specialists, more than 100 positions, mostly for Far

Eastern posts, remained unfilled. By October 30, the lack of personnel had grown so acute that Streibert ordered his staff to drop their regular work and spend the day recruiting people for the information program.[72]

Nonetheless, USIA had survived its darkest days. On December 2, after the 1954 mid-term elections resulted in the loss of seventeen Republican seats, the Senate finally mustered the courage to censure Joseph McCarthy by a vote of 67 to 22.[73] With the furor of domestic anti-communism subsiding and the Cold War spreading into developing nations, U.S. propagandists were poised to sell democratic capitalism harder than ever.

Cultural Exchange and "The Spirit of Geneva"

In early 1955, as Georgii Malenkov, Nicolai Bulganin, and Nikita Khrushchev vied for control of the Soviet government, Eisenhower decided to confront the Soviets' "peaceful co-existence" rhetoric.[74] On March 22, he urged Republican congressional leaders not to cut his $88.5 million appropriations request for the USIA. Noting that the Soviets expended $2 billion a year on propaganda operations, Ike declared it "ridiculous" that the United States spent so little. "The Russians are spending more money in Germany for their propaganda than we are spending in the entire world." America needed a strong information program, Eisenhower asserted, in order to convince people that "we are working for peace and not trying to blow them to kingdom come with our atom and thermonuclear bombs."[75]

The president pushed for an expansion of the exchange program. Under the Malenkov coalition, the USSR had eased restrictions on travel to and from the Eastern bloc. More than 100 American citizens visited the Soviet Union. At the same time, the United States remained reluctant to admit visitors from communist nations. Pointing to the inconsistencies in U.S. policies favoring freedom of travel, both Eastern and Western journalists had begun accusing the United States of maintaining the Iron Curtain.[76]

On March 26, the National Security Council (NSC) asked the U.S. Attorney General to redress the situation. Seeking to maintain the reputation of the United States "as a mature leader and a believer in freedom," the NSC concluded the propaganda advantages of a more fluid admissions policy outweighed the risks of communist spies posing as tourists. Accordingly, the security advisors asked for a modest broadening of U.S. immigration laws toward the Soviet bloc. The revised policy contained several safeguards. Only short-term visas would be granted. Internal safeguards would be established. Admissions were based on reciprocal numbers of Americans being admitted to the Soviet bloc. And, finally, communists could visit the United States only to participate in "bona fide cultural, educational, religious, scientific, professional, or athletic activities."[77]

Both superpowers sent mixed signals. In May 1955, after West Germany joined NATO, the Soviets announced the creation of the Warsaw Pact, a defensive alliance of the USSR and the satellite nations. However, they also accepted Eisenhower's invitation to a summit meeting and agreed to sign the Austrian peace treaty.[78] In July, British, American, French, and Soviet leaders met in Geneva, but the negotiators deadlocked on the question of German reunification. Premier Bulganin refused to address American demands for the liberation of the satellite nations. First Party Secretary Khrushchev rejected Eisenhower's "Open Skies" proposal for mutual inspections of military facilities.[79]

Discussions on cultural exchange proved more fruitful. On July 22, Eisenhower proclaimed the need for peaceful trade and a "free and friendly exchange of ideas and of people" between the USSR and the U.S. The following day, the four national delegations agreed to examine East-West contacts in a future meeting of their foreign ministers.[80] When Eisenhower returned to the United States, he told the American public that the four powers had reached the "greatest possible degree of agreement" on the desirability of increased interactions between the East and West.[81]

The USIA responded carefully to the "spirit of Geneva." On August 24, Acting Director Abbott Washburn sent a circular letter to all USIS posts. He argued that the ebb in Cold War hostilities gave the USIA's role "heightened significance and urgency." He warned of the challenges posed by the new Soviet regime. During the Stalinist era, "questions of international right and wrong were reasonably well-defined." But recent Soviet declarations on "peaceful co-existence" and eased restrictions on the press and travel "are serving to blur the basic moral and political issues in many people's minds." "This," Washburn asserted, "makes our job both more difficult and more necessary."[82]

In an August 31 report to the NSC, CIA Director Allen Dulles and Streibert voiced skepticism about the Kremlin leadership. The Soviet government, Dulles and Streibert argued, did not "intend to relinquish effective control of the captive territories or peoples." Western willingness to negotiate at Geneva had created cynicism and despair behind the Iron Curtain. Eastern Europeans, bombarded by Soviet propaganda, now feared that the United

States would abandon their interests and leave them consigned to communist domination.[83]

Dulles and Streibert proposed a counterstrategy. U.S. information strategists could reiterate demands for individual liberty and national independence in the Eastern bloc. They could also continue to criticize Soviet failures, such as their agricultural policies. While U.S. policymakers exposed "Soviet responsibility for communist efforts at subversion, dissension, and disorder throughout the world," they could simultaneously attempt to negotiate in good faith with the same leaders they blamed for the worldwide communist conspiracy. While patiently waiting for the Soviets' actions to reflect their rhetoric, Dulles and Streibert concluded, the United States should implement a program for "breaking down the isolation of the captive peoples from the West, by penetrating Eastern Europe with books, magazines, and newspapers, by exchange of personal visits, and by elimination of communist jamming of Western radio programs."[84] Within days, Eisenhower approved the plan to keep the Soviets on the propaganda defensive by pushing for more open cultural exchange. The British and French also joined these efforts.[85]

In late October 1955, when the foreign ministers gathered at Geneva, the chances for improving Western-Soviet cultural relations appeared slim. The committee of experts studying East-West contacts reached no agreements. Western officials refused to compromise on trade issues. Soviet negotiators rejected Western requests for information exchanges. Although both sides expressed interest in wider cultural and scholarly ties, neither initiated an accord. John Foster Dulles quickly blamed the Soviets for the impasse. Molotov retorted that the Soviets had vetoed proposals on jamming, censorship, and tourism because they interfered with the internal affairs of the USSR.[86]

Stalinism Exposed

Despite the failure of the meeting, Eisenhower asked congressional leaders for a 50 percent increase in the USIA budget. Meeting at the White House on December 13, 1955, the president emphasized the importance of an aggressive information program as a part of U.S. diplomatic, military, and economic policies abroad. "I am personally convinced," Eisenhower declared "that this is the cheapest money we can spend in the whole area of national security. This field is of vital importance in the world struggle." Streibert then explained the administration's proposed "Program for World Understanding."

He listed a $10 million campaign to publicize American peace activities, a low-priced book program, and a $4 million expansion of USIA television operations.[87] Expecting no significant changes in the USSR, USIA continued to stress the oppressive nature of life under communism.[88]

But, in a stunning turn of events, Khrushchev himself transformed the dynamics of the Cold War. In February 1956, in a dramatic "secret speech" before the 20th Communist Party Congress in Moscow, Khrushchev denounced Stalin's crimes while cleverly concealing his participation in some of them. He blamed Stalin's "cult of personality," not the Communist Party, for the purges. Without repudiating the Five Year Plans and collectivization, Khrushchev advocated a liberalization of the communist political and economic system. The speech solidified Khrushchev's support among military leaders and discredited his more conservative opponents, Malenkov and Molotov.[89]

American officials rushed to interpret Khrushchev's motives.[90] When the NSC met on March 22, Allen Dulles speculated that the Soviets were attempting to win respect abroad by breaking with their past—a ploy he expected to fail. Indeed, he and Eisenhower thought the attack on Stalin accorded the United States "a great opportunity, both covertly and overtly, to exploit the situation to its advantage." Publicizing the extent of Stalinist atrocities, they argued, could force the Soviet regime into political suicide.[91]

Accordingly, the CIA leaked the text of Khrushchev's secret speech to the *New York Times*, which published it on June 4. On June 7, Streibert directed the USIS missions to let the document "speak for itself." He recommended disseminating basic points like, "We can believe [the] present regime has repudiated Stalinism only when it supplements denunciation [of] certain Stalin excesses [with] cessation [of the] methods of Stalin dictatorship."[92] By confirming Stalin's crimes, U.S. officials hoped to expose Soviet despotism and to promote the eventual liberation of the satellites.

East-West Exchanges

East-West exchanges played a vital role in this strategy. On June 6, the State Department recommended the initiation of greater interaction with the USSR. The United States stood to benefit from a more open relationship with the Soviet Union. If Soviet citizens were able to make more informed judgments of the outside world, they could be inspired to demand intellectual freedom, personal security, and more consumer goods. U.S. officials took it for granted that communists would prefer the American political, legal, and economic system.[93] Sharing this belief and eager to capitalize on foreign interest in U.S. consumer products, Congress subsidized international exhibits that highlighted the standard of living in the United States. These included demonstrations of a typical furnished house, manufactured goods and appliances, and mail-order catalogues, as well as television and motion pictures.[94]

At the same time, USIA leaders asked U.S. diplomats to evaluate Eastern European curiosity about American trade and culture.[95] Alexis Johnson, an official at the U.S. embassy in Czechoslovakia, reported that members of the communist regime "are noticeably making an effort to put themselves on better personal terms with representatives of the United States." The Czechs were encouraging American tourists to visit. Communist officials were seeking the restoration of most-favored-nation trading status. Furthermore, the Czech government had sponsored several American cultural displays, including performances of *Porgy and Bess*, appearances by pianist Julius Katchen and singer Hubert Dilworth, and exhibitions by U.S. skating and tennis stars. In return, the Czechs sought an American tour for the Smetana Quartet.[96]

Johnson wondered why the Czechs were permitting these visits. While calling for "peaceful co-existence," the Czech government still prohibited Western publications and continued to jam VOA. Nonetheless, Johnson maintained that local communist leaders, like much of the general populace, "are sick of the isolation forced upon them in the Stalinist period and are glad to come out into the light of contacts and exchange with the West." Therefore, he concluded, the United States should continue efforts to increase American influence in Eastern Europe.[97]

Selling the American Way of Life

Encouraged by such feedback, the USIA aggressively promoted democratic capitalism and American mass culture. Through its new "People's Capitalism" campaign, the agency was making progress toward debunking the Soviet stereotype that Wall Street financiers ruled America. The USIA was publishing ten and fifteen cent translations of twenty-six "Classics of Democracy." The monthly USIA television program, "Report from America" was a hit in Great Britain. "Music U.S.A.," a daily two-hour program of American jazz and popular music drew 1,000 fan letters a month from its European listeners.[98] In September, the administration launched the "People-to-People" program, an elaborate public-private partnership that mobilized individuals, nonprofit groups, and corporations in international publicity efforts for the United States.[99] In October, following months of negotiations with the Soviets, USIA resumed distribution of *Amerika* in the USSR.[100]

Field officers offered additional suggestions for materials that would resonate with local audiences. The USIA office in New Delhi, for example, expressed concern about the lack of a "good basic Americana pamphlet." While new booklets on presidential elections, racial integration, and disarmament had been well-received, publications with strong anticommunist themes had "minimum impact [on] Indian audiences." Instead, Indians craved "straight, informational material about American life, culture, [and] heritage." Accordingly, the information officers suggested the production of "new high intellectual material" that explained the dynamic aspects of "the American way of life" and U.S. foreign policy.[101]

Tumult in Eastern Europe

While supervising these activities, USIA leaders closely monitored protests in Eastern Europe. On October 19, after weeks of unrest, Khrushchev granted Poland domestic autonomy in exchange for continued membership in the Warsaw Pact and loyalty to Soviet foreign policy.[102] Just days later, Hungarians began demanding freedom of the press, increased contact with the West, and reform of the centralized economy. Although the Soviets agreed to a regime change, bloody anti-Russian riots erupted. Soviet military forces killed hundreds of protesters.[103] Unable to suppress the tumult without drawing global condemnation, the Soviets agreed to negotiate with the new Hungarian leader Imre Nagy.[104]

As the uprisings intensified, USIS posts implored their leaders for instructions. On October 25, Aldo D'Alessandro, the director of VOA's European headquarters, fired off a desperate cable to the USIA policy office. Amid chaos in Budapest, he explained, VOA was still broadcasting Americana. He could not understand how the USIA could tell the Hungarians "about the *Globemaster* landing on [the] Arctic shelf, activities of Soviet election observers, and cancer research while people were dying in the streets." Since British announcers were giving sharp news commentaries on the Soviet response, D'Alessandro inquired, why was VOA not doing the same thing? Were VOA announcers hamstrung by "overconcern with policy implementation and apprehension over [the] possibility of unfavorable reaction?" His staff needed a plan for reporting events in Poland and Hungary in a way that conveyed sympathy for the Eastern Europeans and condemnation of the Soviet suppression. "Could you give us some indication," D'Alessandro implored, "of when we can expect revised Soviet orbit guidelines?"[105]

Unwilling to intervene militarily, the Eisenhower administration searched for appropriate ways to endorse the resistance movements. On October 20, the president announced his hopes that the Polish people would "have the opportunity to live under governments of their own choosing."[106] On October 26, a special committee on "Soviet and related problems" discussed U.S. options in Hungary. Having lost contact with the U.S. embassy in Budapest, the policymakers had a difficult time assessing developments. Because the U.S. government would not foment open rebellion, the committee adopted a risky strategy. It directed Radio Free Europe (RFE) to link its antennae to the local radio stations controlled by Hungarian rebels. If the freedom fighters then chose to incite their people, the U.S. government could abdicate responsibility.[107]

On November 4, Nagy's decision to withdraw Hungary from the Warsaw Pact persuaded Khrushchev to crush the revolt.[108] Cognizant that the West was focused on the crisis in the Suez Canal,[109] Khrushchev sent 60,000 Soviet troops into Budapest. They seized Nagy and installed a new puppet regime led by Janos Kadar. In the ensuing pandemonium, Soviet soldiers slaughtered more than 22,000 Hungarian insurgents and almost 170,000 people fled the country. Over the next two years, Kadar reinstituted the purges, arrests, deportations, and executions of the Stalinist era. Throughout Eastern Europe, the USSR halted its de-Stalinization policy and tightened its control over the satellite regimes.[110]

The Hungarian crisis marked the death knell of the U.S. liberation policy. Despite years of rhetoric on the rollback of Soviet power, U.S. officials provided only humanitarian assistance to Hungary and did not overtly challenge Soviet domination of the East bloc. If the price of an independent Eastern Europe was war with the USSR, they concluded, the cost was too high. From now on, the United States would promote "peaceful evolution" through increased cultural and economic contacts with communist nations while simultaneously bolstering U.S. propaganda efforts in the "free world."[111]

Following the Hungarian revolt, disturbing allegations about Radio Free Europe and Voice of America arose. West German and French journalists claimed American propagandists incited the rebels. Several delegations to the United Nations levied the same charges. On November 13, RFE Information Director Frank J. Abbott vehemently denied the accusations. Privately, both the USIA and CIA found Hungarian refugees willing to attest that neither VOA nor RFE fomented the rebellion.[112] Insisting VOA "neither encouraged nor discouraged the Hungarian freedom fighters," Washburn assured Eisenhower that its "calm, factual, and objective" broadcasts had omitted material that "might have had an incendiary effect on the Hungarian audience."[113]

Such denials rang hollow to many Hungarian rebels. On November 19, the U.S. embassy in Budapest granted temporary shelter to Bela Kovacs, a top leader of the Hungarian insurgency. While conversing about the rebellion, Kovacs maintained that the United States misled the Hungarians into believing that they would receive assistance if the Soviets intervened. If American anti-communism was purely defensive, Kovacs fumed, Voice of America and Radio Free Europe should have focused on the USSR and left the East European states alone. Kovacs made crystal clear his opinion that the United States had "cynically and cold-bloodedly maneuvered the Hungarians into action against the USSR."[114] Although fearful of exposing of RFE's connections to the CIA, Allen Dulles contended that RFE did not incite armed revolt or promise U.S. military intervention. He conceded, however, that there was some evidence of "attempts by RFE to provide tactical advice to the patriots as to the course the rebellion should take and the individuals best qualified to lead it."[115]

While refuting allegations about RFE and VOA, the Eisenhower administration tried to exploit the Hungarian calamity. Throughout the world, USIS posts screened films of Soviet tanks killing people in Budapest. On November 8, Eisenhower announced the United States would admit 5,000 Hungarian victims of "the brutal purge of liberty" inflicted by "imperialist communism." Henry Cabot Lodge, the U.S. ambassador to the United Nations, supported resolutions dispatching international observers to Hungary.[116] After the Kadar regime rebuffed the UN overtures, the United States granted asylum to an additional 15,000 Hungarian refugees.[117] The State Department ordered U.S. visa officers to ask the escapees for their impressions of U.S. government pamphlets and radio programs. Although several émigrés resented the implication that they had not orchestrated the demonstrations themselves, U.S. policymakers claimed the uprisings proved that U.S. attempts to promote democracy abroad were working.[118]

Targeting the Developing World

The Hungarian debacle brought American-Soviet cultural interaction to a screeching halt. On November 13, the State Department suspended the East-West exchange program and U.S. participation in international trade fairs. In accordance with Eisenhower's wishes, the decision remained confidential. The president did not want to jeopardize communication with Bulganin or scare satellite nations still interested in increased contact with the U.S. Cultural performers and tourists who wished to visit the USSR were quietly advised of the revised policy.[119]

At the same time, Soviet prestige tumbled to unprecedented lows. On January 8, 1957, the USIA completed a survey of Western European public opinion about the USSR. In explaining their overwhelmingly negative opinions of Soviet foreign policy, respondents cited the massacres in Hungary. Of the 6,830 people surveyed, 80 percent felt that the Soviets' use of force was unjustified. Very few respondents thought the UN or NATO should have intervened militarily.[120]

Capitalizing on the Soviets' diminished popularity, the Eisenhower administration focused on developing nations. The Suez crisis proved the changing nature of the Cold War. European colonialism was collapsing throughout Africa, the Middle East, and India. In addition to providing economic assistance to the Third World, Eisenhower concluded, the United States must prevent the spread of communism to these regions. On January 5, Eisenhower asked Congress for authorization to grant military and financial aid to the Middle East. Additionally, he requested permission to deploy the U.S. armed forces to help any Middle Eastern country resist communist military aggression. Known as the Eisenhower Doctrine, the proposals would give the president sweeping power.[121]

The USIA played an active role in explaining Ike's new policies. The new USIA director Arthur Larson, the former undersecretary of labor, welcomed the challenge. Inheriting an agency invigorated by Streibert's financial and political skills, Larson launched a counteroffensive against Egyptian and Soviet propaganda in the Middle East. Through VOA broadcasts and printed materials, the agency publicized Eisenhower's interest in the region.[122] On February 18, VOA began its first English broadcasts to Africa.[123]

On February 25, Eisenhower honored VOA's fifteenth anniversary with a global appeal for peace, justice, and freedom. The speech marked the first time that all of VOA's worldwide facilities had been used to carry a single message. Hoping to gain support for his foreign policy initiatives, Ike told the people of the Middle East that international communism "could smash all their hard-won accomplishments overnight." The communist system of "control and conformity," the president warned, would "destroy totally the religion, governments, institutions, and traditions of the Christian world, the Buddhist World, the Islamic World, the Judaic world, and the world of every religion and culture." Impressed by the president's zeal, Congress passed the Eisenhower Doctrine in early March.[124]

U.S. information experts also tried to deflect criticism of American race relations. Donald B. Cook, chief of the State Department's Special Projects Division, defended the African American jazz trumpeter Dizzy Gillespie's recent journey to the Near East and Latin America. Although the tour cost $141,000, Cook asserted, it offset reports of racial prejudice in the United States by "indicating that it is possible for Negroes in this country to attain pre-eminence in the field of the arts." With the persistence of racism and segregation in the U.S. South drawing international attention, the State Department and USIA were finding it increasingly difficult to defend America's civil rights record.[125]

Congress Assails USIA (Again)

Larson soon complicated matters further. The author of *A Republican Looks at His Party*, Larson extolled the moderate Republicanism favored by the president. But the Democrats who controlled Congress were not impressed. On April 12, John J. Rooney (D-N.Y.), chairman of the House Subcommittee on State Department and USIA appropriations, slashed 26 percent of USIA's $144 million budget request. Asserting "the mere appropriation of more funds is not the answer," Rooney suggested that USIA divert money from less important countries and programs. Rooney then assailed the information program's "fiscal irresponsibility" as evidenced by actions like providing the 644 members of the British Parliament with free subscriptions to the *New York Times* and the *New York Herald Tribune* and the State Department paying Dizzy Gillespie $2,100 a week.[126]

Four days later, the politically inept Larson sealed USIA's fate. In a speech at a Republican fundraiser in Hawaii, Larson blasted the Roosevelt and Truman administrations for importing "a somewhat alien philosophy" from Europe. Democrats and many liberal Republicans were enraged.[127] On April 17, after the House approved the reduced USIA budget, Eisenhower deplored the move as "the worst kind of economy." Having proposed the largest peacetime budget in history to a Democrat-controlled Congress, the president found himself locked in a nasty political fight.[128]

Rooney's oversight of the USIA budget inspired divergent responses from U.S. information officers. Burnett Anderson, deputy director of the USIA Press and Publication Service from 1955 to 1957, considered Rooney "the scourge of the foreign affairs establishment."[129] But other information officials attributed the congressman's actions to other motives. Edgar T. Martin, chief engineer of VOA, applauded Rooney's close scrutiny of the USIA budget. Rooney would cut "anything that looked half-assed," Martin claims, but "if you could make a case and he sensed that you knew what you were talking about, you got it."[130] In 1958, after Rooney blasted VOA for restructuring its broadcasts to the Baltic states, VOA director Henry Loomis quickly realized that Rooney, a staunch Irish Catholic who represented an ethnically diverse New York district, was trying to please his many Lithuanian constituents. According to Loomis, "domestic U.S. politics" was the deciding factor in the number of hours VOA could devote to a language service, "not . . . the ability to reach the country, or the amount of time that would make sense to the country, or the political importance of the country." Armed with this knowledge, Loomis later secured Rooney's approval for several new VOA transmitters and stations.[131]

Many legislators targeted USIA for special abuse. Because USIA materials and broadcasts remained unavailable within the United States, the American public knew little about the agency. Having drawn rancor from members of both parties, Larson's appeals for additional funds drew little support. Yet he persevered. On April 30, he began two weeks of testimony before the Senate Appropriations Committee. Larson emphasized how communist propaganda expenditures dwarfed the USIA budget. Radio Moscow carried twice as many broadcasts as VOA. Communist films and books were flooding the Free World. Larson promised USIA administrators would not waste money and disputed the charge that the agency competed with private news agencies. The senators were not impressed. On May 9, committee chairman and Senate Majority Leader Lyndon B. Johnson (D-Tex.) contended that USIA "wastes more money than any agency I know." Even Senator J. William Fulbright (D-Ark.), the information program's biggest fan, questioned the necessity of agency operations in friendly nations. Pointing to the dismal state of the NATO alliance, Senator Allen J. Ellender (D-La.) claimed USIA must be failing in the Middle East and Europe. Larson conceded, "We have to work harder."[132]

But the senators were relentless. On May 14, the Senate Appropriations Committee trimmed USIA's budget to $96.2 million—16 percent less than the fiscal 1957 budget. The committee recommended that the State Department absorb the USIA and that the Senate Foreign Relations Committee investigate the agency. The legislation also ordered the USIA not to provide films and press materials in nations where private U.S. news agencies sold similar services. Two hours later, an agitated Eisenhower warned that congressional budget cuts jeopardized the security of the United States. Stressing the vital role USIA played in American foreign policy, the president asserted: "We tell the truth about freedom and the rights of man and seek to win adherents to those concepts." Still not persuaded, the Senate dramatically cut several other areas of Eisenhower's budget. With the Republican leaders defecting to the Democrats, the lawmakers handed the administration a stunning defeat.[133]

USIA leaders braced themselves for the cuts. Throughout the summer, top information officials shaped new plans and determined the areas most vital to combating communism. Although direct broadcasts behind the Iron and Bamboo Curtains remained unchanged, the agency dropped a third of its programming in Western Europe and virtually eliminated its use of television; and 900 USIA employees received dismissals.[134] Convinced that entertainment programs undermined VOA's credibility, Larson ordered his broadcasters to place greater emphasis on news.[135]

Soviet-American Cultural Exchanges Resurrected

While the Eisenhower administration was fighting with Congress, the Soviets resumed their quest for increased interaction with the United States. In late May, Stuart Novins of the Columbia Broadcasting System (CBS) traveled to Moscow to interview Khrushchev for *Face the Nation*. On May 31, as approximately five million Americans watched, Khrushchev addressed several topics. But, when asked to identify the "most pressing" issue in Soviet-American relations, Khrushchev responded, "There must be more contacts between our peoples, our businessmen." He then challenged the United States to "do away with your Iron Curtain" and stop opposing cultural and trade exchanges with the USSR. Four days later, the Soviets announced a proposal calling for a variety of technical, cultural, and scientific exchanges between the U.S. and the Soviet Union.[136]

The move surprised the Eisenhower administration. On June 6, both the president and Dulles downplayed the Soviet overture. But several senators, including Johnson and Fulbright, welcomed Khrushchev's offer. The United States should push for more open communication with the Soviets, Johnson declared, because most Americans would flatly reject communist propaganda. Two weeks later, the State Department proposed a monthly swap of radio and television programs with the USSR. On June 27, Vice-President Richard Nixon dismissed as "hypocritical double-talk" Khrushchev's contention that the United States was impeding East-West contacts. Nixon challenged the Soviets to back their rhetoric with action. Khrushchev, Nixon argued, should demonstrate "his good faith" by ending jamming and censorship, allowing Western broadcasts and publications into the USSR, permitting Soviet citizens to visit the United States, and removing travel restrictions within the Soviet Union. If the Soviet leadership refused to implement such measures, Nixon concluded, they alone would bear responsibility for "blocking the road to peace."[137]

The Kremlin, however, could also play hardball. In late July, the Soviets announced their willingness to discuss East-West contacts "in conjunction with other problems in the development of broad ties between the Soviet and American peoples." They derided the provision of U.S. immigration law requiring the fingerprinting of anyone applying for a visa. Wary of the criticism directed at the policy, Congress amended the legislation in early September. The revised statute allowed the secretary of state or the attorney general to waive fingerprinting for temporary visitors.[138]

Little Rock and Sputnik

Immersed in the tumult attending school desegregation, Eisenhower hardly noticed the policy change. Throughout his presidency, Ike wavered on racial issues. In August, his ambivalence allowed Congress to pass the toothless Civil Rights Bill of 1957. But events in Little Rock forced Eisenhower to take a firm stand for integration. After Arkansas Governor Orval Faubus ordered the National Guard to block the admission of nine African American students to Central High School, the administration persuaded Faubus to withdraw the Guard. On September 23, a vicious mob surrounded the school grounds. Three hours later, local police removed the black students from the campus. Determined to uphold federal law, Eisenhower dispatched Army paratroopers to Little Rock.[139]

The administration was deeply concerned about international perceptions of the controversy. On September 24, Dulles warned U.S. attorney general Herbert Brownell that the situation was "ruining" American foreign policy. "The effect of this in Asia and Africa," Dulles declared, "will be worse for us than Hungary was for the Russians." Reporting the Little Rock incident as straight news, the USIA claimed that the unruly protesters were not typical of the community. Hoping to offset the damage inflicted by photographs and films of the mobs, the agency released several pictures of interracial activities. Despite USIA's efforts, most foreign audiences believed Little Rock exemplified rampant American racism.[140]

Eisenhower's problems worsened. On October 4, the Soviet Union launched the first artificial satellite, Sputnik. Though USIA broadcasters did not belittle the Soviets' success, they concentrated on the overall scientific superiority of the United States. But neither foreigners nor Americans were convinced. All over the globe, people lost confidence in the superiority of U.S. technology and education. They worried about the military ramifications of Soviet missiles. Communist propagandists exploited this anxiety. On October 10, acting Secretary of State Christian Herter assured U.S. diplomats that the USSR still lacked the ability to mount a long-range strike on the United States. But State Department officials admitted that *Sputnik* had dramatically increased Soviet prestige. In December, the dismal failure of the American Vanguard rocket made the Soviets look even better.[141]

Jolted by communist successes and the Little Rock disaster, Eisenhower strengthened the USIA. On October 16, he replaced Larson with George V. Allen, a veteran Foreign Service office. A former ambassador to Greece, Allen had supervised the information program while serving as assistant secretary of public affairs from 1948 to 1950.[142] On November 21, the president established closer coordination between the USIA, the NSC, and the State Department. Eisenhower agreed to meet with Allen once a month and Dulles began inviting the USIA director to weekly policymaking conferences.[143]

The Lacy-Zaroubin Talks

The administration also decided to expand Soviet-American cultural relations. On October 28, Soviet and American delegations began meeting in

Washington to discuss technical, scientific, and cultural exchanges. The U.S. leader, Assistant Secretary of State for East-West Affairs William S. B. Lacy, gave a brief introductory address. The United States, Lacy asserted, still considered greater East-West contacts essential in decreasing international tensions. After reminding the Soviets of American interest in exchanges at Geneva in 1955, Lacy criticized communist radio and press censorship. He offered few specific suggestions for improving U.S.-Soviet interactions.[144]

But Georgi N. Zaroubin, the head of the Soviet delegation, presented several proposals and adopted a less antagonistic tone. Like Lacy, Zaroubin argued that exchanges could contribute to détente. Zaroubin, however, also stressed the economic benefits of fostering American-Soviet trade. He recommended agricultural exchanges of animal scientists and horticulturists. The Kremlin desired interchanges in medicine, radio, sports, education, and culture. More daringly, Zaroubin suggested a mutual visitation program between members of Congress and the Supreme Soviet and the establishment of direct air routes between the United States and the Soviet Union.[145]

Although several of Zaroubin's proposals were self-serving, they formed the basis of subsequent negotiations. For the next several weeks, the delegations discussed a wide variety of possible programs while permitting little publicity. They reached agreement on industrial, scientific, and cultural exchanges, but two areas proved more problematic. Zaroubin's delegation insisted on the direct air flights while the American group demanded the right to present U.S. television and radio shows in the USSR.[146]

USIA Struggles

At the same time, USIA leaders lamented their continuing fiscal limitations. On November 13, Washburn informed Sherman Adams, one of the president's top advisors, that the Bureau of the Budget had trimmed USIA's fiscal 1959 budget request from $108.4 million to $102 million. The Bureau had also imposed a hiring freeze and decreased funding for Project Gamma, a new radio transmitter designed to improve penetration of the USSR. Articulating the frustration shared by many of his colleagues, Washburn declared:

> At a time when the Communists are stepping up their propaganda
> in virtually every country in the free world, at a time when U.S.
> prestige abroad is at its lowest ebb in a decade, at a time when we

should be doubling our efforts to regain confidence following the body-blows of Sputnik and Little Rock, and in the face of the enormous task of making clear to peoples overseas the fact of U.S. leadership in peace and disarmament—this action is shortsighted in the extreme.[147]

Once again, conflicting opinions of propaganda, partisan politics, and differing notions of what constituted "America" converged and U.S. information experts would continue to sell the richest nation in the world in the cheapest ways possible.

While inadequate funding created USIA's biggest challenges, other problems stemmed from the culture of the agency itself. Former U.S. information officers provide myriad examples of equipment shortages, illogical personnel assignments, and cumbersome bureaucratic policies that seriously impeded America's propaganda efforts. In recounting his work on the mobile units used to screen films in remote areas, Alan Fisher asserts, "The only problem was that were no tires for them, there wasn't a single spare part. You couldn't even get a headlight lamp." During his tours in Brazil, seven of the nine units were unusable.[148] G. Lewis Schmidt, executive officer of USIS-Tokyo from 1952 to 1956, reports similar problems and calls the French-made vans "monstrosities."[149]

USIA alumni offer startling tales of field offices staffed by people lacking important linguistic skills and professional training. In a 1991 interview with Robert Amerson, Albert Hemming describes arriving in Berlin not only unable to speak German but also having "absolutely no experience in dealing with the press, or any first-hand knowledge of an Information Officer's duties." In response, Amerson declares such practices "standard operation for the Agency in those days. They weren't testing for demonstrated capability then. They assumed that if a guy made sense, give him a try."[150]

Robert Lochner encountered similar issues. After serving with the Strategic Bombing Survey in 1945, Lochner joined USIS and worked in several capacities in Germany. From 1955 to 1957, he became a public affairs officer in Saigon and felt "totally out of place." He supervised a large staff of thirty-two Americans and two hundred Vietnamese who were essentially the information ministry for the new Diem government. They prepared newsreels, radio broadcasts, and pamphlets. But only one American official, John Donnell, could speak Vietnamese. Lochner joked to the U.S. ambassador, "You know you really could send me and the 30 other Americans home because this one guy speaking Vietnamese is so much more effective than all of us put together."[151]

Lochner was less amused with the USIA performance review process. At overseas posts, USIS officials and their wives underwent a rigorous annual evaluation. A wife found to be insufficiently "socially active" could harm her husband's rating. In 1959, after Henry Loomis assumed the directorship of Voice of America, he instituted a comparable review system for U.S.-based officials. Lochner, then head of the Western European division of VOA, was given the unpleasant task of assessing Alexander G. Barmine, the formidable head of the VOA Russian Service. Although Barmine was known to be quite "difficult" and "obstreperous," VOA leaders had always given him glowing reviews that focused only on his Russian expertise. When Lochner provided a more balanced assessment, Barmine "hit the ceiling" and demanded a hearing. "It led to nothing," Lochner contends, and "just caused a lot of hard feelings and three of the most miserable days I had during my three years in Washington."[152] However disruptive or flawed the evaluative process, U.S. information officers knew that selling democracy abroad meant being subject to the vicissitudes of democratic politics at home.

The 1958 U.S.-Soviet Exchange Agreement

An historic cultural accord between the United States and the Soviet Union highlighted these realities. Signed in January 1958, the compromise agreement—the first-ever U.S.-Soviet accord—established reciprocal cultural, educational, technical, and athletic visits throughout 1958 and 1959. The two nations scheduled future negotiations on the establishment of direct air routes and exchanges between Congress and the Supreme Soviet. The Soviets, however, refused to stop jamming VOA or to abolish restrictions on free travel within their borders. Although the nations agreed to swap radio and television programs, the texts of all broadcasts were subject to prior government approval. The United States relinquished its demands for freedom of information, but the Soviets gained virtually everything Zaroubin originally proposed. Both sides immediately tried to capitalize on the agreement. Khrushchev renewed his appeal for an East-West summit meeting. Eisenhower suggested bringing 10,000 Soviet students to the United States for a year—regardless whether the Soviets reciprocated.[153]

The State Department offered a cautious assessment of the agreement. On January 29, State Department officials concluded that the accord "should be soberly portrayed as a mutually advantageous arrangement, reached after long and detailed diplomatic negotiation." But suspecting that the communists would use the agreement as evidence of their growing respectability, the State Department ordered U.S. diplomats not to exaggerate the importance of the pact. While emphasizing the utility of academic and medical exchanges, U.S. officials also publicized continuing Soviet restrictions on information and travel.[154] Whatever its limitations, the agreement ushered in an era of unprecedented openness in American-Soviet relations.

With USIA leaders struggling to shore up America's declining prestige, the pact was well-timed. Testifying before the Senate Foreign Relations Committee on February 26, USIA Director George Allen conceded that the agency had fostered "too glorified a picture" of American technological prowess. This mistake, Allen argued, had increased the impact of Sputnik. He admitted that much of the world accused the United States of imperialism, racism, and militarism. But, steadfast in his belief in democratic capitalism, Allen contended:

> The pressure for immigration into the United States has not lessened in the slightest since Sputnik went up or since any other event has happened. There has never been in the history of the world a country which has been subjected to so much pressure, by people who want to come and to live in it. . . . This includes people of every color and creed, and the picture has not changed since Little Rock.[155]

Because America had "a better product to offer," Allen averred, the United States would triumph over communist propaganda.

America's Prestige Declines

Others did not share Allen's optimism. In late March, after Nikita Khrushchev assumed the Soviet premiership and announced a unilateral suspension of nuclear tests, renewed accusations that America was losing the Cold War arose.[156] Allen resented such defeatist sentiments. Appearing on *Meet the Press* on April 6, he urged Americans to "grow up" and not get "too excited" about the allegation that the Soviets were winning the Cold War. He reminded the audience that the USSR grossly outspent the United States on propaganda activities. While admitting that the Eisenhower administration had stumbled on the nuclear testing issue, Allen pointed to USIA successes like the Atoms for Peace exhibits. America, Allen insisted, remained popular abroad.[157]

Once again, Allen misspoke. Throughout May 1958, vicious displays of anti-Americanism gained worldwide attention. Arab nationalists burned the USIS libraries in Tripoli and Beirut. A huge mob attacked Vice President Nixon's motorcade in Caracas, Venezuela. Enraged by former Venezuelan dictator Marcos Pérez Jiménez's presence in the United States, the communist-led demonstrators pelted Nixon's limousine with dozens of rocks. Vowing to protect the vice president if necessary, Eisenhower deployed 1,000 U.S. paratroopers to the Caribbean. Although the unrest in Latin America subsided, pan-Arabist activities continued in the Middle East. On July 13, Iraqi nationalists overthrew the Hashimite monarchy. The following day, 14,000 U.S. Marines invaded Lebanon in support of the faltering pro-U.S. government. The American intervention drew heavy criticism in the United States and abroad.[158]

By midsummer, America's prestige was plummeting. In July 1958, USIA researchers discovered widespread contempt for the United States among Western Europeans, Japanese, and Indians. Little Rock confirmed images of American racism. In the wake of Sputnik, international regard for U.S. military and scientific capabilities remained low. America's reputation for making serious efforts toward disarmament had waned. Contrary to Allen's rosy assessments, the United States had suffered significant losses on the propaganda front, even among its staunchest allies. At the same time, the Soviets were recovering dramatically from the nadir of the Hungarian uprising.[159]

Not surprisingly, these events did little to improve congressional opinions of the USIA. In late July, Eisenhower requested a supplemental appropriation of $22.3 million for the acquisition and construction of radio facilities for the USIA. On August 20, the legislators vigorously debated the proposal. Walter H. Judd (R-Minn.) and John Taber (R-N.Y.) resurrected the charges that VOA was worthless and pro-communist. Critical of the fact that the Soviets jammed most of VOA's broadcasts behind the Iron Curtain, Frank T. Bow (R-Oh.) suggested providing $10 million for a high-powered direct transmitter in the eastern United States but denying funds for overseas improvements such as additional radio boosters. Although Congress approved Bow's amendment, the politicians scheduled an investigation of the USIA[160] (Figure 4).

Figure 4. Voice of America leaders considered listener mail a reliable gauge of how foreign audiences responded to the U.S. ideological offensive. In the early Cold War, VOA averaged 25,000 listener letters per month—more than enough to keep volunteers like these busy. National Archives.

USIA Defends Itself

Agency leaders fought back. Allen warned that communist radio facilities were overpowering VOA in the Near East, the Middle East, and Africa. Citing the testimonials of communist escapees and audience mail, Allen and Henry Loomis, director of VOA, disputed Bow's contention that VOA failed to reach the satellite nations. But Allen and Loomis conceded that American "broadcast capabilities in several languages have definite limitations because of signal inadequacy, personnel problems, or audience listening habits." The new focus on English broadcasts, Allen insisted, would overcome these weaknesses and circumvent communist jamming.[161]

Privately, Allen was less sanguine. Responding to a letter from Sigmund Larmon, president of Young and Rubicam, Inc., vice-chairman of Citizens for Eisenhower, and member of the 1953 President's Committee on International Information Activities, Allen pinpointed two sources of popular and congressional criticism of USIA. The first stemmed from "suspicion . . . that there is something fundamentally evil and un-American about a propaganda agency." The second problem reflected the "intimate relationship between our national policies and actions and our information successes and failures." "I do not believe that," Allen asserted, "if we had the best, most expensive equipment in the world and the shrewdest experts in the United States, we could make a foreign people believe that a policy is really in their best interest when it obviously is not."[162]

While weathering the latest congressional onslaught, U.S. information strategists attempted to capitalize on the popularity of U.S. culture and to counter resurgent anti-Americanism. On September 21, Allen announced an expansion of USIA's programming. In addition to straight news on American foreign policy, the agency would begin stressing "not only music, art, and drama, but also America's educational processes, its democratic political institutions, its social customs, its religious interest and practices, and its record of reliability and responsibility as a nation."[163] By late March 1959, he reported many achievements. Agency estimates showed that VOA reached between 7 and 10 million people living behind the Iron Curtain every day. He cited improved circulation of *Amerika* in the USSR and the success of a new Polish-language edition of the magazine. 130,000 people had studied English at 185 agency-sponsored cultural centers. Additionally, 4,500 teachers participated in USIA English instruction seminars.[164] Most important, the United States and the Soviet Union agreed to host massive exhibitions highlighting their opponent. The USSR exhibit in New York and the American National Exhibition in Moscow permitted each superpower to demonstrate its industry, culture, and society. Undaunted by political or financial constraints, U.S. information strategists prepared to score their biggest propaganda victory.

The Moscow Exhibition

On July 24, 1959, Vice President Richard M. Nixon and Soviet Premier Nikita Khrushchev attended the opening of the American National Exhibition in

Moscow's Sokolniki Park. Strolling through the elaborate displays, the two men argued the merits of capitalism, summit meetings, international trade, and the free exchange of ideas. As the pair entered the model American home, the debate grew more heated. Nixon suddenly led Khrushchev into the kitchen and pointed out a built-in washing machine. Unimpressed, Khrushchev retorted, "We have such things." After Nixon claimed Americans aimed to make the lives of women easier, Khrushchev asserted that the Soviets did not share "the capitalist attitude toward women." Clearly misunderstanding Khrushchev's implication that communist women enjoyed equality of opportunity, Nixon replied, "I think that this attitude toward women is universal. What we want is to make more easy the life of our housewives." Abandoning the topic of gender relations, the two leaders then discussed the cost and variety of American housing. Although Nixon and Khrushchev resolved nothing, the "Kitchen Debate" gained worldwide attention.[165]

During the following six weeks, almost 3 million Soviets streamed through the 30,000 square-foot display marveling at frozen foods, radios, color televisions, phonographs, and other consumer goods. They read placards describing American cultural, scientific and technical achievements. They admired automobiles and full-scale models of typical U.S. homes. They cast mock ballots on a voting machine. They peppered USIA guides with thousands of questions about unemployment, race relations, living standards, and other aspects of the United States. For these reasons, U.S. information leaders declared the exhibit a "corner of America" in the USSR.[166]

The American National Exhibition in Moscow potently illustrated the ideological dimension of the Cold War. It demonstrated how American propagandists articulated the material advantages and intangible values of democratic capitalism. Rather than focusing exclusively on geopolitical, military, and economic factors, U.S. officials projected a vision of the United States they sought to protect from communism: rewarding employment, happy families, comfortable homes, political and religious freedom. These were the things worth fighting for. And the Moscow exhibit abounded with examples of the way of life U.S. policymakers hoped to defend.

In 1958, when the two superpowers nations agreed to stage national exhibitions on the other's soil, both sides elected not to censor the products and literature distributed at the fairs. They agreed to omit political materials from their displays.[167] U.S. officials welcomed the chance "to strengthen the foundation of world peace by increasing understanding in the Soviet Union of the

American people, the land in which they live, and the broad range of American life, including American science, technology and culture."[168]

The conciliatory rhetoric notwithstanding, organizers of the U.S. Exhibit in Moscow were eager to highlight the superiority of democratic capitalism.[169] The Eisenhower administration appropriated $3.6 million for the Moscow Exhibition, a figure equal to the amount spent on eighteen U.S. trade exhibits in 1958. The president appointed Harold C. McClellan, a wealthy paint manufacturer and former assistant secretary of commerce, to direct the Moscow project.[170] U.S. propagandists formulated extensive plans for the exhibit. They consulted journalists on the best means for reaching the Soviet people.[171] USIA officials scoured universities and language schools looking for Russian-speaking Americans to serve as guides.[172] The White House selected four art experts to select works for a display on American culture.[173] Barbara Sampson, home economist for the Bird's Eye division of General Foods, and Marylee Duehring, product counselor for General Mills's Betty Crocker line, planned a massive cooking demonstration in the main exhibition hall. Using a Whirlpool gas kitchen, Sampson, Duehring, and a team of six Russian-speaking women would serve 110 varieties of food including beef pies, fish dinners, biscuits, and Boston cream pie.[174] Maimonides Hospital of Brooklyn, New York loaned a heart-lung machine to a special display on American health and medicine. The presentation consisted largely of photographs documenting progress in physical rehabilitation, prosthetics, geriatrics, and mental health.[175] By late June, more than 800 private American firms had donated materials and services to the exhibit. McClellan's staff heavily publicized America's support for the upcoming Moscow fair.[176]

Construction of the exhibits proved a less cooperative enterprise. Beginning in late March, a joint Soviet-American crew began building the geodesic dome and enormous glass and steel hall housing the U.S. displays. Although American workers expressed dismay when Soviet women lugged rocks on stretchers or operated jack hammers, they also complained bitterly about the laziness of Russian laborers. They derided the simple tools and outdated methods used by the Soviet crews. The criticisms of Soviet craftsmanship proved valid. Just days after the exhibit opened, the concrete floors crumbled, filling the demonstration halls with thick dust.[177]

Political controversy marred other displays. Despite the prohibition on political content, USIA leaders attempted to insert affirmations of democracy and capitalism into some exhibits. In the original version of the fashion show, wedding scenes featured an African American bride with white attendants and then a white bride with African American attendants. After 250 fashion reporters viewed the revue, 41 signed a petition protesting the unrealistic depiction of U.S. race relations. Claiming the show ran too long, exhibit officials immediately eliminated the wedding sketches.[178] Following a preview of the U.S. model home, *Tass*, the official Soviet news agency, asserted, "There is no more truth in showing this as the typical home of the American worker than, say, in showing the Taj Mahal as the typical home of a Bombay textile worker or Buckingham Palace as the typical home of an English miner." Pointing to the home's wall-to-wall carpet, TV sets, hi-fi stereo, radios, and "beautiful contemporary, automatic General Electric appliances," *Tass* alleged that the home's furnishings cost far more than the $5,000 claimed by the American retailer Macy's. In response, U.S. officials declared the home's $14,000 price well within the budget of most U.S. laborers, and Macy's executives released an itemized price list of all merchandise contained in the home. It totaled $4,938.19.[179]

The Exhibition rekindled long-standing debates about "American" culture. After the art committee announced the selection of forty-nine paintings and twenty-three sculptures that highlighted American artistic trends from 1918 to the present, Representative Francis E. Walter (D-Pa.) claimed that more than half of the chosen artists had "records of affiliation with Communist fronts or causes." Wheeler Williams, sculptor and president of the American Artists Professional League, dismissed most of the selections as "childish doodles" that brought "discredit" on the United States.[180] In response, President Eisenhower suggested the addition of artistic works that reflected "what America likes," but refused to censor the Moscow art show—a stand that won wide praise from leaders in the U.S. artistic community.[181] On July 8, USIA announced the shipment to Moscow of approximately twenty-five paintings by nineteenth-century American masters including Gilbert Stuart, John Singleton Copley, Mary Cassatt, Frederic Remington, and George Caleb Bingham.[182]

A dispute over the content of the American book exhibit was not resolved as amiably. Having failed to screen closely the books donated by American publishers prior to their arrival in Moscow, McClellan and other U.S. officials acquiesced to Soviet demands that eighty Russian-language texts, several of which were hostile to the USSR and communism, be jettisoned. Yet the battle continued. On July 24, as Khrushchev and Nixon stood nearby verbally sparring over the meanings of "freedom," three Soviet censors poured over the 8,000 volumes in the U.S. display. Arguing that the 1958 Soviet-American cultural exchange agreement banned books unrelated to "American culture," the trio removed more than one hundred English-language texts, including the 1959 *World Almanac*, several volumes on the Soviet Union, and monographs on foreign policy. Eventually, Exhibition officials returned seventy of the books to the display, but placed them behind a plastic shield.[183]

Eisenhower's recent approval of a "Captive Nations" resolution in support of the oppressed peoples living in Eastern Europe added more intensity to Soviet-American feuds over freedom of expression. When Nixon arrived in the USSR on July 23, Khrushchev sarcastically welcomed the vice president to the land of a "captive people." After accusing American "imperialists" and "monopolists" of interfering in communist affairs, he challenged Nixon to listen the ideas of the "real people here." Nixon called Khrushchev's bluff. After several hecklers disrupted his speech that evening, Nixon engaged them in an impromptu discussion of free speech.[184] Ironically, Soviet newspapers retaliated by printing only perfunctory accounts of Nixon's remarks.[185]

Attempts at censorship, however, did not diminish the popularity of the exhibition. Soviet women vied for free haircuts, makeovers, and manicures from U.S. stylists. Long lines formed at a Pepsi-Cola soft-drink stand. Crowds eager for souvenirs pocketed hundreds of books, toys, utensils, and food products. Rampant theft forced the temporary closure of the fair's bookmobile. After four *Monopoly* games vanished, the American toy manufacturer Parker Brothers rushed additional copies to Moscow.[186] Soviet teenagers enthusiastically discussed American jazz at the hi-fi exhibit.[187]

The Soviets proved especially fond of the RAMAC computer demonstration. Designed by the International Business Machine Cooperation, the giant device answered 4,000 preprogrammed questions about a wide variety of topics. "What is the typical wardrobe of an American woman?" "What is the present direction in the development of American jazz?" and "How much do American cigarettes cost?" were among the most frequent. But the most popular inquiry was "What is meant by the American dream?" RAMAC responded:

The American dream is the fundamental belief by Americans that America has meant and shall always mean that all men shall be free to seek for themselves and their children a better life. Americans interpret this in terms of a demand for freedom of worship, freedom in the expression of belief, universal suffrage, and universal education.

Not surprisingly, the computer offered equally laudatory depictions of democracy, capitalism, consumerism, social programs, and race relations.[188]

Disturbed by the tenor of the American Exhibition, Soviet journalists published blistering attacks on the fair. An *Izvestia* article entitled, "The Reds Did Not Turn Green," derided the fair's abundant consumer products. *Literary Gazette* contended the Soviets had found "nothing usual" about the items displayed. The communist youth paper *Komsomolskaya Pravda* quoted a Moscow man claiming, "Much can be learned from the Exhibition about the things we do not have: unemployment, racial discrimination, pensions which the individual has to pay for himself—a great many things which do not trouble people living under a socialist system." *Moskovskaya Pravda* asserted:

> Exhibition organizers supposed that John Doe of Moscow or Gorky, on seeing the glittering kitchen equipment, elegant shoes, textiles, and the non-typical "typical home" of the American, would come to the conclusion that life is better under the capitalistic system. This was a miscalculation. Soviet people expected dependable information about the American way of life, more about technical and scientific achievements, about engineers and scientists. They did not find this. The exhibition did not satisfy them.[189]

In early August, after an announcement that Khrushchev and Eisenhower would exchange state visits, Soviet journalists moderated their anti-American tone.[190] They remained, however, critical of the Exhibition.[191]

But most Soviet visitors were highly impressed by the Moscow fair. If anything, U.S. officials underestimated the appeal of consumerism and democracy to the average Soviet person. In striving to present "a true picture of American life," Exhibition creators disappointed visitors to whom the United States exemplified wealth, creativity, and ingenuity. When presented with simple shoes, toys, housewares, and clothing, they often replied, "Why haven't you shown us your best?" or "This is a meager show." Rather than downplaying American affluence, U.S. information strategists realized that future exhibits should emphasize the economic opportunities that democratic capitalism afforded U.S. citizens.[192]

To the average Soviet, items like television and automobiles signified a comfortable, secure life rarely available in the Soviet Union. Through countless conversations with the exhibit guides, many visitors realized that "real" Americans were intelligent, articulate, and polite, the antithesis of their image in communist propaganda. Through Edward Steichen's "Family of Man" photographs and the Circarama 360-degree film displays, Soviet citizens witnessed the diversity and humanity of the American people. Fair visitors wanted more souvenirs like buttons and brochures and expressed great disappointment when told that exhibit items were not available for purchase. They clearly associated the Exhibition with the individualism, freedom, and contentment desperately lacking in their own lives.[193]

Dismayed by the popular response to the Moscow Fair, Khrushchev boasted of the productive capacity of the Soviet Union and the superiority of communism. Because the Soviet people already enjoyed a high standard of living, Khrushchev insisted, they would never accept capitalism. While visiting the United States in September 15–27, 1959, he blamed the United States for the continuing Cold War and called for world peace and total disarmament. With the world watching, Khrushchev demonstrated that the Soviet Union was a global power recognized and respected by the United States. In a stroke of propaganda genius, he offered the possibility of a détente between the superpowers.[194] But the Eisenhower administration greeted Khrushchev's pronouncements with extreme skepticism. They dismissed the premier's peace overtures and disarmament proposal as pure propaganda.[195]

After Khrushchev returned to the Kremlin, the Soviet Union and the United States continued their ideological conflict. The risk of nuclear holocaust made direct military engagement decidedly unappealing. Profound philosophical and economic differences made U.S.-Soviet trade highly unlikely. Facing these limitations, the superpowers ardently waged the cultural war. On November 21, the U.S. and USSR signed an agreement on East-West contacts for 1960–1961. The two sides made virtually no progress in expanding exchanges of publications and in establishing direct air flights between the two countries. The Soviets continued to jam Voice of America broadcasts.[196] Both superpowers viewed the ideological war as the best means for advocating and protecting their respective ways of life.

Conclusion

But cultural and information activities did not halt the militarization of the Cold War. Although the superpowers signed exchange agreements, neither halted its military spending, espionage, or armament. In May 1960, the U-2 incident shattered any pretense of a U.S.-Soviet détente. The following year, the construction of the Berlin Wall and the Bay of Pigs debacle further illustrated the hostility between the superpowers. In May 1962, the Cuban Missile Crisis provided terrifying affirmation that the Cold War was raging unabated.

Throughout the Truman and Eisenhower years, U.S. policymakers attempted to ensure national security by relying on preponderant military and economic strength. Although they also recognized the power of ideology and culture as weapons against communism, they seldom accorded information activities status equal to other tools of U.S. foreign policy. Consequently, U.S. information specialists repeatedly found themselves whipsawed by sudden shifts in international relations or domestic politics. Despite an inordinate amount of rhetoric stressing the value of propaganda activities and several attempts to reorganize U.S. information programs, neither the Truman nor Eisenhower administrations successfully reconciled the frequent gaps between the messages used to promote the American way of life abroad and the actions of the nation itself.

But these limitations do not negate the significance of U.S. propagandists' efforts to sell and defend America abroad. While U.S. officials and politicians bitterly debated the content and operations of U.S. information programs, they rarely questioned the superiority of democratic capitalism. They expressed little doubt that "American" liberty, tolerance, and affluence would resonate throughout the world.

These shared beliefs deeply inform the visions of democratic capitalism produced by U.S. information officials. However intense the political opposition and turf wars they faced at home, their portrayals of American life remained remarkably consistent and surprisingly liberal throughout the postwar era. While foreign audiences did not passively or universally accept their messages, U.S. propagandists frequently succeeded in making the American way of life appealing and in affecting international perceptions of the United States.

CHAPTER THREE

Defining Democracy: Images
of the American Political System

THROUGHOUT THE 1950S, USIS motion picture units showed the film *Social Change and Democracy* to foreign audiences. Using an apt metaphor for America's efforts to instruct the world about itself, the film begins with a teacher lecturing his class about the horrors of World War II-era totalitarianism. Images of jack-booted Nazis and Stalinist *gulags* accompany his narration. The film then cuts away from this conflation of fascism and communism to a homey story about a group of fishermen who prevail upon their city council to protect local waters from pollution. The men win redress peacefully and are not imprisoned or killed for challenging figures of authority. Their triumph, the film concludes, demonstrates how democracies craft solutions in which "all people are considered" and that enable "communities to flourish because the people flourish."[1]

Such tales about democracy are the most common feature in U.S. propaganda of the early Cold War years. While information experts interwove additional themes about American life, their promotion of democracy formed the foundation on which the entire U.S. ideological offensive against communism rested. American propagandists articulated elaborate comparisons between democratic and communist governments. Through publications, radio broadcasts, films, cultural exhibitions, and other methods, they enunciated visions of the freedom and equality inherent in the American political ethos. These depictions of democracy, therefore, provide an invaluable lens for exploring how U.S. policymakers understood and valorized the political culture they represented and defended.[2]

In the aftermath of World War II, U.S. information experts expressed dismay at international distortions of American democracy. On February 26, 1946, Assistant Secretary of State for Public Affairs William B. Benton told the House Appropriations Committee:

> The nature of the American democratic system, with its disagreements and its individual liberty, is bewildering to a world emerging from the throes of authoritarianism. It is easy for foreigners, without knowing the real situation, to get the impression that this is a land of strife and discord, with race set against race, class set against class, religion set against religion, the rich oppressing the poor, the poor revolting against the rich, gangsters roaming the streets of our cities, cowboys shooting up wild west saloons, and Congress weltering in a whirl of filibusters and cocktail parties.[3]

Confronting communist expansionism, U.S. propagandists recognized the need to convey the advantages of the American democratic system.

U.S. information officials considered freedom the most appealing element of democracy. Echoing rhetoric found in the Truman Doctrine speech and NSC-68, they distinguished the national and individual liberties of the Free World from the "slavery" of communist countries. On April 7, 1948, Benton, while serving as a U.S. delegate to a "Freedom of Information" conference at Geneva, asserted:

> I find it not at all ludicrous that all around the clock and in several languages Soviet propagandists appropriate, degrade, and bastardize the words which are the hard-earned and world-accepted currency of free men. Liberty, equality, fraternity, independence, justice, freedom, democracy. For these, brave men have died at the hands of tyrants for thousands of years.
>
> Now the USSR insists with a thousand amplified voices that repression is freedom, and that true freedom elsewhere in the world is slavery; they insist that the police state is democracy, and that democracy in other countries is dictatorship by monopoly capitalists.[4]

By equating democracy with freedom, American propagandists imbued their proclamations with implied moral superiority.

When attacking communism, U.S. officials broadly defined democratic freedom. They simultaneously advocated national self-determination and individual liberty. They stressed the freedom of worship, freedom of assembly, and freedom of speech fostered by democratic government. They demonstrated how democracies protected civil rights, personal property, and individual dignity. They presented the United States as a pluralistic society characterized by widely dispersed power and the reconciliation of conflicting interests. By extolling these liberties, U.S. policymakers hoped to gain adherents to the democratic way of life and to discredit communism.[5]

At the same time, Soviet officials proclaimed the virtues of communism and the evils of democratic capitalism. Like their U.S. counterparts, they defined the Cold War as a struggle between slavery and freedom. Communist propagandists accused "Wall Street capitalists" and "American imperialists," of "enslaving" U.S. workers. They denied that the United States protected freedom and individual rights. For example, on February 14, 1950, Radio Bucharest announced:

Wall Street tolerates and encourages the Ku Klux Klan, lynchings, and the indescribable misery of the Negroes. [Abraham] Lincoln opposed exploitation of slaves but Wall Street daily intensifies the bloody exploitation of U.S. people and other peoples kneeling under Yankee imperialism.[6]

The United States, communist officials contended, was an oligarchic, racist, imperialist, and immoral nation unconcerned with the lives of "the people." In a direct attack on U.S. political discourse, they adopted the phrase "people's democracy" when advocating communism.[7]

To counteract communist distortions of democracy, U.S. information strategists employed a variety of propaganda tactics. Most materials were simple. In 1950–51, USIS officers distributed more than 500,000 copies of *Herblock Looks at Communism* in English, Chinese, German, Indonesian, Malay, Telugu, Spanish, Tamil, Thai, and Vietnamese. In the preface, editorial cartoonist Herbert Block wrote, "If liberty existed in communist lands there probably would have been no occasion to draw the cartoons in this pamphlet—and we would all be living in a happier world." In several drawings, Block mocked the communist "peace offensive." In another section entitled "Life in a Communist State," Block derided Soviet efforts to censor musicians, scientists, art, literature, and architecture. Throughout his cartoons, Block flatly denied that the Soviet government valued individual freedom, world peace, or political debate.[8]

U.S. propagandists also created cartoons that bitterly satirized the communist system. In 1951–52, the USIS released 500,000 copies of *Glossary of Soviet Terms*, a booklet of sardonic pictures. "Classless society" depicted the "people's commissariat" riding in a limousine past two Soviet beggars. "People's democracy" showed two Soviet policemen forcing a couple to enter a detention camp. "Democratic elections" featured an armed soldier guarding a single ballot box labeled "yes." All the cartoons in the *Glossary* attacked communist attempts to usurp democratic rhetoric.[9]

Some drawings aimed to inspire popular resistance in communist nations. In 1954, the series *Little Moe: His Life Behind the Iron Curtain* featured one man's defiance of communist authority. One picture showed Moe throwing an anchor to a drowning communist official. Another depicted Moe training his dog to rip the seats out of the pants of communist guards. He then uses the swatches of cloth to make upholstery, draperies, and blankets. All the Little Moe cartoons ridiculed the lack of consumer goods and absence of political freedom behind the Iron Curtain.[10]

United States Information Agency (USIA) publications also extolled U.S. democracy. In *A Picture Story of the United States*, the agency quoted famous U.S. historical figures describing freedom in the United States. Roger Williams declares, "I'll start a settlement where ALL can worship as they please, government must never interfere with a man's belief!" John Peter Zenger asserts: "The press must be free to print the truth, no matter whom it offends!" Other cartoons portrayed abolitionism, women's rights, and the rise of organized labor. After illustrating the growth of American industrial and economic power, the booklet defended the capitalist system stating, "But with all this material progress and prosperity, Americans did not lose sight of the foundations on which their blessings rested; free education for all, the free spread of knowledge and ideas, the right to worship as they chose." Overall, the pamphlet presented the United States as a nation of diversity, equality, and morality.[11]

In presenting such messages to specific countries, USIA often linked famous Americans and figures revered by local audiences. A host of events and publications commemorating the 150th anniversary of Abraham Lincoln's birth provide good illustrations. In February 1958, USIA officer Manning H. Williams expressed concern that if the agency did not make "a major effort on Lincoln" the following year, "we may well find that the Soviets have stolen our own show." Manning warned that the Soviets "outdid us on the recent 250th anniversary of Benjamin Franklin." In order to rebut Soviet propaganda suggesting that the "America of Washington and Lincoln" differed from the current "American reality," Manning urged his superiors "to demonstrate that the democratic and humanitarian ideals of Lincoln are revered in the America of today, but overlooked in the Soviet Union."[12]

Acting on Manning's suggestion, the USIA organized global celebrations of Lincoln throughout 1959. USIS motion picture units screened *In Search of Lincoln*, a short biographical sketch of the fifteenth president superimposed over images of fawning crowds at the Lincoln Memorial and somber shots of books and artifacts connected to Lincoln.[13] In the spring, the USIS office in Madras hosted an exhibit entitled, "Lincoln-Gandhi, They Belong to the Ages." Large photographs of Lincoln and Mahatma Gandhi were placed on a simple yellow wall. A sculpture of Lincoln sat in the center of the hall. Attendants distributed pamphlets and posters. A majority of visitors responded positively to the exhibit. The statement of a salesman was typical: "May Mr. Lincoln's and M. Gandhi's teachings help us preserve our national solidarity and freedom."[14]

The architects of the "Classics of Democracy" series had similar objectives. While touring Southeast Asia in late 1955, Representatives Barratt O'Hara (D-Ill.) and Michael A. Feighan (D-Oh.) were distressed by the number of communist bookstores and reading rooms drawing large crowds. Concluding that "books are one of the major weapons with which the United States will either win or lose" the Cold War, they sponsored legislation creating a USIA program for disseminating inexpensive paperbacks about "American democracy." After the bill passed, O'Hara asked Thomas B. Stauffer, a humanities instructor at Wilson Junior College, and Dr. Harold Fey, editor of *Christian Century*, to convene a selection committee. The group sent out 3,500 questionnaires asking for book recommendations. O'Hara proclaimed their top choices "above partisanship and controversy" and "immortal documents of American history."[15] By September 1957, USIA had distributed 20,000 copies of thirteen different volumes to audiences in Africa and Asia. Selections included Henry David Thoreau's *Selected Writings on Nature and Liberty*, *The Political Writings of John Adams*, *The Autobiography of Benjamin Franklin*, and *From the Declaration of Independence to the Constitution: The Roots of American Constitutionalism* by Carl J. Friedrich and Robert G. McCloskey.[16]

Through texts like those in the "Classics of Democracy" collection and many others, American information experts explained the mechanics of the

U.S. democratic system. *America Today*, for example, devoted several pages to the Constitution, federalism, and the separation of powers. The booklet highlighted the fact that voters selected the president, Congress, governors, and dozens of state and local officials. Secret ballots, recall, referenda, and initiatives accorded voters additional power and protection. The Bill of Rights defended individual rights.[17]

VOA broadcasts and USIA films also stressed the merits of democracy. In the fall of 1951, VOA aired a multipart series entitled "Giants of Democratic Thought" that discussed the origins and evolution of democracy throughout the world.[18] The aforementioned film *Social Change and Democracy* showed how democracy benefited ordinary people. When fishermen discover their catches of shrimp precipitously declining, they hire water analysts to study the waste disposal systems of a new factory located on the shoreline. When they confront the plant managers with evidence that the factory is pouring pollutants into the bay, the factory officials dismiss them, saying no law requires them to stop such practices. When the angry fishermen depart, some of them contemplate violence, but one young World War II veteran stops them. After declaring that everyone had enough fighting in the war, he points out that the Constitution accords them the right to have their grievances heard by the city government. After the board of selectmen thoroughly investigate the matter, they not only pass a law requiring sanitary disposal of industrial wastes, but also call for a publicly financed sewage treatment facility to accommodate the needs of the growing community. Businessmen, fishermen, selectmen (all white men) leave the hearing satisfied, and USIA demonstrates democracy's balance of power between large and small interests and preservation of community well-being and individual rights.[19]

In addition to championing civil liberties, U.S. policymakers advocated independence for all nations. Determined to counter Soviet accusations of U.S. imperialism, U.S. propagandists denied that Wall Street financiers dominated American politics.[20] They defined the United States as an anti-colonial power with genuine interest in the principle of national liberation. But communist propagandists repeatedly accused the United States of atavistic territorial ambitions. When reestablishing the Comintern on October 6, 1947, the Soviets derided the global division between the "Soviet Union and other democratic countries" and "the camp of imperialism and anti-democratic forces whose chief aim is the establishment of a worldwide American imperialist hegemony."[21] Voice of America broadcasters retaliated by publicizing the 1939 Nazi-Soviet plan for carving up continental Europe.[22]

U.S. information strategists assailed the Soviet Union for exploiting weaker nations. In late 1949, the State Department released *Russia the Reactionary*, a booklet denouncing Soviet attacks on national and individual liberties. A chapter entitled "Russia Destroys National Independence" condemned the Soviets' seizure of land and personal property for collective farms. After recounting the communist annexation of Eastern Europe, the text asserted:

Throughout the USSR and the satellite countries, the entire educational, informational, and legal structure has been used to wipe out every culture, every belief, every person that stood in the way of complete conformity to the Moscow party line. Experiences of all nations under the domination of the Kremlin prove that only one way of life is tolerated among those nations—the Soviet way of life. National independence and love of country must be subordinated to allegiance to the Communist Party. There can only be one kind of patriotism—Soviet patriotism.[23]

The Soviets, U.S. officials argued, completely disregarded legitimate aspirations for national independence among Eastern Europeans. Instead, communist authorities created police states that consigned satellite peoples to lives of poverty, desperation, and subjugation.[24]

After the eruption of war in Korea, U.S. policymakers became increasingly sensitive to Soviet accusations of imperialism. On August 9, 1950, U.S. officials warned that "charges of Yankee imperialism" regularly appeared in communist propaganda. The State Department retorted:

We not only have voluntarily abandoned our control over many areas but also have encouraged other western powers to do likewise. For example, we have granted independence to the Philippines, are giving greater measure of self-government to other territories, took the lead in eliminating extra-territoriality in China, have sponsored good-neighborliness . . . in the Americas, and have refrained from interference in the internal affairs of all countries. Moreover, we have used our influence to preserve the independence of Thailand and to hasten the independence of India, Pakistan, Burma, Ceylon, Indonesia, the Associated States of Indochina, and other countries. We are using our influence to promote a greater degree of self-government in dependent areas. That is a creditable record by any

standards. It becomes all the more creditable when compared with
the undeniably aggressive imperialism of the USSR.[25]

Despite these protestations, U.S. policymakers knew that communist attacks
on American foreign policy were appealing to much of the global audience.
Hence, they attempted to deflect communist accusations of U.S. territorial
and economic imperialism. Whenever possible, they stressed the "reckless nature of Soviet policy and its consequences." They pointed to Stalinist excesses
and the isolation of Eastern Europe as evidence of Soviet political oppression
and territorial ambitions.[26] USIS distributed hundreds of thousands of copies
of *Who Is the Imperialist?* The booklet listed population and mileage figures
for all the territories and nations annexed by the USSR beginning in 1939.
It also described communist "imperialism" in North Korea, Poland, North
Vietnam, and Tibet.[27]

The Soviets depicted the United States as hostile to national struggles for
liberation. On March 2, 1955, the NSC reported the success of the Soviet
campaign to present the U.S. as "another Western colonial power."[28] In response, the USIA stressed America's desire to "assist subject peoples to attain
independence by peaceful methods" and to support newly independent states.
In order to demonstrate this mutuality of interests, USIA publications publicized the colonial heritage of the United States in order "to establish a basis of
America's understanding and sympathy with subject peoples."[29]

Not surprisingly, American policymakers rushed to exploit the 1956
Hungarian Revolution. USIA officials showed the film *Hungary's Fight for
Freedom* to audiences all over the world. The agency printed a special edition
of its subtly named journal, *Problems of Communism*, exposing the Soviet attack on democratic reforms in the East Bloc.[30] USIS centers circulated the
pamphlet, *Bitter Harvest: The October Revolution in Hungary and Its Aftermath*, which described the Hungarians' quest for free elections and multiparty
government. By crushing legitimate demands for representative government,
Bitter Harvest concluded, the Soviets had exposed the fraudulent nature of
their support for national liberation movements.[31]

When presenting images of the American government, U.S. information
officials offered a meticulous depiction of the benefits fostered by democracy.
They celebrated America's participatory democracy, laws, welfare programs,
and commitment to peace and freedom.[32] In contrast to the ruthless destruction of personal liberties by Soviet authorities, the USIA stressed the dignity

of individuals living in the United States. Cognizant of the tremendous role of spirituality in the lives of people everywhere, U.S. information strategists extolled religious freedom and spiritual practices. Although diplomatic historians have often neglected the role of religion in U.S. foreign relations,[33] American propagandists emphasized Americans' religiosity as a means not only of discrediting communism but also of demonstrating the multiculturalism, tolerance, and community that flourished under U.S. democracy.

U.S. information experts publicized communist persecution of religious leaders and suppression of religious practices. They highlighted the persecution of Soviet Jews and Catholic clergy like Cardinal József Mindszenty of Hungary, Archbishop Alojzije Stepinac of Yugoslavia, and Archbishop Joseph Beran of Czechoslovakia. On December 27, 1948, when the Hungarian communist regime announced the arrest of Mindszenty and thirteen others on allegations of conspiracy, espionage, treason, and illegal currency trading, the State Department directed VOA to treat the case as a symbol of the "destruction of human liberties" behind the Iron Curtain.[34] VOA used similar language in exposing Soviet closures of mosques, refusals to permit Muslims to attend world congresses or make holy pilgrimages, and purges of Islamic leaders in the USSR.[35] By late 1954, the NSC claimed that the USSR had curtailed its suppression of religion as a result of VOA broadcasts on the anti-religious actions and statements of Soviet leaders.[36]

In the earliest stages of the Cold War, American information officials had no formal policy on religious programming. Instead, they abided what Charles Thayer, chief of the VOA Russia desk, described as an unwritten agreement to make "no special pleading for the Christian church"; to celebrate "the political concept of freedom of religious worship"; and to commemorate important religious holidays and festivals.[37] For example, on Easter Sunday 1950, Voice of America broadcasts to Eastern Europe included a special statement from Cardinal Francis Spellman, archbishop of New York. Adopting an ecumenical tone, Spellman declared:

> This is a message from America, from a land of liberty where free men of every faith live in peace and harmony together. All are enjoying freely their God-given rights. . . . With you we are mourning over your enslavement and over your misery, praying for your delivery from persecution and suppression, beseeching God that you also may enjoy the blessings with which we are blessed in America.

Figure 5. Freedom of religious expression was a key element of U.S. attempts to explain and export democratic capitalism. National Archives.

Spellman urged his audience not to lose faith "in this hour when the voice of God is silenced in all the churches, your schools closed, and your press muzzled, your prelates, priests, brothers of the orders, nuns jailed or exiled."[38]

Spellman was only one of dozens of Americans who addressed religious freedom in U.S. propaganda. VOA aired speeches of a spiritual nature made by Presidents Truman and Eisenhower as well as other public officials. Holiday broadcasts included a wide variety of religious music. The State Department republished religiously themed stories such as the chaplain's role in Congress and the history of the Quakers in the United States. Additionally, *Air Bulletin*, a weekly news digest on American life and culture, carried articles like "Books of the Spirit," "Church Women's Aid," and "Salvation Army, Flying Missionaries"[39] (Figure 5).

After the outbreak of the Korean War, Voice of America began regularizing its religious output as part of the Truman administration's "Campaign of Truth." A committee on religion and VOA identified the promotion of spiritual values as a means of combating communist allegations of American materialism, demonstrating the complexity of U.S. life, and showing the importance of human rights in democratic societies. Members recommended a half-hour weekly religious program devoted to Protestantism, Catholicism, and Judaism, "the three major religious faiths in the United States." In order to avoid violating constitutional provisions mandating the separation of church and state, VOA rebroadcast domestic radio religious programming instead of producing its own content. It allotted time on the basis of a faith's representation in the U.S. population. Although State Department policymakers worried that the new show would alienate smaller religious groups, they concluded that a bigger risk inhered in not challenging "ungodliness" behind the Iron Curtain. "A Nation at Worship" began airing in English in October 1950.[40] Monsignor Thomas J. McCarthy of the National Catholic Welfare Conference, Isaac Franck of the Jewish Community Council of Greater Washington, and the Reverend Edward Hughes Pruden of the American Baptist Convention served on the advisory panel reporting to Roger Lyons, VOA's director of religious programming.[41]

By early 1951, U.S. information experts had formulated a strategy on "moral and spiritual factors" in American propaganda. First, they described the role of religion in the United States. They underscored the absence of a national religion and explained the separation of church and state. They extolled the diversity of U.S. religions as well as the right to be irreligious. Second, they appealed to religious peoples abroad. Careful to avoid favoring the Judeo-Christian tradition, U.S. propagandists invoked general principles such as "freedom of conscience, respect for human life and the human spirit, love of one's neighbor, truthfulness, honesty, and loyalty to one's convictions."[42]

By the late 1950s, U.S. information officials had successfully interwoven religious freedom into their larger narrative about American life. In April 1959, USIA director George Allen assured Senator Thomas J. Dodd (D-Conn.) that no exhibition about the United States would be complete without demonstrating the "pervasive influence of religion" as evidenced by

> the role of church and church-affiliated groups in community affairs, the pride we take in our traditional and modern ecclesiastical architecture, typical American families exercising their right to worship as they please in accordance with our constitutional provisions for freedom of worship and the separation of church and state.[43]

Two months later, USIA issued policy guidelines that identified religion as "a vital force in American society." In crafting materials about American life and culture, U.S. information officers were directed to demonstrate how "in America followers of many faiths without sacrificing their religious principles live and work together in an atmosphere of toleration and cooperation."[44] In praising these freedoms and exposing atheism and religious persecution in the USSR, U.S. policymakers aimed to create international support for democratic capitalism.[45]

For maximum efficacy, U.S. officials tailored materials for specific religious groups. Materials directed at Muslims are a good illustration. USIS outposts in Muslim nations avoided depictions of religious taboos such as eating pork and drinking alcohol.[46] During Ramadan, VOA Arabic broadcasts included daily readings from the Quran by well-known imams and special talks on the relation of Islam and democracy.[47] In the early 1950s, U.S. policymakers made demonstrating the incompatibility of the Muslim faith and Marxism one of their top propaganda objectives in Arabic countries. For example, the booklet *Red Star over Islam* asserted that "Communists fear Islam" because "it is a way of life that stands for everything the Communists hate—family ties, love of one's fellow man, respect for the individual, freedom of worship."[48] In January 1953, the VOA Arabic Service carried daily commentaries by Mrs. Zeinab al-Ghazali al-Gobeili, an Egyptian delegate to the Communist-inspired Vienna Peace Congress. Obviously disillusioned by her experience, she declared:

> I think and believe that it is in the interest of the Communists to
> destroy both Christianity and Islam. Therefore it is the duty of
> Moslems and Christians to be aware of the moral degeneracy of
> these people and cling firmly to their faith. There is afoot today a
> plot to destroy all religion.[49]

Four years later, USIS struck similar themes in *Communism v. Islam.* Through a partnership with Front Anti-Komunis, an anticommunist group led by Indonesian Muslims, USIS ensured that copies of the pamphlet reached pilgrims traveling to Mecca. The agency also regularly distributed its publications and films through Islamic schools, organizations, and institutions and placed unattributed news articles about the United States in predominately Muslim countries throughout the Middle East and Asia.[50]

USIA authorities also crafted messages designed to resonate in certain geographic regions or individual nations. Careful not to ignore the Jewish population of the Middle East, the VOA Hebrew Service carried broadcasts celebrating "the integration of American Jews in the pattern of American life."[51] Disseminated throughout Southeast Asia, *Buddhism Under the Soviet Yoke* described communist persecution of Buddhist monks and nuns, seizure of Buddhist temples, and banning of incense, candles, and other articles of worship.[52] In *An Asian Looks at Communism*, J. R. Jayewardene, finance minister of Ceylon, warned of the ramifications of accepting a communist government:

> The Marxist parties—any support for them, or seating them in power, would be not only a change of individuals, not merely an attempt to solve our economic difficulties by socialist methods, but the wiping away of all that the people love and cherish today. . . . It also means that the great religious and cultural heritage which is ours will be swept away; that the right to practice the religions of our choice, whether we are Buddhists, Christians, Muslims, or Hindus, will no longer be conceded; that an age of religious persecution, as experienced in Russia and her satellite countries, will prevail here.[53]

On July 4, 1954, a VOA broadcast to Latvia began with a sermon by the Reverend Richard Zarins, an émigré who led the Latvian Lutheran Church in New York City and who was renowned for his commitment to fellow Latvian refugees.[54] Zarins interwove an explanation of Independence Day, invocation of biblical verses, and praise for a recent congressional resolution adding "under God" to the Pledge of Allegiance. He concluded by exhorting, "Living with the laws of America, let us wish that the Latvian people are also standing firm under God, inseparable from God, and are expecting freedom and justice in their native country."[55] This fusion of nationalism, religion, and political ideology proved a powerful tool in the U.S. ideological assault on communism.

U.S. propagandists assailed other communist restrictions on freedom of thought and expression. They claimed that democracies permitted ideas to flourish unfettered. In 1952, the USIS released *Soviet Communism Threatens Education*, a pamphlet urging foreign educators to resist communism. The booklet warned:

> One of the targets of a Communist regime would be the school system. The Communists realize that to survive they must destroy free

thought. While democracy works through a free people, Communism must have blind, unthinking obedience. Communists secure that obedience through controlled, regimented instruction and the brutal suppression of free thought.[56]

Other USIS publications ridiculed Soviet attempts to censor scholars, artists, and writers. In *It's a Great Life, Comrades*, U.S. information strategists used satirical photographs with captions such as: "I will not compose bourgeois music" and "Who cares about facts? I'm an historian."[57]

U.S. policymakers attacked the one-party ballot system, absence of representative legislatures, and persecution of political dissenters behind the Iron Curtain.[58] In January 1947, Walter Bedell Smith, the American ambassador to the USSR, offered this blistering commentary on recent "democratic" elections for members of the Supreme Council of the Soviet Union:

> Soviet elections are not [a] contest as in a democracy but [a] carefully staged spectacle. Ruling party, controlling government, press, police, utilizes services of its millions of members and of entire state machinery to get one hundred percent vote for its picked slate of candidates. In these elections, public has no choice either of candidates or of issues. . . . This is government of the party, by the party, for the party.[59]

In April 1954, the VOA Persian Service echoed these themes. Broadcasters mocked Soviet news stories portraying the Supreme Soviet as a "democratic legislature at its best." VOA continued:

> It is hard to understand in what way it is democratic, since there is no debate, and since the deputies have been chosen in an election which offers the voters only a single slate, handpicked by the Communist party. It is hard to understand why it is even called a legislature, since the deputies are not asked to propose laws but merely to rubber stamp actions already taken by the Politburo or the Council of Ministers.[60]

Such realities made it easy for American propagandists to expose the undemocratic nature of the communist political system.

In contrast, U.S. officials celebrated the political freedoms characterizing democratic societies. They praised the multiparty elections and diversity of political opinion in the United States. For example, during the 1948 presidential campaign, VOA broadcasters portrayed the Dixiecrat rebellion and the growth of the Progressive Party as evidence of the vitality of American democracy.[61] Four years later, VOA leaders crafted elaborate guidelines on presenting the 1952 presidential campaign to international audiences. They directed their editorialists not to voice personal opinions of candidates or to make predictions about the campaign's outcome. Instead, commentators were to focus on the "color and significance of the U.S. election drama and . . . processes of arriving at free democratic choice."[62]

But such rules did not shield VOA employees from accusations of Democratic bias. Barry Zorthian, then working for the VOA English service, contends that most of his co-workers were Democrats, something he found "not particularly surprising . . . [because] we had just gone through sixteen years of Democratic administrations." Zorthian claims that members of the incoming administration criticized VOA "for not being enthusiastic enough in the central news room about the Eisenhower victory. And that was thrown in our face many times thereafter."[63]

Partisan disputes at home notwithstanding, U.S. propagandists highlighted the laws that protected the American democratic tradition. In September 1950, Voice of America broadcasts to the USSR included an extensive segment on the judiciary. Asserting "No one man, no one group, no one organization or party can hold complete power in the United States," the first narrator praised the checks and balances system. A second narrator then explained the role of the Supreme Court in handling litigation filed by states and individual citizens, verifying the constitutionality of acts by the executive and legislative branches, and resolving disputes between the federal government and state and local administrators. He then detailed the importance of the Court's majority and minority opinions. The publication of these contrasting views, he argued, demonstrated that the Supreme Court "does not consider itself to be a super-human authority and does not claim infallibility"—a critical difference between "free democracies" and "communist autocracies." He challenged Soviet allegations that the Court defended only the interests of big business and monopolies and claimed that the justices were invalidating "the remains of racial inequality." He celebrated decisions abolishing child labor, setting minimum wages and maximum working hours, and establishing old-age pensions, unemployment insurance, and collective bargaining. Although some reforms had evolved slowly in the United States, he insisted:

> They are secure; they cannot be revoked arbitrarily by some dictator. The American Constitution and its interpreting organ—the Supreme Court—protect human and civic rights in the widest sense of the word: the right to life, liberty, and the lawful acquisition of property. In countries of communist autocracy, human and civil rights are recognized on paper only. In actual fact, the communist authorities violate these rights at every step.[64]

Not surprisingly, American propagandists exposed such abuses whenever possible.

U.S. information leaders excoriated communist police states. In May 1951, VOA blasted the communist regimes of China and Poland for issuing decrees mandating the death penalty for a long list of "political crimes" including "cooperating with imperialism," corruption, insurrection, and espionage.[65] Two years later, the USIA released *You Can't Win!* and *This Is the Story of Sergei.* The former was a list sarcastically defining the thirty-seven ideological "crimes" punished under East German law. "Pacifism" indicated a "failure to see that the USSR maintains the world's largest army in order to 'liberate' nations like Czechoslovakia." "Imperialism" encompassed "any opposition to the policies of the Soviet Union." The sarcastic tone of the pamphlet illustrated U.S. disdain for the communist legal system.[66] *This Is the Story of Sergei* featured a man with "one terrible misfortune"—living under communism. The cartoon depicted Sergei protesting Soviet housing conditions, censorship, and "re-educational methods." Soviet authorities murder Sergei for these offenses.[67]

In publications like the "Facts About Communism" series, the USIA denigrated the Soviet justice system. Contrary to communist rhetoric venerating individual rights, Soviet "law" controlled "all phases of human life" and cowed people into silence about government malfeasance. By outlawing "crimes" such as changing jobs without permission or being late for work, Soviet law made it virtually impossible for otherwise innocent people to remain law-abiding. Those convicted of petty crimes like stealing a loaf of bread or a piece of lumber could be sentenced to twenty-five years of slave labor. More hypocritically, USIA also criticized the Soviets' use of the death penalty.[68]

U.S. propagandists found attacking the USSR much easier than defending the actions of Joseph McCarthy. In February 1950, when the senator first alleged that communists had permeated the State Department, VOA did not broadcast the story overseas because it was "primarily of domestic interest" and cast unfavorable light on the U.S. political system. But, as Congress began investigating McCarthy's charges, the news gained worldwide attention. U.S. information leaders concluded that if Voice of America failed to report the hearings, the credibility of U.S. propaganda would plummet. Furthermore, they viewed VOA coverage as essential to counteracting the torrent of communist materials on McCarthyism. Nonetheless, VOA broadcasters restricted their comments to "factual, brief, temperate, and balanced" descriptions. For example, on March 9, 1950, U.S. newscasts to Europe declared, "A Senate subcommittee continued its investigation into the charges of Senator Joseph McCarthy of communist infiltration into the State Department."[69]

Until Congress censured McCarthy in late 1954, U.S. information strategists faced a losing battle in defending and explaining the senator's anticommunist crusade. Many foreigners, especially Western Europeans, found McCarthyism irreconcilable with democratic values. They abhorred the senator's attempts to censor the holdings of USIS libraries and castigated the "hysteria" pervading American political culture.[70] In response, U.S. policymakers attempted to downplay militant anti-communism in the United States or to present it as a defensive measure against the Soviet threat. In May 1954, a VOA Russia broadcast about U.S. political parties claimed that low popularity of the Communist Party of the United States stemmed from the fact that the American people did not sympathize with the party's ideas, actions, or "complete subjugation to the Kremlin." Nonetheless, the "liberality" of the American legal system, VOA argued, accorded the party "equal terms with other parties" and "all the rights and opportunities existing in a free country."[71] Given the extent of anti-leftist laws then in effect in the United States, these assertions stretched credulity.

USIA rarely resorted to such outright distortions. Instead, the agency defended repressive manifestations of domestic anticommunism like the Internal Security Act of 1950 that required federal registration of "communist action" groups and permitted the deportation of individuals with "subversive" political beliefs. Despite the anti-democratic nature of these policies, the USIA pamphlet, *Communists in the Daylight*, supported the legislation, asserting:

> The Internal Security Act of 1950 reflects the determination of the people of the United States to protect their country and its free institutions against the threat of international communism while

avoiding the repressive methods which are inherent in the communist doctrine.

In short, Americans would resort to extreme measures to protect their unique
political system and to ensure national security.[72]

Communist propagandists claimed McCarthyism illustrated the true na-
ture of U.S. democracy. Pointing to the Smith Act and the Internal Security
Act, they denied the existence of freedom of speech in the United States. On
December 27, 1951, Soviet broadcasters declared:

> The Smith Law legalizes the campaign against all progressive ele-
> ments and all defenders of peace in the United States, as "conspira-
> tors." The McCarran Law permits the police to carry out mass
> arrests. On the basis of these draconian laws, thousands of people
> are being put on punitive lists.

A nation too cowardly to permit its citizens to discuss Marxist-Leninism, the
announcers asserted, most certainly did not believe in freedom of speech.[73]

Rather than resorting to hostile attacks on the USSR, U.S. policymakers
attempted to maintain a calm, factual tone when contrasting democracy and
totalitarianism. On May 22, 1952, the USIS circulated *Communism Is Losing*,
an indictment of the Soviet political system focusing on its victims, not its
rulers. The booklet claimed that people everywhere were rejecting Marxism
because "communist promises are meaningless words, used only to conceal
the ambitions of Stalin and the men in the Kremlin." The pamphlet then
listed statistics on the declining status of communism in "free" nations:

> Since 1946, one-third of the Communist Party members in the Western
>   world have abandoned the party.
> In Italy, the Communists have lost over 150,000 members since 1947.
>   . . .
> In Japan, there has been a 28% decrease. In Brazil, a 69% decrease since
>   1947. . . .
> In 1949, the International Confederation of Free Trade Unions
>   (ICFTU) was formed by the free workers of the world as a protest
>   against Communist domination of the World Federation of Trade
>   Unions. By the end of 1951, the ICFTU had 54,000,000 members in
>   70 countries.[74]

As proof of popular discontent behind the Iron Curtain, the USIA pointed to the hundreds of thousands of people fleeing the so-called "paradise of the workers." "These are the men, women, and children who have lived under communism. They have heard the Communist promises. They have seen Communism in action. They have witnessed the tragic results. They offer the best proof that Communism cannot survive," the pamphlet concluded.[75]

Communist escapees in the post-1945 era served as powerful, pro-Western propaganda. On March 3, 1953, the Voice of America's Russian service noted that more than 2 million refugees had fled from the Soviet zone of Germany at the rate of 20,000 a month. Broadcasters described the exodus as follows:

> Seeking freedom from serfdom are peasants, whom the Stalinist whip-wielders in East Germany are forcibly herding into *kolkohozes*. Factory and plant workers, not wishing to be turned into robots, deprived of all rights and subjected to a cruel exploitation by communist state capitalism, are fleeing to the free world. Deserting are young people whom communist militarism has forced into the army, hypocritically named the "People's Police."[76]

Despite these strong accusations, U.S. officials were reticent to use communist refugees as American propagandists. On July 16, 1948, Secretary of State George Marshall asserted that most émigrés should not be employed as VOA commentators because their former countrymen sometimes resented them. Moreover, refugees often voiced political opinions contrary to U.S. foreign policy.[77]

The USIA, however, eagerly publicized the achievements of notable escapees from totalitarianism. In 1954, USIA published *They Escaped to Freedom*. Using a comic book format, the pamphlet profiled thirteen individuals who had made daring getaways from communist nations. Karel Havelik, a young Czech lawyer, led thirteen men out of a labor camp by crawling through an abandoned mine shaft and traveling thirty-five miles into West Germany. Dr. Jing-Chi, a physician horrified by the North Korean army's disregard for human life, surrendered to the United Nations command rather than remain in his communist homeland. These "average people," USIA concluded, were "deprived by communism of their freedom, their faith, their heritage" and were "unhappy human beings desperately seeking to regain, by even the most hazardous means, the cherished rights and privileges which only free men enjoy."[78] USIS films like *Dance to Freedom* profiled individuals who defected in order to fulfill their artistic ambitions.[79] In March 1957, USIS distributed 65,000 copies of *In Quest of Freedom*. The pamphlet described the lives of individuals who fled Nazism, fascism, and communism and found in America "a climate of freedom in which his particular talent flourished." The list included conductor Arturo Toscanini, inventor Igor Sikorsky, biologist Selman Waksman, composer Sergei Rachmaninoff, architect Walter Gropius, and physicist Albert Einstein. The booklet then extolled U.S. programs for resettling people displaced by totalitarian oppression, war, or disaster.[80]

In upholding the dignity of individuals, the USIA discounted Soviet largess to impoverished nations. In May 1952, the USIA broadside *By Their Fruits Ye Shall Know Them* asserted:

> For too long has the Kremlin talked of its concern for the unfortu-
> nates of the world. For too long has the Soviet Union orated about
> its self-proclaimed benevolence. For too long have Communist
> claims of championing the underdog gone unchallenged.

The pamphlet pointed out that the USSR had contributed nothing to the United Nations International Children's Emergency Fund, the International Refugee Organization, or the World Health Organization. The United States, of course, had provided generous assistance to all of these organizations.[81] Special USIA packets directed at women abroad frequently included stories about American charities and government programs for the needy. At the same time, the agency printed articles like "Aid to Blind Denied by Communists" claiming that Czech authorities refused to supply "seeing eye" dogs for "non-communist blind, or those who have not sufficiently proved their loyalty to the communist regime."[82] Not only did American democracy offer greater individual freedom, the USIA argued, but the U.S. government also cared more about the welfare of people.

U.S. policymakers drew stark distinctions between democratic and communist nations. Where democracies permitted patriotism and individuality to flourish, communist states compelled nations and peoples to abandon their identities. Where democratic countries allowed multiparty elections, representative government, and open political debate, communist societies deprived their citizens of genuine political participation. Where democratic legal systems protected civil liberties and personal property, communist laws authorized widespread police surveillance, detention camps, and dramatic re-strictions of individual liberties.

U.S. information strategists presented the United States as a nation that valued its citizens, its families, and its tradition of freedom. They appealed to patriotism and individualism. They celebrated dignity, spirituality, and creativity. They promoted pluralism, tolerance, and respect. They defined democracy as a political system, an ideology, and a way of life worthy of victory in the Cold War.

CHAPTER FOUR

Selling Capitalism: Images of the Economy, Labor, and Consumerism

IN 1960, ECONOMIST Walt Whitman Rostow published *The Stages of Economic Growth: A Non-Communist Manifesto*. Explicitly challenging Karl Marx's portrait of capitalism as an oligarchic and unstable system, Rostow defended capitalism as the surest path to political freedom, personal fulfillment, and economic security. Rostow outlined an economic progression in which "traditional" societies reached a "take-off," attained "maturity," and then entered an "age of high mass-consumption." Not surprisingly, Rostow identified the United States as the exemplar of enlightened modernity and democratic values.[1]

Like most of his contemporaries, Rostow fervently believed in American exceptionalism. Americans have long viewed themselves as a free and prosperous people whose nation inspires admiration throughout the world. They are convinced that the United States can spread its vision of democratic capitalism abroad without imperiling the standards of living and political liberties making America special. In the words of historian Michael Hunt, the United States can "transform the world without itself being transformed."[2]

Such views pervaded U.S. foreign policy in the 1940s and 1950s. U.S. officials like Rostow preached a gospel of modernization in which economic development fostered political and social freedoms. They fused a benevolent conception of American national identity to the pursuit of U.S. economic and political objectives abroad. Although they denied imperial ambitions, U.S. policymakers declared that all nations that adopted democratic capitalism could attain the superior way of life found in the United States.

The Stages of Economic Growth, advertisements, and U.S. propaganda materials produced during the early Cold War show striking parallels and similarities. While U.S. information officials did not use the term "modernization," their efforts to promote democratic capitalism echoed modernization theorists. This is not surprising, given that many social scientists who espoused modernization theory, including Rostow, Alex Inkeles, and Daniel Lerner, worked as consultants to America's psychological warfare and propaganda programs. So did leading advertising executives such as Sigmund Larmon of Young and Rubicam, William B. Benton of Benton and Bowles, and T. S. Repplier of the Advertising Council. Drawn together by a collective vision of American national greatness, public and private individuals crafted propaganda that claimed that the United States not only could but should lead the world to modernity, liberalism, democracy, and capitalism. Through linking the social, spiritual, and political benefits of capitalism to its economic advantages, they offered a powerful alternative to communism. Propagandists, advertising executives, and modernization theorists worked separately to achieve the shared goal of a global order governed by American standards of freedom, productivity, and rationality.[3]

At the end of World War II, the United States was poised to make itself the world's political, economic, cultural, and strategic superpower. Many foreigners viewed the United States as the epitome of modernity. America's industry, technology, mass culture, efficiency, consumerism, and progress were widely admired and occasionally feared by international business people, intellectuals, and mass audiences.[4] U.S. officials worried that "less fortunate" countries would resent—and perhaps sabotage—America's economic and political success. In order to avert such suspicion and resistance, U.S. policymakers dedicated themselves to explaining the U.S. economic system to foreign audiences. From the inception of the postwar information program, American propagandists linked the defense of liberal capitalism to the preservation of world peace and freedom. In articulating the material and immaterial values democratic capitalism accorded individuals, they defined American national identity and defended U.S. strategic interests to a world facing the threat of communism.

These attempts to promote American consumerism and free enterprise abroad won wide support from corporate and labor organizations. Throughout the Great Depression and World War II, business and labor often clashed on issues such as the connection between government and the economy, the functions and scope of the welfare state, and the role of unions in workplace management. By 1948, following passage of the Taft-Hartley Act and a back-lash against New Deal liberalism, business-labor relations became less acrimonious. As unions surrendered their demands for economic planning and government regulation, industry awarded wage and benefit increases. Labor and business embraced the notion that the federal government should ensure sustained economic growth and minimal expansion of the welfare state. This consensus included shared beliefs in individual freedom and opportunity, "classlessness," productivity, and a dynamic economy. Although corporate and labor leaders struggled to maintain this accord throughout the 1950s, these common assumptions inspired both sides to assist U.S. international information programs promoting liberal capitalism, free trade, and consumption.[5]

In the aftermath of World War II, the distorted and unfavorable picture of the United States being propagated by the Soviet Union greatly disturbed U.S. officials. In September 1945, Assistant Secretary of State for Public Affairs William B. Benton declared:

> The war has dramatized once more the superlative economic strength of the United States. The advent of atomic power, with American science in the forefront of research, means that we have become—temporarily at least—the most powerful military nation on earth. Such strength could easily generate suspicion and dislike abroad. Thus we face one of the great challenges of our history. Morally, spiritually, and intellectually we must rise to the responsibilities inherent in our economic and political strength. And we must make clear to all the world that we propose to use our strength and the force of our example, constructively and in the interest of the well-being of all mankind.[6]

But not all America's motives were altruistic. U.S. officials also believed that nations familiar with American technology and production methods were more likely to purchase U.S. goods and services. American propaganda on economic issues, therefore, protected commerce as well as national security.[7]

On January 20, 1946, Averell Harriman, U.S. ambassador to the USSR, described widely disseminated communist accounts of strikes, unemployment, crime, and racial discrimination in the United States. The Soviets saw communism, not democratic capitalism, as the most progressive political and economic system in the world. Rather than attacking the Soviet government—a strategy that risked sparking an anti-American backlash—Harriman urged his superiors to embark on a "vigorous and intelligent" American information program that explained the virtues of the American way of life to foreign audiences, especially those in communist countries.[8]

Other U.S. officials made similar recommendations. In November 1947, General Walter Bedell Smith, Harriman's successor, warned that "the myth of Communist paradise" was impeding U.S. attempts to promote the Marshall Plan. Smith offered detailed instructions for countering Soviet propaganda. He suggested publicizing the regimentation of the Soviet economy in which "labor loses individuality and becomes like a draft animal to be used where boss thinks best." He pointed to child labor, low productivity, and the poor standard of living as further ways to undermine communism. Giving a factual account of American working conditions and the realities of capitalism, Smith argued, would generate support for the Marshall Plan among Europeans.[9]

U.S. policymakers also hoped to combat anti-Americanism in the developing world. In July 1948, Secretary of State George Marshall directed American diplomats to use all of their resources to challenge the distorted views of the United States held by people in "third countries." According to Marshall, the most pervasive stereotypes included

- The belief that the United States and its citizens have unlimited wealth.
- The belief that the United States government is run by "Wall Street" and by "the monopoly capitalists."
- The belief that Americans are wholly materialistic, have no culture worthy of mention, and judge everything by its value in dollars.

Finally, Marshall warned that many foreigners believed that American democratic principles were used to conceal widespread racial and economic discrimination and oligarchic practices.[10]

As the ideological battle between capitalism and communism intensified, U.S. information leaders escalated their efforts to promote the American economic system abroad. In 1950, as part of Truman's "Campaign of Truth," the State Department began a "Labor Information Program" under the auspices of its Office of International Information (OII) and Office of Educational Exchange (OEX). Charged with "winning the support of the working people of foreign countries for free institutions and against totalitarianism," a new labor advisor began coordinating projects with the Psychological Strategy Board (PSB), the Department of Labor, the Economic Cooperation Administration

(ECA), and American and international trade union organizations. The State Department *Wireless Bulletin* started issuing *Labor Air Bulletin* each week. Film strips, photo exhibits, cartoons, and motion pictures highlighting labor themes were also planned. Voice of America hired a labor editor and aired interviews with labor leaders.[11]

American propagandists insisted that the United States did not view itself as a model for all nations. A 1959 USIA policy paper read, "The Agency does not attempt to 'sell' the American economic system as a blueprint for other countries to follow."[12] This disingenuous disclaimer notwithstanding, U.S. information officials, advertising executives, and modernization theorists were quite willing to advocate American economic ideals and to extol the virtues of life in a capitalist democracy. They viewed the American standard of living and mass consumption as evidence that the U.S. economic system represented the pinnacle of economic development and modernity.

U.S. information authorities hoped to capitalize on the high level of international curiosity about living conditions in the United States. Consequently, they carefully designed programs that stressed three basic elements of the American economy: free competitive enterprise, free trade unionism, and limited government intervention. In creating this picture of capitalism, USIA administrators emphasized that the American economic system, unlike socialism or communism, did not leave laborers beholden to an uncaring bureaucracy. "We do insist," information leaders asserted, "that the economy should exist for the benefit of the citizen, not for the state." Therefore, their portrayal of the American economy emphasized "related themes" such as the quest for social justice, the equitable distribution of income, "the growing classlessness of our society," the potential growth of the U.S. economy, and the thriving culture of the United States.[13]

U.S. information strategists meticulously interwove the economic and social benefits capitalism could produce.[14] Information packets prepared for distribution in all American embassies featured stories like "Labor's Drive for Guaranteed Annual Wages," "Union Plan Opens New Careers for Disabled Miners," "Wider Employment Opportunities for Women," and "Profit-Sharing Plans in U.S. Industry." Overall, U.S. propagandists accented harmonious labor and management relations, movement toward racial and gender equality in the workplace, and the material benefits capitalism afforded the typical worker, especially when juxtaposed to his or her Soviet counterpart.[15]

In advocating the American economic system, U.S. policymakers had to overcome negative international perceptions of capitalism. Soviet propagandists bombarded foreign audiences with reports of widespread labor unrest, insoluble social problems, economic instability, and high unemployment in the United States.[16] These accounts resonated abroad. Even after war-torn nations began to recover, American officials noted that misconceptions about the U.S. economy persisted. In early 1951, State Department analysts described how European "managerial elites" were exploiting loopholes in their national tax and trust laws. Although the United States forbade similar practices, the officials reported, much of the European populace linked the abuses to the American free enterprise system.[17]

Many foreign workers, even those living in capitalist nations, did not wish to emulate the American economy. A 1952 State Department analysis revealed that many foreign workers possessed few of the benefits U.S. laborers enjoyed and therefore viewed capitalism as "a system that protects management, yields inordinately high profits to the employer and does not give the employee a fair return for his day's work." They assumed that U.S. capitalism differed little from their own economies. Accordingly, they did not "view America as the answer to their prayers, or as a country that it is to their advantage to support or imitate."[18]

In some nations, conceptions of capitalism remained those put forth by Marx in the 1848 political treatise *The Communist Manifesto*. Using Great Britain as a case study, Marx alleged that capitalism led to poverty, instability, and exploitation. Over a century later, American propagandists in the State Department and the United States Information Agency (USIA) struggled to disprove Marx's charges. For example, a 1956 survey of 1,665 entrepreneurs in India revealed generally unfavorable attitudes characterizing capitalism as a system marked by worker exploitation, high unemployment, oligarchy, and "a general lack of social responsibility." For these reasons, Indian businessmen concluded that capitalism was not an acceptable system for their nation.[19]

U.S. information leaders addressed these criticisms by differentiating U.S. capitalism from its European "cartel-like or feudalistic" variations. They praised the American "mixed economy" characterized by federal regulations, individual freedom, collective bargaining, and economic competition. They stressed the purchasing power of the American consumer and his or her ability to choose among competing goods and services. Legal authorities and consumer groups protected the public from unfair and dangerous business practices and products. The spread of private pensions, insurance plans, and social security programs gave U.S. workers "the floor of security for the individual which a dynamic, urbanized society requires."[20] The U.S. economy was stable and productive.[21] Yet even some USIA officials resisted this portrayal. One complained, "I don't think you're going to get any successful preaching of that point because the average government employee, the average bureaucrat, no matter how sincere, would not" accept a completely affirmative version of U.S. capitalism.[22]

The communists of course flatly rejected this vision. Determined to defeat capitalism, Soviet propagandists derided the American economy as immoral, imperialist, and materialistic. Communist officials claimed that the "socialist" system of the Sino-Soviet bloc provided the "only pattern for rapid industrialization and economic growth which will benefit the many instead of a select few."[23] Soviet authorities contended the average U.S. worker stood powerless in the face of pervasive malnutrition, severe unemployment, and an oligarchic political system. Furthermore, they claimed Wall Street financiers intensified the arms race "for the purpose of reinforcing the dictatorship of monopoly capital" and "to convince workers that a militarized economy means full employment." Capitalism, in short, fueled the Cold War.[24]

In response to such attacks, U.S. information experts assailed the Soviet "worker's paradise." When State Department analysts identified the principal weaknesses of the Soviet economy, they argued:

> While all labor in the Soviet Union is in effect forced since "the happy workers" cannot leave the country and must work, the concentration camp system as such probably constitutes the Soviet Union's principal psychological vulnerability since it runs entirely counter to Russian ideals of solidarity and fraternity and since it is the living proof of the evils inherent in trying to force an unworkable system to work.

Furthermore, the analysts suggested publicizing the low standard of living and poor housing conditions in the USSR. They recommended emphasizing the economic disparity between the average Soviet citizen and communist bureaucrats who enjoyed "dachas, good clothes, good food and other luxuries."[25]

U.S. propagandists stressed the impact of communism on individuals and families. Some USIS publications, such as *The Truth Crushes Commie Lies*, bluntly attacked communist labor laws. "Communism means no freedom for workers," the pamphlet declared. The text pointed out that Soviet workers could not bargain collectively, choose or quit their jobs, strike, or form their own unions.[26] The provocative USIS comic book *It Happened to Us!* portrayed communism's deleterious effect on a Soviet family. One of the cartoons depicts the young daughter, Louise, at a communist indoctrination center. A matronly teacher tells her, "Home-making and raising children are inferior occupations." Not yet modern enough to accept nontraditional gender roles, the USIA implied that only an economically backward nation created women who valued careers more than motherhood.[27]

U.S. information officials frequently criticized slave labor in the USSR and China. Through stories like "Slave Labor Follows the Russian Flag" and "The New Slavery," they contrasted oppressive working conditions in communist nations with the freedom and prosperity found among American laborers.[28] Pamphlets such as *The Road to Serfdom* and *Slave Labor* described how the collectivization of agriculture devastated farmers living in North Korea and the Soviet Union.[29] Communism, U.S. information officials maintained, destroyed families and devalued workers.

In contrast, capitalism enabled individuals to fulfill their ambitions and to live in comfort. In the early 1950s, the USIS distributed more than a million copies of *Meet Some Americans at Work*, a lengthy pictorial essay portraying a variety of U.S. workers. All appeared content. Not a word about racial and gender discrimination, wage inequities, or labor unrest accompanied the photographs.[30] In April 1953, Voice of America offered this glowing profile of "the American farmer":

> The freedom he enjoys and the non-interference of the federal and state authorities in his affairs have made him a citizen conscious of his role. The American farmer is the wealthiest farmer in the world. His farm is equipped with the most modern agricultural tools; the soil's production comes in with abundance; his family is healthy and happy.[31]

In October 1955, USIA guidelines on the American economy stressed the salary increases, investment opportunities, stock purchases, and fringe benefits available to productive U.S. workers.[32] The 1957 USIA pamphlet *Thomas Brackett* emphasized the lifestyle of the average American. Brackett, a Ford Motor Company employee, owned a car and a house stocked with appliances. He planned to send his four children to college. His high wages enabled his wife to remain at home. "There are millions of American capitalists like the Bracketts," the booklet concluded.[33]

Juxtaposing the gains in wages and benefits won by American unions to the existence of forced labor camps behind the Iron Curtain, USIA administrators sought to define unions as a force protecting workers in democratic nations.[34] The USIS booklet *American Labor Unions: Their Role in the Free World* exemplifies these efforts, asserting:

> American workers know how difficult is the struggle for security and justice. Through their unions, they triumphed after many failures. . . . Capitalism in a democracy uses its forces not in a negative way, to depress and exploit the masses, but to expand production, to create new ideas and new wealth.[35]

In October 1958, USIA guidelines on labor information activities identified "militant and responsible free trade unions" as "the symbol of the democratic movement through which workers in all free countries are making or can make real progress toward a better life with peace and freedom."[36] USIA authorities frequently cited American labor leaders in order to demonstrate widespread domestic support for the objectives espoused by the U.S. information establishment.[37] They pointed to union programs for women and African Americans as examples of progressive, democratic attitudes.[38]

The role of organized labor, however, formed only a portion of the larger image of the American worker crafted by the USIA. The agency rarely focused on white collar workers in materials directed at foreign laborers. For example, a December 1955 article called "An American Worker's Family" featured Ray Bellingham, a mill operator at General Electric's locomotive and car equipment department in Erie, Pennsylvania. The Bellinghams discussed Ray's wages, mortgage payments, workday, and taxes. His wife, Helen, described her attempts to maintain a budget while feeding and clothing their family of six.[39]

The Bellinghams exemplified how the "classlessness" of U.S. society enabled individuals to reap the benefits of capitalism. The gains included profit-sharing, paid vacations, sick leaves, company-sponsored scholarships, and health insurance. Job security, workman's compensation, and unemployment stipends demonstrated the existence of an American social welfare system.[40] Like the modernization theorists, U.S. propagandists attacked the Marxist claim that capitalism only helped the wealthy.

In contrast to the dignity and decent standard of living accorded American workers, USIA materials showed "Soviet drones" locked in a despotic system plagued by sinecures, forced labor camps, and oppressive working conditions.[41] Under communism, "classlessness" was a chimera. Despite its rhetoric about worker equality, the Soviet government lavished Communist Party officials, military leaders, and secret policemen with higher salaries, better housing, posh vacations, and luxury items.[42] Communist unions, American information officials alleged, existed only to ensure worker discipline and production quotas set so high that no worker could ever meet them.[43] Simple factual accounts of Communist slave labor camps provided USIA policymakers with propaganda more effective than anything they could create.[44]

But countering Communist allegations that capitalism served only rich, white men was a great challenge for USIA officials who considered racial issues "America's major point of vulnerability, especially when dealing with non-white peoples."[45] USIA information packets frequently included stories acclaiming an African American for his or her achievements in order to demonstrate that racial discrimination did not impede careers.[46] They also emphasized the progress made by U.S. companies in eradicating racial inequities.[47] By "put[ting] the Negro problem in perspective," USIA officials could focus on advantages of democratic capitalism.[48]

In order to deflect attention from the status of African Americans, information leaders pointed to the economic success of other minority groups. For example, a May 1951 VOA broadcast in Hebrew addressed the financial standing of Jews in the United States. After explaining that most American Jews held commercial and professional jobs, VOA declared that "this phenomenon of occupational concentration is one of the characteristics of the different immigrant groups and their descendants in this country." Italians dominated the building trades while Greeks gravitated toward the flower and restaurant industries. Early Jewish settlers worked as peddlers or in garment factories. Not surprisingly, VOA did not mention how anti-Semitism and nativism affected these workers. Instead, the broadcast lauded the hard work that enabled these immigrants to rise out of poverty as well as the leadership of Jews in the American labor movement.[49]

It proved more difficult for U.S. propagandists to illustrate capitalism's positive impact on American Indians and Hispanics. Cognizant of the dismal conditions on most reservations, USIA could offer few examples of Indian economic success. For example, a June 1953 labor packet examined a small band of Aleuts working in the Alaskan seal fur trade. At the height of U.S. efforts to deport illegal Mexican immigrants, the same publication stressed that "wetbacks" were not "forced to work involuntarily."[50] Such assertions, one speculates, did little to improve the international reputation of the American free enterprise system.

USIA had a much easier time demonstrating how capitalism benefited women and children. U.S. information administrators exposed the Soviet "workers' paradise" as one in which women operated drop forges and worked as stevedores while their children languished in state-run day care. U.S. propagandists hoped to shatter Communist claims of gender equity and equality of opportunity.[51] USIA women's packets often featured stories about the economic status of women behind the Iron Curtain. In August 1953, June S. McIlvaine, an American journalist, recounted her recent visit to the USSR. In a tour of the Stalin Auto Workers, McIlvaine recalled:

> I saw many women working in the foundry. Without goggles, fireproof gloves or any of the safety devices Americans would regard as essential, they were pouring molten metal. . . . I saw girls who didn't look more than 14 years old mopping floors in the subway, laying bricks and even lugging loads of bricks up ten flights of steps.[52]

True concern for the role of women, U.S. information officials implied, necessitated protecting their roles as homemakers and mothers, not as manual laborers. USIS materials stressed U.S. laws safeguarding women from hazardous jobs. Most important, they emphasized that the high wages earned by American men allowed mothers to raise their children at home.[53]

This emphasis on domesticity created some fascinating contrasts between Communist and American propaganda. Using articles like "Help for Housewives with Heart Disease" and omitting women perceived as too career-oriented from Agency materials, USIA officials countered Soviet portrayals of American working women as immoral and greedy.[54] By presenting women like Mrs. Gail Forster of Philadelphia as typical Americans, U.S. information leaders hoped to instill images of selflessness and devotion extending beyond the family. In an April 1953 USIA packet aimed at foreign women, Mrs. Foster described not only her child-rearing activities and household chores, but also her involvement with her church and a community housing committee.[55] American women best typified Agency ideals by achieving in the home, not at the workplace.

In addition to written materials and radio programs, international trade fairs highlighted the U.S. economy. In the aftermath of World War II, private business leaders and government officials began collaborating on international trade exhibits and exchange programs in the hope of generating foreign support for American-style capitalism, especially in developing nations. The rise of the Cold War gave new urgency to these efforts as the United States strove to prove the superiority of its economic system over that of the Soviet Union. In 1954, lagging far behind the USSR in participation in international trade fairs,[56] the Eisenhower administration earmarked $2 million in "emergency funds" to begin expanding the U.S. presence in international trade exhibits. They aimed to persuade the "free and captive" people of the world that "the United States' great productive capacity" was dedicated to "the preservation of peace and the improvement of mankind's standard of living" and "basic principles of human dignity and freedom."[57]

U.S. displays directly linked consumption, democracy, and the American way of life. The Commerce Department and USIA worked closely with private businesses in determining what types of products and displays best demonstrated the wonders of consumer capitalism. U.S. exhibits usually featured a typical furnished house, manufactured goods and appliances, mail-order catalogues, as well as television and motion picture shows.[58] For example, at the Constitution Fair in Bangkok, Thailand, in December 1954, representatives from more than 140 American firms displayed their products under the general theme of "The Fruits of Freedom." Their wares included the latest construction and road-building equipment, a Chevrolet Corvette, toys, household goods, medical supplies, and air conditioning. The message that the Soviet Union could not match such material bounty, political freedom, and cultural vibrancy was hardly subtle.[59] By 1960, more than 60 million people had attended ninety-seven U.S. trade exhibits in twenty-nine countries.[60]

But American trade exhibits produced mixed results. On April 25, 1956, USIA researchers released a survey of visitors to U.S. exhibits in the Far East, South Asia, Europe, and Latin America. The survey revealed that audiences were "predominately male, young to middle-aged, medium to well-educated, and in business or white collar occupations." U.S. exhibits were no more popular than those of the USSR and, in fact, less appealing than those of China. Although audience members ranked displays of Chinese creative arts materials and Soviet heavy machinery highly, they were also intrigued by demonstrations of American technology. Televisions, electric trains, airplanes, sewing machines, and sports cars drew crowds at U.S. pavilions. It proved more difficult to substantiate whether the trade fairs affected audience opinions about the United States.[61]

U.S. policymakers recognized that American material wealth was not necessarily a propaganda asset. Communist propagandists regularly seized on international displays of U.S. consumer goods as evidence of materialism and immorality in the United States. To deflect such distortions, U.S. propagandists tied the success of American economy to its democratic system. Communism, they insisted, destroyed individual initiative.[62] On April 23, 1953, William L. Grenoble, an administrator of the International Motion Picture Service, explained:

> One of our biggest jobs—this is of course directly related in antipathy to the Communist line—is to demonstrate that although the average American has a good deal more of the material things of life than many people throughout the world, he has attained those by the application of hard work and ingenuity, and other people can do the same.[63]

Americans, in short, were not lazy. They had earned their possessions by performing well in an economy that valued productivity and creativity.

The USIS film *The Pursuit of Happiness* illustrates these themes. Bill Johnson, an auto worker, dreams about buying his own motel. As he and his wife peruse brochures on inn-keeping, the narrator declares, "Bill did not feel like a member of the working class." But, after he completes a course on auto mechanics and gets a promotion at his factory, Bill abandons the idea of becoming his own boss. The film then segues to Paul Abbott, an executive at a shoemaking plant. Paul has worked his way up to management from the assembly line. He now wants the factory to adopt new machines and make more styles, but he understands that he must consult his workers, his shareholders, and his vendors. After bringing his suggested improvements in marketing and manufacturing to these stakeholders, Paul successfully introduces changes that result in a more profitable, efficient, and inventive operation. Individual initiative and management-labor harmony prevail. Such tales of success, the film concludes, "are not merely a pattern of buildings, production, and technology," but the results of the dignity accorded American workers.[64] It was difficult to miss the implication that nations that did not emulate American modernization were inferior.

Because foreign audiences noticed these value judgments, even accurate portrayals of typical U.S. workers could produce undesirable results. Although broadcasts extolling capitalism generated fan mail, some of the letters contained sarcastic comments like, "I listen to the Voice of America everyday. Please send me a Buick automobile. Yours sincerely."[65] Some audience members were intimidated by accounts of American economic performance. In December 1954, Clifton B. Forster, the public affairs officer of the USIA post in Fukora, Japan, recounted his difficulties in reaching Japanese laborers. When presented with factual representations of "the daily activity of an American laborer which show him driving to work in his own car, eating a steak by a Westinghouse Refrigerator, etc.," Foster explained, the Japanese expressed strong resentment and feelings of inferiority. "You are much too advanced over there," one labor leader commented.[66]

Yet foreigners were fascinated by U.S. consumer goods. Mail-order catalogues from U.S. stores ranked among the most popular materials at USIS libraries. In Finland, U.S. embassy officials claimed back issues of the Sears, Roebuck & Company catalogue "have been worn out through use, rebound with stronger covers and put back into circulation." In West Berlin, USIS authorities chained the catalogues to the tables as Germans crowded four deep to glimpse the illustrations. An airport bookstore in Djakarta, Indonesia reported selling the catalogues for $20 each despite currency restrictions that prevented Indonesians from ordering the items featured.[67]

Communist authorities were often stunned by the popularity of American products. When Yugoslav officials obtained a stolen copy of the film *The Grapes of Wrath*, they fully expected their audiences to be horrified by its vivid depiction of poverty in the United States during the Great Depression. But not only did viewers claim that far worse conditions existed in contemporary Yugoslavia, they were also mesmerized by the jalopies driven by the Okies. One audience member declared, "This can't be such a bad country if even these laborers, those workers there, can drive away in their own automobiles."[68]

These events inspired U.S. propagandists to respond assertively to Soviet distortions of the American economy. Certain that the Soviet Union could not match U.S. levels of productivity, State Department analysts expressed little concern over improvements in the Soviet standard of living.[69] Accordingly, USIS materials emphasized the comparative work time required to buy certain items in the United States and the Soviet Union. For example, an April 1953 pamphlet featured a chart showing the buying power of an average Moscow worker as far lower than that of a laborer in New York. "For a pound of bread, he has to work twice as long as the American worker; for potatoes, he has to work about three times as long; for beef, 5 times; for eggs, about 7 times; and for sugar, 25 times."[70] USIA researchers noted clothing, housing, and food shortages in the USSR[71] (Figure 6).

COMPARATIVE WORKTIME REQUIRED TO BUY BASIC FOOD ITEMS

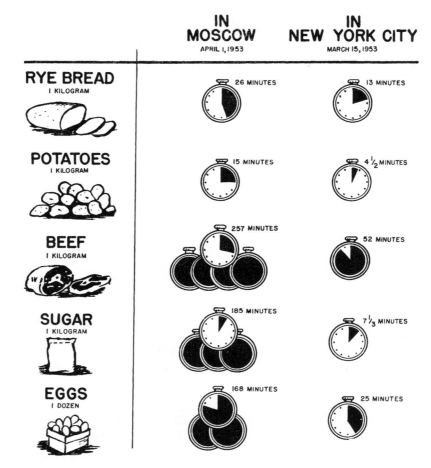

	IN MOSCOW APRIL 1, 1953	IN NEW YORK CITY MARCH 15, 1953
RYE BREAD 1 KILOGRAM	26 MINUTES	13 MINUTES
POTATOES 1 KILOGRAM	15 MINUTES	4 ½ MINUTES
BEEF 1 KILOGRAM	257 MINUTES	52 MINUTES
SUGAR 1 KILOGRAM	185 MINUTES	7 ⅓ MINUTES
EGGS 1 DOZEN	168 MINUTES	25 MINUTES

Figure 6. U.S. information experts drew stark contrasts between the lives of American and Soviet workers. This chart, prepared for the USIA by the U.S. Department of Labor, explained purchasing power in terms average people could understand. National Archives.

Nothing exemplifies the U.S. effort to promote democratic capitalism and modernization better than the "People's Capitalism" campaign. In August 1955, after completing a six-month tour of USIA facilities worldwide, T. S. Repplier, president of the Advertising Council and an advisor to President Eisenhower, claimed that the United States needed propaganda to counter communist gains in the underdeveloped world. Intentionally appropriating communist rhetoric, Repplier suggested "People's Capitalism" as the campaign's slogan. Impressed with Repplier's recommendations, Eisenhower ordered U.S. information strategists to plan an unprecedented global effort to explain capitalism to foreign peoples. In conjunction with private citizens in the advertising and public relations fields, American officials carefully designed written texts, films, and exhibitions that debunked Marxist rhetoric and promoted democratic capitalism.[72]

Privately, the creators of "People's Capitalism" expressed deep faith in democratic capitalism and modernization. On November 28, 1955, USIA research officer Henry Loomis argued that capitalism allowed individual nations to progress without violent revolution.[73] In January 1956, while explaining the campaign to the U.S. Department of Commerce, USIA Deputy Director Abbott Washburn praised "People's Capitalism" for emphasizing that "the people own the capital and the people share the benefits."[74]

At the same time, propaganda advisors tested the themes of "People's Capitalism" before American audiences. On October 27, 1955, Repplier spoke to the Business Paper Editors of America and stressed the urgency of finding a way to explain "the American way of life." After candidly admitting that "People's Capitalism" sounded "Russian," Repplier asserted:

> like "democracy," "freedom" and other words which were bequeathed to us in the founding documents, the word "people's" has been kidnapped by the Russians. Yet no word is more American. The U.S. Constitution begins with "We, the people," and an immortal and inspired definition of democracy is Abraham Lincoln's "government of the people, by the people, and for the people." It is high time we liberated this noun from the Russians. We cannot let the Soviets steal all our good words. At long last, let us turn the tables on them. Let us take back a word as American as apple pie.[75]

A few weeks later, Sherman Adams, another of Eisenhower's advisors, made a similar appeal on the Mutual Broadcasting System radio network.[76]

Before sending "People's Capitalism" abroad, USIA leaders held a public preview of the exhibit. On February 14 and 15, 1956, almost 25,000 people, including 100 invited foreign journalists, filed through the main hall of Washington's Union Station to preview "People's Capitalism." Celebrated as a "means of bringing information about America to the world and counteracting the falsehoods of communism," the display highlighted two homes: the common dwelling in 1776 and a modern, prefabricated steel house stocked with new furniture and labor-saving appliances. Another display featured a contemporary nail-making machine creating 16,000 in an hour, an amount one thousand times greater than the average Revolutionary era artisan making nails by hand. Visitors learned that "people's capitalism," unlike previous economic systems, enabled most workers to own property and to profit from the results of increased productivity through higher wages and greater availability of consumer goods. "The people themselves," the exhibit declared, "are the capitalists."[77]

But "People's Capitalism" meant different things to different people. Visitors to the exhibit offered their opinions. President Eisenhower suggested the incorporation of additional material on the religious and cultural life of the typical U.S. worker in order to illustrate that capitalism fostered freedoms beyond the workplace. Others remarked that the homes "looked too good" to represent typical workers. After evaluating the comments made by USIA officers and visitors to the exhibit, the Agency made minor revisions.[78] In an attempt to evoke more humble Americana, a revised version of the display used a log cabin similar to Abraham Lincoln's childhood home. And, striving to achieve a more "lived-in" look, USIA officials replaced the new furniture and appliances in the modern house with used ones.[79]

The revised script for "People's Capitalism" offers cogent insights into the methods and motives for the campaign. Boldface titles alerted visitors to important themes including "THE REWARDS WERE SHARED WITH THE WORKERS," "AMERICA BECAME A MIDDLE-INCOME NATION," "ALMOST EVERYBODY BECAME A CAPITALIST," and "WEAKNESSES TEND TO BE ONLY TEMPORARY." Anticipating many of the points later made by Rostow, the exhibit defined capitalism as much more than an economic system. Contrary to Marx's economic determinism, "People's Capitalism" encompassed political, spiritual, and cultural elements as well as economics. Although communists presented themselves as the guardians of working people, only capitalist nations gave their citizens "*complete freedom* to choose their jobs, to work where they wished, to invest, to start a business or a labor union." Where Marx predicted monopolies, instability, and low wages, "People's Capitalism" proved the vitality of capitalism. Under a competitive economic system, American wages *increased*. Instead of concentrating property in the hands of a few, U.S. capitalism made it possible for almost everyone to own property. Rather than abusing their workers, U.S. companies protected them through generous insurance policies and pension plans. In contrast to communist censorship of culture and religion, Americans enjoyed rich intellectual and spiritual lives. USIA leaders were certain this portrait of democratic capitalism could counter even the most strident communist propaganda.[80]

In November 1956, "People's Capitalism" opened in Bogota, Colombia. During a two-week run, 235,000 people attended the exhibit. When the display reached Guatemala City, 94,000 people, a third of the city's population, came. After making stops in Chile and Bolivia, "People's Capitalism" traveled to Ceylon, where another 50,000 people saw the exhibit. While USIA considered "People's Capitalism" a smash hit, budgetary and logistical problems forced the Agency to suspend the exhibits for 1957.[81]

Although "People's Capitalism" drew impressive crowds, it is difficult to assess whether it changed foreign perceptions of capitalism. Throughout the campaign, audiences complained that USIA officials did not adequately acknowledge economic problems in the United States. This criticism was well-founded. At a time when one in five Americans lived in poverty, the "People's Capitalism" pamphlet proclaimed that the United States "has left far behind the indifference to the public, the lack of concern for the workers, the ruthless preoccupation with profits which many critics in the past considered inevitable in a capitalist society."[82] Such explanations rang hollow even in foreign nations allied with the United States. In December 1956, USIA officials reported that a majority of 4,205 Western Europeans surveyed did not believe that U.S. capitalism provided great opportunities for individual advancement or economic security for the elderly. While they lauded the productivity of the American economy, they expressed skepticism that capitalism was the sole reason for U.S. efficiency and standards of living.[83]

Convinced that they could not answer such criticism directly without undermining "People's Capitalism," U.S. information officials tried to divert attention to the positive features of democratic capitalism. In March 1957, responding to an official Soviet request for information about the "People's Capitalism" exhibit, USIA Director Arthur Larson ordered his staff to prepare materials on unemployment, installment buying, and Wall Street capitalists.

To correct Soviet distortions of U.S. unemployment, Larson urged USIA officials to emphasize the number of vacant jobs, the seasonal nature of some jobs, and the existence of unemployment compensation. Because of the social welfare programs in America, Larson reminded his colleagues, unemployment "quite definitely should not and does not necessarily mean breadlines, soup kitchens, squalor, starvation."[84] To counter communist accusations that financiers controlled the United States, USIA officials explained the benefits and liabilities of the use of credit, the structure of American corporations, and buying power of American consumers.[85]

Larson and other USIA administrators claimed that the charge of materialism directed at Americans was not usually "an emotionally significant one." Consumerism therefore remained a prominent feature of American international information programs. USIA officials remained confident that as long as depictions of luxury items were omitted, international audiences found purchasing power an important factor distinguishing American and Soviet workers.[86] At the 1958 Brussels World's Fair, U.S. propagandists claimed that the Soviet industrial exhibits stressed scientific advances and heavy machinery in order "to divert attention from the area of communist economic weakness—[the] production of consumer goods." U.S. information leaders criticized "the well-advertised Soviet posture that the USSR can serve as both a model for industrialization of the underdeveloped countries and a source of "aid without strings."[87]

Foreshadowing Rostow's emphasis on mass consumption as evidence of economic "maturity," U.S. propagandists maintained that consumerism improved Americans' daily lives without eroding their social values. They shared Rostow's belief that no society lacking genuine social welfare programs, mass consumption, and social and political freedom was a good model for modernization. And, like the modernization theorists and advertising executives, they ignored the stinging critiques of conformity and consumerism coming from scholars such as David Riesman, William Whyte, Vance Packard, and John Kenneth Galbraith.

Presented in these sanitized terms, "People's Capitalism" signified a more fulfilling, comfortable life for the individual. In choosing the word "people's," U.S. propagandists sought to appropriate communist discourse in showing how the American economy allowed individuals to flourish as citizens and consumers. Capitalism granted the average worker dignity as embodied in personal buying power and fringe benefit programs. American information officials had little difficulty making the image of a typical U.S. housewife more attractive than that of a Soviet woman working on the railroad or the Communist man suffering in a labor camp. Through skillful crafting of propaganda materials, they placed less appealing aspects of American society in a better light. In articulating the material advantages and intangible values of modernization, U.S. officials fused their notions of national identity to the imperatives of national security.

CHAPTER FIVE

"The Red Target Is Your Home":
Images of Gender and the Family

ON SEPTEMBER 12, 1947, the State Department's *Air Bulletin* contained an article entitled "Mr. and Mrs. America." Drawn from eleven years of Gallup polls, the profile depicted the "typical" American man and woman. The average U.S. male, the study noted, "spends fifteen minutes traveling two miles to work, gambles occasionally, and says he loses more than he wins." Six-tenths preferred brunette women, only three-tenths blondes, the rest redheads. "Mr. America" considered married men happier than bachelors and valued his wife's companionship, intelligence, and homemaking talent more than her beauty. He thought women nagged too much, and opposed the idea of a woman president. The poll then described an average American female. She "swims and walks for exercise, plays cards for fun, thinks she eats too much for her health, and wants to be her husband's partner in household finances and prefers marriage to a career." Although "Mrs. America" would excise the word "obey" from the marriage ceremony, she wanted deferential courtesies from men. She most appreciated her husband's kindness, good temper, and consideration.[1]

The archives of the State Department and U.S. Information Agency (USIA) contain scores of documents like "Mr. and Mrs. America." While such materials may appear trivial, images of gender and the family were valuable tools in explaining the American way of life to foreign audiences. Many scholars have examined the importance of gender in shaping the discourses of power in international relations. They have demonstrated that policymakers often allow their notions of gender to influence their decisions. For example, an official unwilling to be perceived as "weak" will adopt a "tough" line. Accordingly, a narrowly proscribed "masculinity" affects foreign policy. Such assumptions are particularly evident during the early Cold War. In this era, many Americans embraced domesticity and traditional gender roles as an antidote to anxieties unleashed by atomic weapons and political instability.[2] Sharing similar elite backgrounds, most U.S. political leaders extolled the nuclear family as the embodiment of democratic values.[3] At the same time, U.S. information strategists recognized that ideals of gender and family life could be used to discredit the communist economic and political system. While the Soviets denigrated American morality and culture, U.S. propagandists emphasized the freedom and comfort among citizens of the United States. In contrast to communist atheism, exploitation, and misery, U.S. information experts promoted the spiritual, physical, and emotional fulfillment available in the United States. Fighting communism, they implied, involved much more than guarding concrete interests. It meant defending American families and their way of life.

In attempting to stigmatize communists, U.S. information officials revealed their own biases and views of the United States. "America," to these overwhelmingly male bureaucrats,[4] meant that men were able to take care of their wives and children. In "America," women devoted themselves to their families and their communities. In "America," the state protected families. Although narrowly defined, this "America" presented an attractive alternative to life behind the Iron Curtain. Through idealizing American political culture and daily life, propagandists justified U.S. dominance in international affairs.

Immediately following World War II, some U.S. policymakers were alarmed at international stereotypes of American citizens. In December 1945, Assistant Secretary of State for Public Affairs William B. Benton derided unflattering foreign images of U.S. women. "Too many people think that every American housewife has a 40-foot living room and a maid to wait on her," he explained. Without an information program to correct such falsehoods, Benton argued, poorer nations would continue to resent American wealth and resist trade with the United States.[5]

Like Benton, U.S. ambassador to the Soviet Union Averell Harriman found stereotypes of the American people and economy distressing. On January 20, 1946, he explained how the Soviets were capitalizing on the fact that millions of American women were receiving dismissals from their wartime employers and were often barred from unemployment compensation. *Komosomol*

Pravda, the communist youth newspaper, claimed "that educated girls seek any kind of work, they become housemaids and live mannequins in store windows; and that need and unemployment are driving American girls into prostitution." Harriman echoed Benton's call for an information program designed "to correct this grotesque and slightly sinister conception of the USA presented to the Soviet people by their rulers."[6]

Determined to correct such images, U.S. information strategists argued that democracies valued individuality and families more than communist societies. In late 1949, the State Department's *Russia the Reactionary* assailed Soviet laws barring marriages between citizens of the USSR and foreigners. In contrast, free nations allowed their people to marry whomever they chose.[7] In 1951, the USIS released more than 1.3 million copies of *The Free World Speaks*, a pamphlet celebrating liberties found in noncommunist nations. The caption of one picture states, "The Free World cherishes the sanctity of family life." Communist governments, however, divided families in order to fill distant factories, collective farms, and the military.[8]

In May 1953, the USIA women's packet included *Democracy Begins in the Home*. The booklet praised the benefits democracy granted U.S. families. "Democratic families" were cooperative and considerate. In contrast to the crowded living conditions and police surveillance in communist nations, democracies protected individual dignity and privacy. This emphasis on individuality, the pamphlet asserted, was the "key difference" between democratic and totalitarian societies. Rather than forcing people to conform, democracies celebrated and protected their diversity. By cherishing the family, the text concluded, democracies created a formidable bulwark against "dictatorship and intolerance, mind-slavery and statism."[9]

U.S. propagandists ridiculed Soviet claims of gender equity. On May 13, 1953, John Albert, the chief of USIA's German service, articulated these sentiments:

> In the Soviet Zone in Germany, as in all the satellite countries, the women have equality. They have the equality to work in coal mines, work night shifts in heavy work. They can do everything which nobody in a free country would ask a woman to do. There is only one thing they can't do. They can't have time to raise their children, to provide for their home and take part in community life, because they are much too tired for it.

Albert, like most of his agency colleagues, believed that American consumer goods enabled U.S. women "to have a decent life, to have a job, to bring up children and still take time out for cultural and economic life." Convincing people behind the Iron Curtain of the possibility of a better family life, Albert concluded, inspired them to continue resisting the Soviets.[10]

Accordingly, USIA experts attempted to build support for democratic capitalism among foreign women. In the 1952 pamphlet, *The Women in Communist Countries*, agency writers asked Italian women, "Do you remember the food ration cards, the black bread, the long waiting lines in front of the shops, and other wartime inconveniences?" All these hardships, the treatise declared, had returned to "all the countries ruled by communists."[11]

The Soviets responded with broad indictments of the shortcomings of the United States and capitalism. Communist propagandists frequently mentioned U.S. laws barring the employment of married women, disparities between the wages of American men and women, and job discrimination on the basis of race.[12] In November 1951, Valentin Zorin, a radio broadcaster for the Soviet Home Service, averred:

> Capitalists want to deprive the working woman of the happiness
> of motherhood. When an American woman worker gets married
> and has a child, the owner immediately throws her out into the
> street. . . . The propagandists for the American way of life, who
> describe the beauties of the American paradise, forget to tell their
> listeners that . . . at least 225,000 women in the United States give
> birth to children without medical assistance. . . .The women of
> America suffer in the chains of permanent poverty, trying in vain to
> make ends meet.

Rejecting U.S. propaganda claims, Zorin dismissed as "utter absurdity" the notion that American women were happy.[13]

Rather than trying to prove the contentment of U.S. women or denying the inequities among American workers, U.S. information officers exposed degrading working conditions in the Soviet Union. "Emancipated" Russian women performed heavy labor in mines, construction sites, and shipyards.[14] In the USSR, equality of opportunity "allowed" women to work as stevedores, street cleaners, and forge operators.[15] In 1950, State Department analysts listed the exploitation of women as one of the principal "psychological vulnerabilities" of the USSR. They described the low wages and high prices that forced the majority of Soviet women to work. They urged their superiors to publicize the plight of communist women—but without suggesting women belonged at home.[16]

Within two years, American information experts implemented this strategy. They emphasized U.S. labor laws safeguarding women from dangerous occupations. For example, a 1952 edition of *Labor Air Bulletin* declared:

> In contrast with conditions in communist countries, where the much advertised equality and rights of women means the right to work in coal mines, the United States has shown a growing concern for the health and welfare of working women because of their role as home makers and future bearers of children.

Labor laws regulating hours, wages, and working conditions indicated a higher regard for women and children. The United States, the article implied, cared too much about its women and children to permit equality in the workplace.[17]

The presentation of the American family abroad involved more than a defense of capitalism. U.S. information experts also sought to convey the quality of life in the United States. USIS libraries distributed material on American health, nutrition, and education.[18] They celebrated the political and social freedom fostered by democracy. Frequently, USIA pamphlets quoted communist émigrés impressed by the United States. An August 1954 women's packet included an article, "What America Means to Me," written by Tamara Chernashova Gilmore, a former Russian ballerina. She told the poignant story of her eleven-year courtship with Eddy Gilmore, a Moscow correspondent for a U.S. newspaper. Soviet authorities repeatedly refused to allow her to marry an American citizen and even tried to keep the couple from seeing one another. In desperation, Eddy asked his friend Wendell Wilkie, the 1940 Republican presidential nominee and an acquaintance of Stalin's, to intervene. Wilkie complied and the couple married in 1943. It took another ten years for Soviet officials to grant the Gilmores and their two children exit visas enabling them to move to the United States. The agency directed its public affairs officers to use the piece "to stress the hospitable attitude of Americans to visitors, to indicate their people-to-people friendliness and to emphasize individual freedom in the United States as contrasted, by implication, with communist repression."[19]

Interviews with communist refugees revealed deep admiration for the American people and their lifestyles. Not persuaded by Soviet distortions of the United States, many émigrés fled Eastern Europe in hopes of attaining U.S. political and social freedoms. In a 1953 survey, Hungarian escapees articulated some of the reasons why they found the U.S. appealing. One woman asserted:

> To me, the most attractive aspect of the U.S. is that people there can strike; they can write what they want in newspapers; the churches are free; there isn't any caste system of society. There is time for recreation, too; the women may dress elegantly without anyone accusing them of being bourgeois.[20]

Another man relished the freedom to meet girls and talk to them without worrying about being reported to the authorities for voicing anti-state sentiments. Armed with this knowledge, USIA experts began emphasizing U.S. leisure and recreation activities. They realized that the freedom to dine and relax could "sell" America as effectively as the freedom to vote and strike.

It proved more difficult to convey the moral values of Americans. In July 1948, Secretary of State George Marshall urged his staff to "use all our resources to correct, as far as possible, the false or distorted stereotypes concerning the [morality of] the United States." Many foreigners, especially those in developing nations, believed Americans were "immoral," had little "family life," and condoned "loose living."[21] Soviet propaganda fueled these perceptions. On March 17, 1950, Radio Prague derided the objectification of American women. The communist announcers told their Greek audience that U.S. advertisements "always depict a woman's body usually stripped to the waist."[22] In 1956, communist television portrayed American men as "half-criminals, roughnecks, and immoral beings" and characterized American women as "on the verge of prostitution, slovenly, ugly, and silly."[23]

In response, U.S. propagandists alleged that communist governments undermined human rights and morality. American officials drew careful distinctions between communist rulers and common citizens. They blasted the Soviet regime for rejecting "truth, mercy, pity, charity, love of family, and hospitality"—"basic values" that the Soviet people "held in common with the people of the free world."[24] On November 28, 1951, VOA commentator Arthur H. Burling accused Chinese authorities of "making a determined effort to wipe out all romantic and passionate love." To keep young people focused on Mao's political vision for China, officials barred American love songs and issued guidelines on love and marriage. One pamphlet declared:

> Communist love is somber, intellectual, and definitely revolutionary. When choosing a life mate, the Communist youth should look first for correct political thoughts, and only afterwards for education, temperament, health and good looks.

Burling sarcastically noted that the expression "life mate" was misleading because "reactionary or counter-revolutionary thoughts" were grounds for divorce under Communist Chinese law. The government wanted no individual "to love their mate as much as their local Party cadre." Only a "cruel, backward-looking despotism," Burling concluded, would impose such restrictions.[25] In April 1952, VOA editorialist Edward Jelenko echoed these themes. Maoism, he alleged, obliterated traditional Chinese reverence for ancestral and familial ties. Couples viewed relationships entirely through the lens of party ideology. Jelenko quoted a Hong Kong student declaring, "We have no time for such trash as love. You will never see a boy and a girl pair off to look at the moon or whisper to each other in typical petty bourgeois manner"[26] (Figure 7).

In February 1953, VOA's Mandarin Service attacked China's efforts to enforce state marriage law. Although the 1950 statute aimed "to achieve equality between men and women by promoting freedom within marriage," VOA claimed that the Chinese were pursing "unbridled freedom" or "freedom without responsibility." Rejecting "recognized concepts of the free world," the Communist Chinese now legally sanctioned divorce and adultery. As result, VOA alleged, "more than 5,000 years of Chinese civilization have been destroyed" and "suicides and homicides among the unhappily-married" were increasing.[27]

VOA also used satirical music to impart its messages about the corrosive effects of communism upon marriage. On November 21, 1954, the VOA Polish service broadcast an evening of parodies set to the tunes of Polish hit parade numbers. One song featured Comrade Gebert serenading his wife Krystyna with the following ditty:

> I and my wife, two charming words!
> Hubby asks for a kiss—and wifey informs . . .
> I and my wife.

Figure 7. Happy couples like this one demonstrated U.S. propagandists' claims that marriage, love, and family thrived in democratic capitalist societies—and withered under communism. National Archives.

Everyone knows the truth about us!
The husband is not his wife's type
So she informs on him
And the idyll continues . . .
I and my wife.
Without keeping track
My wife reports me to the U.B. [Urząd Bezpieczeństwa—Polish secret
    police]
I and my wife:
For me she'll give up life itself (my own).

Although Mrs. Gebert musically blames this sad situation on the U.B., she warns her husband that she will be forced to inform on him again.[28] In the American propaganda narrative, communist police states easily tore asunder the banns of matrimony.

By contrast, marriage flourished under democratic capitalism. In April 1952, VOA-Persian proclaimed that "The basis of American family life is a happy marriage." Once Americans got married, they sought to buy their own homes as soon as possible. Because of the thriving U.S. economy, young couples enjoyed upward mobility and a high standard of living. Unlike meddlesome communist governments who intruded on people's intimate lives, Americans could choose their own spouse. "Parents do not interfere in this matter and do not permit others to interfere in this important decision of their children." Americans had long life expectancy and a low infant and child mortality rate. If a married couple did not get along, they could "end their marriage, instead of being subjected to moral strain and tension."[29]

Children were another critical element in U.S. portrayals of family life under communism. In March 1951, VOA broadcasts in Cantonese and Mandarin condemned *Little Friend*, a magazine published in Shanghai. The magazine, VOA contended, was "a propaganda directive," not light entertainment for young people. Like Hitler, the Maoists attempted to warp the minds of children, to divide them from their parents. But VOA predicted this "monstrous" strategy would fail because there "is no greater beauty than the beauty between members of a family." Family ties were stronger than any political philosophy.[30]

On June 15, 1952, VOA Russia made similar claims. Eviscerating a recent issue of *Pravda* that contrasted the happy lives of Soviet children to "the cruel fate of children in America and in other free countries," the broadcaster thundered:

> Any sensible person . . . realizes that the condition of children in the Soviet Union . . . is the very last concern of the Party and the Government. How can a power, whose path is strewn with the bodies of millions of children, pose as a protector of children? . . . Today, packs of hungry, homeless, orphaned, and abandoned children still fill the railroad stations, streets, marketplaces, and slums of Russian cities. . . . What was the effect on children of the mass seizures utilized to fill Soviet forced labor camps? . . . How and by whom were children cared for, those whose fathers and mothers perished as victims of mass executions, as hostages, as victims of the sham courts of communism, victims of executions without trial?[31]

On a milder note, a 1953 USIA women's packet asserted, "Many Soviet women leave their children in state-run nurseries, and many mothers don't see their

Figure 8. In the U.S. propaganda narrative, young people living under communism could never experience the carefree joy expressed by these American boys watching a baseball game. National Archives.

children from Monday morning until Saturday night."[32] In February 1955, the USIA published "Russian Children to Throw Hand Grenades"—a description of newly established "physical culture tests" in the USSR[33] (Figure 8).

Communism, American propagandists contended, destroyed families. In June 1951, a USIS cartoon entitled "Communism and the Family" stated:

> Communists take your young, but they cast aside the aged. Communism turns sons against fathers . . . and takes daughters for slave labor. Under Communism, she [a mother] loses her loved ones. And gains a "family" of strangers![34]

The 1953 USIA pamphlet *Korea My Home* shows communist soldiers stealing the crops and possessions of a Korean farm family, the Kims. Disgusted by these actions, the father, Chong Kim, declares, "These communists, like locusts, devour everything. They take our food, our sons, our daughters."[35] The

USIS center in Manila distributed 10,000 posters proclaiming, "The Red target is *your* home." The placards featured Communist soldiers forcibly separating two women and a young boy. The text read, "Happy family life cannot exist in the communist scheme of things."[36]

USIA's comic book and animated film versions of *When The Communists Came* vividly depicted these themes. In the first, a Chinese man laments the effect of communism upon the families in his village. When the communists first arrive, they are "well-behaved" and give the struggling residents land, food and water. But over time, the communists seize crops, spy on the populace, indoctrinate the young, and exile or kill "enemies of the people." Because of the actions of local communist authorities, the narrator asserts, "Many families no longer existed. Now the village held only middle aged and older people who lived constantly in fear. . . . It was not safe even to talk in your home with friends. The minds of the children were slowly being poisoned." To escape the "evil" in his village, the narrator flees rather than "be a slave."[37]

The animated film presents a similar story set in a Middle Eastern context. Arnez, a cobbler, narrates. At first, the communists promise modern farm machinery and freedom from landlords. They do not get drunk or mistreat women, and pay well for items they procure. The situation quickly degenerates. After Arnez's grandfather, a respected town elder, challenges the communists, he is imprisoned and later dies. Arnez's brother is so brainwashed by the new regime that he allows his wife and children to starve, devoting himself to the party at the expense of his household. The authorities plunder supplies and close the mosque. "They took away our freedoms, broke up our families, killed our neighbors, stole our property, and left us only poverty, hunger, and misery," a forlorn Arnez declares. Salvation for the village comes only when local rebels oust the communists.[38] U.S. information strategists clearly implied that democratic governments would never permit such abuses. Democracies cherished freedom, families, and the sanctity of the home.

Hoping to undermine extensive communist efforts to indoctrinate young people,[39] US officials directed special programming and publications at youth behind the Iron Curtain. In November 1950, Voice of America initiated a weekly jazz program "for the purpose of attracting young listeners." Heath Bowman, a VOA policy analyst, explained, "Jazz is useful because it keeps alive states of well-being in the young that cannot but be associated with the West, and because it can be made to carry other propaganda freight." But, Bowman warned, jazz was not enough to persuade people under twenty-five of the merits of democratic capitalism.[40]

Hence, VOA broadcasters also blasted communism's effect on young people. In late 1951, VOA Russia lamented the "tragic contradictions" facing Soviet citizens born following the October Revolution. Although the Stalinist government celebrated its educational system, VOA asserted, "The education which the Soviet youth receive is penetrated with backward, anti-scientific communist values and ideas." But VOA saw hope in this dire situation. Because young people would not tolerate the inconsistencies of Soviet life, VOA declared:

> Youth is the grave digger of communism. The youth who has a different faith than "leaders" and teachers. The youth who will not trade in their will for freedom, truth, and brotherly against any Marxist-Leninist-Stalinist hatred. Future and victory belongs to the youth. [41]

Such confidence inspired U.S. policy makers to make young people "a priority target" in their campaign to promote American life internationally.

In April 1953, the USIA inaugurated feature packets aimed at youth. The premiere issue included articles on Rocky Marciano, Louis Armstrong, the Boy Scouts, school safety patrols, public speaking contests, scientific talent searches, and conservation. The series' mixture of politics, business, religion, culture, sports, education, science, and agriculture aimed at the widest possible audience of young men and women living abroad.[42] U.S. information experts chose each selection in order to emphasize one or more of the following themes:

(1) U.S. cooperation with the youth of other free nations.
(2) Respect for freedom of thought and inquiry.
(3) Belief in a divine power and in the inherent worth of the individual.
(4) Appreciation of the culture of other peoples.
(5) Opportunities available to youth under a democratic, free-enterprise system.
(6) Repression of youth in communist countries.
(7) Manipulation of youth to serve the ulterior purposes of the communist leaders.[43]

These goals illustrate these officials' conviction that anti-communism appealed to people of all ages as well as all nations.

According to the USIA, families thrived in democratic capitalist societies. The agency presented carefully crafted images of American families emphasizing community involvement, rewarding employment, and material comfort. In 1955, the USIS disseminated 150,000 German and Spanish copies of *Building the Community Through Family Life.* The lavishly illustrated book featured "families and family life" in Buffalo, New York. It addressed the role of religion for local Jews, Catholics, and Protestants. It described activities and classes at neighborhood schools. It depicted blue- and white-collar workers in their factories and offices and highlighted their earning power. All of the workers shown, however, were male. Denying the economic realities of many American families, the booklet claimed, "Our family income very seldom depends on everyone's working." But families did share household cleaning and child care tasks. *Building the Community Through Family Life* portrayed citizens working to improve their community as a whole. Such actions, the book concluded, helped abolish "deep prejudices against various groups." "Only by sharing with others some of the responsibility for building our whole community do we overcome these fears and cynical conceptions of the way our society works." Americans, the USIA implied, were selfless, contented, and honorable.[44]

To support these claims, U.S. information officials released stories about "real, living American families." In December 1951, VOA announced that the Purdues of Pequannock Township, New Jersey, were the "perfect family" to show the world how Americans celebrated Christmas. Jack, his wife Bunnie, and their four children, Spencer, Pamela, Russell, and Robert recorded the broadcast in their home. The Perdues sang carols and explained their holiday rituals.[45] In July 1952, the VOA weekly program "Of Women's Interest" profiled the McCoys, a midwestern family of five. Mr. McCoy worked as a public accountant. Mrs. McCoy held a part-time job in her husband's firm. While their parents worked, the McCoy children "voluntarily" cooked and performed chores around the house. Mr. and Mrs. McCoy considered giving their children "a sense of family solidarity and the will to serve one's church and community" their "most important" duty. The McCoys actively participated in church choral groups, the Parents Teachers Association (PTA), and fund-raising carnivals. For leisure, the McCoys attended lectures and concerts and played cards. With such balanced lives, it probably surprised no one to learn that "There is no in-law trouble whatsoever in the McCoy family."[46]

USIA also extolled the virtues of American family life. In contrast to their innumerable depictions of Soviet women toiling in misery with no assistance from husbands or relatives, U.S. propagandists stressed the spirit of partnership and division of labor in American homes. In July 1952, VOA features reporter S. C. Chen told Chinese audiences that most Americans performed household chores after completing eight hours at their paid jobs. "Nobody thinks it is beneath him to push a lawn mower, to paint a wall, or to wash dishes."[47] The July 1953 USIA women's packet highlighted a survey proclaiming that sixty-eight percent of U.S. husbands helped their wives with grocery shopping at least once a week.[48] The USIS film *Smalltown U.S.A.* profiled several families in Anamosa, Iowa. While all the families shown are white, the film points out that the town's original settlers came from many nations including England, Germany, Norway, and Syria. Whatever their ancestral background, Anamosa's residents are happy and industrious. Mr. and Mrs. Edgar Mayberry and their three daughters share duties on their dairy farm. While newspaperman Tom Howell and his family eat a jointly prepared dinner of fried chicken and corn, the narrator states, "American families are much together and on Sundays, they worship together." The strains of "Faith of Our Fathers" are heard as images of the family meal give way to scenes of a packed church. The film concludes with all the families joyously watching a 4th of July parade.[49] The USIS blend of domestic harmony and patriotism was sappy but effective (Figure 9).

Profiles of "typical" American housewives were another USIA staple. In April 1953, the USIA women's packet featured Gail Forster, a Philadelphia housewife and mother of three. The Forsters lived well, but not lavishly, on the wages of husband William, a radio engineer. In response to communist criticisms of American wealth and materialism, the USIA emphasized the Forsters' middle-class status. "Like most American families, they have no servants." Mrs. Forster, the text stated, "cooks the meals, cleans the house, washes, irons, and mends the clothes, cares for the children, and works in her flower garden." Despite her heavy workload, Mrs. Forster remained active in her neighborhood. She taught one day a week in her children's cooperative nursery school and volunteered for a housing committee in Philadelphia. Every Sunday, the Forsters attended a Christian church. "Mrs. Forster," the publication concluded, "would never consider herself or her life unusual."[50]

Women like Gail Forster were commonplace in USIS films. In *Women and the Community*, the agency told stories of women with widely different circumstances but shared beliefs in engaged citizenship. The film opens with Mrs. Carter, the wife of a young lawyer, scanning a sample ballot for an upcoming election. Cut to Mrs. Gates sitting with her son in a dentist's waiting

Figure 9. This image of a small community's Independence Day celebration is a good illustration of USIA's fusion of community, family, and patriotism. © Bettmann/ CORBIS

room. Viewers are informed that "she is a widow with three children, but also finds time to take an active part in community life." The film then moves to the local high school where student Mary Collins peers into a microscope. Although Mary will someday be a wife and mother, "she'll be a better one because of her broad education." The scene changes to Mrs. Carter at her League of Women Voters meeting. Since "most members are mothers too," the women take turns watching children "while the other mothers devote themselves to building a better town for the youngsters to live and grow up in." The film then introduces Mrs. Brown, the leader of the local Parent-Teacher Association (PTA). The PTA organizes square dances ("an effective weapon against juvenile delinquency"), hot lunches, and school-based dental exams. Mrs. Brown is described as "an effective force for good in her community, perhaps because she thinks of all children as her children." The film closes with a contemplative shot of Mary Collins and the narrator speculating about the seemingly endless ways Mary will someday serve her community. "Whatever she does as an interested and intelligent American woman," viewers are assured, "she will become part of the floodstream of her community."[51]

U.S. information strategists tried to make their selections carefully. Many families failed to meet the criteria for American propaganda materials. In mid 1951, the State Department rejected the Seymours of Falls Church, Virginia. While preparing a picture story entitled "Home Life in the U.S.A.," the USIS post in London had requested specific photographs of "a typical middle class family." In order to meet the rather exacting requirements, the USIS Photos Branch checked families of agency employees. Finally, a staff member asked a long-time real estate agent for suggestions. The realtor recommended the Seymours. Mr. Seymour had worked for the People's Drug Stores for twenty-four years. He served in the Masons and the Optimist Club. He and his wife had two children. They were active in the PTA and attended Forestville Methodist Church. "The family," Department aides assured Assistant Secretary of State for Public Affairs Edward Barrett, "appeared to be respectable and suitable as subjects for the picture story."[52]

But when the Washington *Evening Star* reported that Voice of America had selected the Seymours as the "typical American family," U.S. officials regretted their choice. Within hours, a Mrs. Simmons, identifying herself as a writer, telephoned the State Department to ask if policymakers could defend their choice of the Seymours as the "average American family" when "he is a divorced man, and she is a divorced woman, and moreover the man does not even have a war record, etc." Stunned at the revelations, information leaders in the United States instructed their London colleagues not to use the picture story until a substitute family was discovered. The State Department took this action, an aide later explained, because "there was a possibility (even though slight) that the communists might get the background facts and use them to good advantage in playing their theme of the USA as a country of moral degenerates."[53]

USIA leaders eagerly made similar charges against the Soviets and zealously publicized the grim realities of Soviet life. In *The Soviet Woman Under Communism*, the USIA declared that for the vast majority of the 100 million in the USSR, "life is an endless round of work and worry, of physical hardship and spiritual dejection." The story depicted some of the difficulties an average Soviet woman experienced in her daily life. The USIA called this woman Nina Saitsev. "She is no one in particular," the pamphlet stated, "but she is representative of every woman in the USSR." Nina was a thirty-year-old, married factory worker. She and her husband Ivan worked in the same plant. They had two young sons, who were cared for by the day care center in the factory. During the week, Nina rose at 4 a.m. and went to the market. Compared to Gail Forster's comfortable life, the housewife in the USSR struggled daily with "the problem of getting enough food to keep herself and her family alive." The USIA showed Nina, waiting in line for an hour or more in order to purchase "milk for her children, a sliver of cheese, a few wilted vegetables (probably cabbage or potatoes), a loaf of black bread, and a little tea." The Saitsevs could rarely afford meat, and when Nina did purchase it, she could not "be sure of its quality or sanitary handling." While the Forsters owned a three-bedroom house, the Saitsevs lived in a four-room apartment shared with three other families.[54]

Nonetheless, the agency presented Nina Saitsev as a strong, if unhappy, woman. She declared it "useless" to complain and focused on keeping her family fed and clean. The USIA subtly blamed communism, not Nina, for her family's depressing situation:

> Frequently, as she waits impatiently in the morning line at market or hurries through the breakfast and housekeeping chores before getting out for the day, Nina wishes that she might stay at home and give her full energy to the job of wife and mother. But for most Soviet women such a wish is impossible.

On her way home at night, Nina picked up the children at the factory nursery where they spent the day. The agency described Nina's concerns for her sons. She wondered whether they would someday betray her and Ivan and if they would become "slaves of the state, captives in body and in soul." She regretted having her children. Nina Saitsev, the profile concluded, "has little faith in promises any more." The "long, bleak days of toil and hardship" had convinced her that "communism is death in life."[55]

Both superpowers employed gender stereotypes in their propaganda. While deriding American women as lazy, promiscuous, and vapid, the Soviets stressed the strength, political commitment, and virtue of communist women.[56] USIA writers retaliated by deriding femininity, motherhood, and fashion behind the Iron Curtain. While the Soviets bragged about the achievements of women lumberjacks, one USIA cartoon mocked such exploits by showing two burly Soviet women lamenting, "Even if we are superwomen, I still wish we had fun like Americans."[57]

Although popular culture of the era was rife with derisive comparisons of fit, slender Americans and unhealthy, husky communists, U.S. information experts rarely discussed the physical bodies of their subjects.[58] USIS film crews avoided using "extreme body-build types" and preferred people who were not "unnaturally thin or fat, tall or short." Determined to avoid the "over-aggressive" and "over-feminine" stereotypes of Hollywood, USIS featured "homogeneous" Americans of average physical build.[59] When America propaganda included images of the body, they were linked to larger political objectives. A good illustration occurred in February 1951. After Representative Walter Judd (R-Minn.) watched a USIS film about the Tanglewood festival that included some footage of female musicians swimming between rehearsals, he publicly objected. Assistant Secretary of State for Public Affairs Edward Barrett quickly defended the "perfectly appropriate and constructive" sequences. Such images, Barrett claimed, exposed "Soviet lies about Americans being a downtrodden, unhappy, boorish people suffering under Capitalism's heel."[60]

While they rarely resorted to pictures of bikini-clad women to illustrate the happiness of life in the United States, U.S. officials often emphasized the grace and good temperament of American women. In May 1954, the USIA instructed its public affairs officers to use the article "Home Is What You Make It" to demonstrate that "American women share the homemaking interests of women everywhere . . . and put time and effort into beautifying their homes."[61] Two years later, agency leaders encouraged USIS posts to stress that "American women have initiative, enterprise, and good taste in designing their own clothes."[62]

In contrast, both superpowers presented men as courageous, intelligent, and hard-working. Neither American nor Soviet propaganda mentioned the clothing or appearance of men. In September 1950, U.S. ambassador to the Soviet Union Grayson Kirk described the "Soviet man" campaign. In juxtaposition to characterizations of American men as boorish and uncultured, the Soviets described communist men as "endowed with graces possessed not even in full measure by the twelve disciples." "This mythical creature," Kirk noted, "has been extolled by Soviet writers as an example of the beneficent effects upon the human race of the Marxist system."[63] Two weeks later, U.S. information officers recommended the publication of a series of biographic sketches of top American diplomats who had "rugged" backgrounds, including "military award winners, ex-football stars, hard-bitten ex-newsmen, as well as pillar of the community types."[64]

The USIA proved more cautious when presenting the achievements of women. *Women in the United States*, a 26-page description of American women in the workplace, at home, and in political and community activities, assured readers, "There has been little militant feminism on the part of American women." The agency claimed that "no shrill antagonism between the sexes" existed in the United States because men and women had worked together on the frontier. The USIA stressed women's role as wives and mothers. After acknowledging that 19 million women in the United States worked outside the home in 442 different job classifications, the agency reminded readers that most women only worked until they got married. "Homemaking," the text stated, "is still the goal of most American girls." Unlike their Soviet counterparts, U.S. mothers rarely worked. They, not the state, raised their children. When describing unmarried working women, U.S. propagandists compared the "love affair" American women shared with the typewriter to the manual labor performed by Soviet women.[65] To deflect criticism of gender wage inequities in the United States, the USIA pointed to the scarcity of Soviet women in managerial and administrative positions. While alleging that no Soviet women held "positions of real power" in the Communist Party, the USIA spotlighted the participation of American women in the United Nations, the U.S. government, parent-teacher associations, pacifist groups, and the League of Women Voters.[66]

The USIS film *American Working Women* took a similar approach. The film examined four women with markedly different jobs, personal lives, and aspirations. Hazel Kennedy balances her duties as a hearing aide assembler and her commitment to her husband Ed and their two children. "Her job is important to her, but not all-important." She and Ed want their children to go to college, to have better lives than their own. Bank teller Joan Morgan intends to work only until she gets married. She wants to earn money, but also wants to have a good time. Martha Hansen, a college-educated biologist, is focused on her career as a cancer researcher. "Martha represents a growing segment of women whose dominant interest is in their vocation, whose life is more or less their work." Finally, Ann Maloney is the head "salesgirl" at a lingerie store. Although she had planned to be a pianist, a family illness forced her to drop out of college. She works primarily to care for her aging parents. After introducing viewers to these women, the narrator praises the fact that American women have many career options other than homemaking. He claims that even those working in factories usually have rest periods, "cheerful and sanitary washrooms," paid vacations, and company-provided health care. While Joan does not aspire to an executive position at the bank, the film is nonjudgmental about women who seek such positions. Indeed, Joan is shown greeting a "fascinating" woman described as "the owner of a thriving business" and one of three women serving in the state legislature. All these women are depicted as valuable workers and contributors to their community.[67] Despite their emphasis on images of middle-class families, U.S. information experts recognized the complexity of American society.

They also tailored their materials for different national audiences. In September 1949, information officers at the Office of the U.S. Military Government in Germany examined the status of women in postwar Germany. American propagandists placed special emphasis on overcoming the isolation instilled by years of Nazi propaganda and censorship. U.S. radio broadcasts highlighted news on the lifestyles of women and interviews with foreign women in order to reconnect German listeners to the outside world. Nonetheless, the report acknowledged the disfranchisement of German women stating:

> The national apathy that has resulted from this swift succession of great effort and great defeat is to be noted particularly in German women, for whom many hardships have persisted until the present day, with no immediate prospect of betterment. Family life has been gravely disrupted; the husband and father has been killed or mutilated, or is still in imprisonment, and the burden of supporting the family has fallen on the wife and mother. Material necessity has forced her to take a job to which she may or may not be suited, and in which she may or may not find satisfaction. In the upbringing and education of the children she stands alone. If her house has been bombed out, or if she is a refugee or expellee, all her strength is absorbed in her efforts to reconstruct her home.

American information strategists recognized the futility of upholding the idealized American family before German women facing these hardships. Instead, U.S. propagandists encouraged German women to become politically active and to think independently. For example, the Radio Frankfurt program *Women and Marriage* dealt with "problems resulting from the large plurality of women over men, from the widespread material distress, from cramped living conditions, and from the frequent separation of married couples owing to the housing shortage."[68]

While often caricatured as insensitive and imperialistic, American information experts were attuned to international cultural mores. In January 1953, the USIA Office of Research described the difficulty of creating propaganda films in underdeveloped nations, especially in the Middle East. The subordinate status and cloistered lives of women made casting them in the films especially trying. Agency films crews complained:

> On the one hand, the particular woman selected may strongly resist what she interprets as an invasion of her personal privacy. Such a thing as dropping her veil, which the crew would almost certainly request, symbolizes such an invasion. On the other hand, the woman is not a free agent even if she herself might be willing. Her behavior is rigidly circumscribed by the constraints of village culture, to say nothing of her husband and family.

Female casting, therefore, remained "a matter of extreme delicacy." Avoiding direct recruitment of women, agency officials asked village or town leaders for suggestions. If a woman was married, the agency asked her husband for permission to photograph the woman. Frustrated by these complications, the USIA recommended using native women "only to the extent to which their appearance is indispensable for the purposes of the film." After all, the agency concluded, "their presence in a film certainly has little 'cheesecake' value."[69]

Such sexist slurs notwithstanding, USIA leaders hoped to capitalize on the increasingly important role of women in international and domestic affairs. On March 31, 1959, the agency revised its audience guidelines in view of the changing social and economic status of women in certain countries. In cultures where men and women had similar educational background, interests, and social roles, the USIA urged its posts to abandon the women's packets and to reach women with "the same themes and procedures as those with male audiences." But in nations lacking extensive interaction between the sexes, the agency recommended the continuation of special programs for women. Significantly, the USIA warned staff members "to avoid using American yardsticks" when analyzing the influence of women in foreign cultures and political systems.[70]

Although USIA leaders recognized that some women were challenging gender stereotypes and inequalities, agency depictions of American women to overseas audiences changed little. On August 13, the USIA summarized its policies regarding the portrayal of American women. The guidelines directed USIS officials to depict the American woman "above all as a thoroughly human, hard-working, feminine person." The agency's primary emphasis remained on the "average" American woman, particularly as wife and mother, but occasionally profiles of outstanding women appeared. U.S. information leaders deplored the persistence of "highly distorted images of the American woman" in many countries. Several foreign audiences, USIA reported, perceived the U.S. female as "an irresponsible glamour girl" or "unfeminine, materialistic being whose main interest in life is her job."[71]

Agency leaders were determined to counter these stereotypes. U.S. propagandists articulated democratic capitalism in a manner that emphasized its benefits for individuals and families. They argued that in almost every culture women represented the family, "the primary stabilizing force that holds society together." Consequently, USIA leaders concluded that negative perceptions of American women influenced international opinions about the United States as a whole. While acknowledging that some American women were poor role models, they asserted, "The great majority of American women are characterized by devotion to family, womanliness and industriousness—qualities with which foreign audiences can identify with sympathy." American information materials therefore continued to stress women's roles as wives, mothers, and homemakers.[72]

USIA policymakers provided field officers elaborate instructions for crafting images of American women. They suggested the incorporation of information on the American woman and family life into propaganda material "on a wide variety of other subjects, such as education, cultural life, religion, minority affairs, and social welfare." "The American woman in her role as a homemaker," agency leaders declared, "should be discussed primarily in terms of her characteristics as a person, rather than shown as a mere user of machines or the passive beneficiary of a high standard of living." Accordingly, they ordered USIS posts to stress the emotional bonds shared by U.S. couples and the efforts of American parents to maintain a close family relationship.[73]

In the late 1950s, despite a decline in U.S. international prestige and rising anti-Americanism abroad, American information strategists saw little reason to modify their ideals of gender and family life in the United States. They remained convinced that communism itself attested to the superiority of democratic capitalism. Communist governments enslaved and exterminated millions of people. Communist regimes monitored and controlled virtually every aspect of private life. Those living under communism paid high emotional and psychological costs. These facts served U.S. propagandists well.

It proved more difficult to explain the complexities of American democracy. Confined by traditionalist conceptions of domestic life, U.S. information officials defined "America" in terms that omitted many Americans.

Segregation, sex discrimination, and poverty were only a few of the issues underplayed or ignored in their vision of the United States. Ironically, communist propagandists foreshadowed many of the criticisms that shattered America's Cold War consensus during the 1960s. As millions of Americans protested social inequities, U.S. political leaders were forced to address the gaps between democratic ideals and democratic realities.[74]

Nonetheless, we cannot dismiss the propagandists' defense of American families as mere rhetoric. In linking individual lives and international relations, U.S. information experts recognized that Man's longings and aspirations fuel political movements. In espousing their views on family life and gender, they articulated deeply held beliefs and political values. While their visions of America may not have adequately encompassed the socioeconomic diversity of the nation, they provide important insights into why U.S. policymakers took the fight against communism so seriously—and so personally.

CHAPTER SIX

"A Lynching Should Be Reported Without Comment": Images of Race Relations

In October 1957, K. A. Gbedemah, leader of the Ghanaian delegation to the United Nations, and his personal secretary, Bill Sutherland, stopped at a Howard Johnson's restaurant near Dover, Delaware. They ordered soft drinks. But when they sat at a nearby booth, the manager asked them to leave. Black customers, he asserted, were not permitted in the dining room. Gbedemah immediately protested, explaining that he was a diplomat. The manager stood fast. Furious, Gbedemah slapped sixty cents on the table, left the drinks untouched, and departed.[1]

After Gbedemah complained to the State Department, the incident received international media attention. Already reeling from the negative publicity attending school desegregation, the Eisenhower administration took immediate action. Secretary of State John Foster Dulles persuaded executives at Howard Johnson's to issue a public apology. President Eisenhower invited Gbedemah to breakfast at the White House. On October 10, officials at the U.S. Embassy in Ghana declared that the quick American response to the affair had "effectively sterilized this wound."[2]

The Gbedemah incident presents a rare instance of U.S. officials successfully countering global condemnation of American race relations in the early Cold War. But the episode also illustrates the central paradox of the U.S. ideological response to communism. While U.S. policymakers asserted that democratic government ensured freedom and equality, the United States permitted systemic economic, social, and political segregation of its African

American citizens. American attacks on communist oppression abroad rang hollow to foreign audiences cognizant of lynchings, race riots, Ku Klux Klan rallies, and white supremacist politicians in the United States. The contradictions between democratic rhetoric and American racism proved particularly troublesome to people of color in Asia, Africa, and Latin America. As the Cold War struggle moved into developing nations, U.S. policymakers recognized that perceptions of U.S. race relations were seriously impeding their attempts to discredit communism in these regions. Accordingly, they began supporting domestic civil rights reform.[3]

When communists vilified racism in the United States, U.S. propagandists retaliated by pointing to signs of American racial progress or by deriding communist oppression of religious and ethnic minorities. Officials at the State Department and the USIA extolled prominent African Americans and praised the U.S. political and legal systems for protecting the rights of minorities. Nonetheless, racial controversies, violence, and segregation continually left U.S. policymakers on the defensive. The rise of revolutionary nationalism among people of color exacerbated this situation. Throughout the early Cold War, American information experts struggled to defend the hypocrisy of a segregated democracy. Their attempts met little success.

In the aftermath of World War II, U.S. intelligence researchers noted a marked increased in Soviet reports on "instances of racial strife and discrimination in America." In radio and press materials directed at domestic and foreign audiences, the Soviets trumpeted the "evils of racialism" in the United States.[4] For example, in January 1947, the Russian periodical *Vokrug Sveta* (*Around the World*) reported:

> Negroes in the South are never jurors, and the courts of the South, never acquit Negroes. Thereafter, if people who have lynched Negroes are accidentally brought to trial, everyone knows that the murderers will be acquitted. Lynching in the South is a picnic, a diversion. People attend lynchings with sandwiches and whiskey. No Negro in the South can sleep quietly—and perhaps in the next hour it will be [he or she] who is hanged from a tree.[5]

Other Soviet publications and radio broadcasts addressed employment and wage discrimination among African American and Mexican American women, substandard health care for minorities, and voting discrimination based on race.[6] In July 1949, the Soviet Home Service aired a lengthy attack on "the desperate situation of the 400,000 American Indians who are doomed to a slow death as a result of a life of semi-starvation, with insufficient medical services and a lack of good agricultural land."[7]

But the Soviets were not alone in attacking U.S. racism. In March 1952, the State Department formed a working group on "racial problems in propaganda." The group soon compiled a lengthy paper describing "foreign attitudes on the Negro problem in the United States." The results were mixed. An analysis of Western European press coverage revealed that although Communist publications took the lead, "flagrant examples of infringements of the civil rights of any American citizens are considered news by papers of all political orientations in most of the countries of Europe." These findings contrasted sharply to those revealed in the Far East, where researchers concluded that "the Negro issue" was not "a significant factor in the formation of area attitudes toward the U.S." In Latin America, treatment varied greatly depending on the political biases of the relevant newspaper and the racial demography of the specific nation. The further left a newspaper leaned politically and the more people of color comprised a local population, the more negative and expansive the coverage of American racial problems.[8]

Although communists of all nationalities presented a broad indictment of U.S. racism, American information officials rarely addressed the plight of Asian Americans, Latinos, or American Indians. Instead, U.S. propagandists focused on black-white relations and insisted that African Americans were making significant strikes in employment and education. In 1948, the State Department issued "The Continuing Advance of Negro Americans," a guide for U.S. information officers fielding press inquires on U.S. racial problems. The paper highlighted *To Secure These Rights*, the 1947 report of the President's Committee on Civil Rights recommending stronger civil rights laws, the abolition of the poll tax, and "an immediate end to all forms of segregation and discrimination in American life." The State Department also stressed the movement of African Americans into the ranks of organized labor, judicial decisions striking down restrictive covenants and segregated professional schools, and strides in improving African American access to health services[9] (Figure 10)

At embassies and libraries throughout the world, U.S. diplomats disseminated glossy publications like *The Negro in American Life* that not only celebrated the achievements of blacks but also placed American race relations into historic context. Created in 1952 in collaboration with the National Association for the Advancement of Colored People (NAACP), the booklet was distributed by USIS in at least fifteen languages. "Over the past fifty years,"

Figure 10. When depicting the lives of African Americans, U.S. information experts suggested that all blacks could attain happiness and affluence. While they did not deny the existence of segregation and racism, they claimed the United States was moving past its troubled racial history. Images such as this one exemplified these claims. National Archives.

the text asserted, "the average Negro has made progress on every front—social, economic, and educational—at a tremendous pace." While the typical African American had not attained the eminence of Nobel Laureate Ralph Bunche or opera singer Marion Anderson, he or she also rarely inhabited the nightmarish world of mob violence, segregation, and poverty found in anti-American propaganda.[10]

The Negro in American Life offered a nuanced examination of American racism. Tracing the origins of prejudice to slavery, the pamphlet argued:

> Those who had moral qualms about enslaving human beings could be persuaded to accept the notion that Negroes . . . were something less than human. And so there began in the United States a theory of racial inferiority which became a key tenet in support of slavery, and later, of economic and social discrimination. . . . From this simple concept of Negro inferiority burgeoned an intricate structure of customs, laws, and habits of thought and conduct which penetrated every recess of life and level of consciousness.

While most blacks reluctantly acquiesced to "the white man's dogma of racial differences," other resisted through slave revolts or participation in the abolitionist movement. The publication rejected a one-dimensional characterization of the Civil War as a conflict "to free the slaves" and acknowledged that the mixed legacy of Reconstruction created a climate where "hooded night riders and flaming crosses burning on hillsides warned Negroes against asserting their new-won freedom."

Rather than whitewash or deny the more objectionable elements of America's racial past, *The Negro in American Life* heavily emphasized the advances African Americans were making in all areas of U.S. life. Deeming education "the most significant index of overall Negro progress," the pamphlet outlined African Americans' increasing rates of literacy, high school graduation, and college enrollment. Such factors were producing a growing number of black lawyers, doctors, engineers, professors, and writers. "An army of community leaders for and spokesmen for the Negro cause" was emerging.[11]

Culture reflected the improving status of African Americans. *The Negro in American Life* argued that cinematic stereotypes of blacks as "ignorant, lazy, irresponsible, and amusing" were disappearing. In 1950, at least six major Hollywood films "sought to portray the modern Negro and his problems and aspirations with earnestness, dignity, and perceptiveness." Furthermore, African Americans were leaving an indelible impact on many art forms. Paul Robeson's work in *Othello* and the late Bill Robinson's vaudeville performances transformed American theater. Ann Petty, Countee Cullen, Langston Hughes, Richard Wright, Zora Neale Hurston, and others were writing about "the realities of Negro life with warm and sensitive insight."[12]

Blacks were also making great strides economically. Although white Americans still earned higher average incomes, the racial wage gap was closing and African Americans were enjoying the prosperity of postwar America. Courts were striking down segregation laws. Since 1900, the percentage of blacks in low-paying agricultural jobs had declined significantly and African Americans were distinguishing themselves in fields like banking, physics, metallurgy, and retail. Expanding black membership in unions, especially the Congress of Industrial Workers (CIO), was generating additional economic gains.[13]

Noting that these improvements did not result entirely from "enlightened white social attitudes," *The Negro in American Life* then delved into "the increasing political effectiveness of the Negro himself." Gifted African American political leaders like Lester Granger of the National Urban League, U.S. Representative Adam Clayton Powell, and educator Mary McLeod Bethune were harnessing the rights accorded them under the Constitution and fighting for racial equality. Pointing to the fact that every black citizen "could vote freely in the North," the pamphlet suggested that U.S. racial problems were confined to the South.[14]

The booklet concluded with photographs showing racial harmony or illustrious African Americans. A black New York teacher beams at her classroom of white pupils. West Point cadet David Carlisle dines with his white classmates. John Wiggins, a black machinist, and William Bogart, his white co-worker, are described as "a highly skilled maintenance team." Edith Sampson, a U.S. delegate to the United Nations; Marian Anderson, "America's premiere contralto"; baseball icon Jackie Robinson; surgeon Charles R. Drew; and judge William Hastie are also pictured. Finally, a dignified but unnamed African American woman is identified as "the greatest contributor to Negro progress: the literate voter."[15] Overall, *The Negro in American Life* told a story in which white and black Americans worked together in overcoming racism and ensuring that everyone shared the blessings of democratic capitalism.

Such narratives of racial progress, however, usually omitted African American family life. U.S. propaganda materials rarely showed blacks in domestic situations or mentioned the spouses or children of notable African Americans.[16] A May 1950 Voice of America broadcast to Yugoslavia is a good example. In a program devoted to African American housewives, VOA profiled three black women from Spencerville, Maryland. But the interviewer focused on the women's public activities in their sewing and canning clubs, not their private efforts to take care of their families. Listeners learn nothing about how racism and segregation affected many black Americans. Instead, they are assured, that "Negro women share this country's efforts to improve the life of the average American family striving towards economic prosperity of everyone regardless of origin, race, or religion."[17] With enough time, patience, and effort, U.S. propagandists confidently declared, democratic capitalism would vanquish racial inequality.

Privately, however, U.S. information officials revealed doubts about their treatment of minority issues. In a June 1953, aides wondered whether they had "overdone the atypical prominent Negro" and accordingly urged more emphasis on middle-class blacks. Furthermore, USIA policymakers suggested that "the seamy side" of American race relations be confined to verbal commentary. Visual imagery of racism was proving too difficult to rebut. Finally, in order to dispel foreign doubts that "central figures are really Negroes if they are too light in pigmentation," USIA recommended the use of dark-skinned individuals or narration that made clear a person's African American status.[18] Some officials even questioned the necessity of an aggressive U.S. response to "the minority question." Pointing to racial problems in South Africa, the British Commonwealth, and India, they rejected the notion that America's racial unrest was uncommon. "The charge that we are all suffering from some psychiatric underlying 'sense of guilt' for our past and present acts of discrimination against minorities in this country," USIA policy analyst Earl A. Dennis asserted, "is, in my opinion, pure tripe, and the sooner we adopt a policy of presenting an honest, forthright picture of the situation to the world at large, the better."[19]

Such dissent rarely filtered into U.S. propaganda about race relations. American propagandists focused on themes of racial progress and remained defensive in the face of international criticism of U.S. racism. USIA materials on the 1954 Supreme Court ruling on *Brown v. Board of Education* requiring the integration of public schools illustrate this point. The Agency presented the decision as a powerful demonstration not only of racial advancement, but also of the conviction that talented and hard-working people—whatever their race—could succeed in the United States. For example, VOA's Chinese branch announced, "There is in reality nothing new in the principle enunciated by the Supreme Court. For more years than most Negro children can remember, their fathers and grandfathers have been improving the conditions under which the Negro has been living."[20]

Minimizing *Brown*'s significance, U.S. information experts claimed most U.S. schools were already integrated and that few Americans supported segregation. In June 1954, the USIA youth packet included "Equal Education for All." The article characterized *Brown* as "only the logical culmination" of a series of steps including the Emancipation Proclamation and previous legal rulings granting blacks "the same rights and opportunities as those enjoyed by white citizens of the United States." Although per pupil expenditures still lagged behind northern schools, southern states were equalizing educational spending on white and black schools. Additionally, many religious organizations, unions, and professional associations were admitting black members. With African Americans flourishing "in every sphere of life and activity," the *Brown* decision embodied "the will of the great majority of the American people."[21] Echoing these assertions, the October 1954 USIA women's packet highlighted "the general acceptance that American women have displayed toward racial equality."[22]

Yet, while USIA applauded integration in its radio broadcasts and printed materials, the Agency was much more reluctant to feature racial themes in its films. According to communications scholar Melinda Schwenk-Borrell, "civil rights, integration, and the *Brown* decision simply do not receive explicit attention" in USIA films of the 1950s. While she opines that this omission may have reflected the conservatism of the director of the Agency's motion picture service, Turner B. Shelton, another plausible explanation is that U.S. information officials recognized the incendiary nature of images exposing American racism.[23]

Global reaction to the rise of "massive resistance" to integration validated such fears. International media coverage of Autherine Lucy's unsuccessful attempt to enter the University of Alabama and the lynching of Emmett Till generated global censure of American racism. In 1957, U.S. prestige tumbled even further when ferocious white mobs prevented school desegregation in Little Rock, Arkansas. In December 1958, with several legal challenges to integration pending, the USIA released exhaustive guidelines for propaganda materials on minorities. Agency leaders directed their subordinates to stress "the gains of non-white Americans, both as individuals and in integrated situations." Rather than dwell on persistent racial problems, they suggested focusing on "the real progress already made and in process." They listed intellectuals, students, labor groups, and journalists as the primary targets for USIA explanations of racial issues.[24] Despite the limited impact of their efforts to convince foreign audiences of America's improving race relations, U.S. propagandists made few changes to their strategy. Beholden to a Congress in which Southern Democrats not only opposed integration but also controlled the USIA budget, American information officers exercised extreme caution when discussing racism and segregation.[25]

While formulating materials on race, U.S. information strategists noted widespread ignorance about the socioeconomic status of African Americans. In September 1953, a USIA survey of 910 French citizens revealed that most of the respondents did not know whether or not Harlem was "an immense slum."[26] A 1959 State Department guide urged American tourists to correct racial stereotypes held by Soviet citizens explaining:

> Some of the Soviets are surprised to hear that Negroes have schools at all, and many are surprised to learn that in Little Rock the troops were on the side of integration, rather than trying to prevent it. It is news to many of them that in most parts of the U.S. children of all races have been attending the same schools for years without significant incidents. Some do not know that "lynch law" is not actually a law, and that lynching is actually illegal everywhere in the U.S.

Many do not know that the Ku Klux Klan is generally condemned, or that Paul Robeson is a wealthy man.[27]

Although the pamphlet recommended sincere and candid responses to Soviet questions about race relations, it urged U.S. tourists to "put the Negro problem in perspective." The booklet even provided a list of "the most important points to make" including that U.S. government opposed discrimination; that most American schools were integrated; and that African Americans were enjoying "greater opportunities . . . in all fields."

Throughout the Cold War, U.S. officials acknowledged racial problems without declaring the United States a racist nation. Although they did not resort to outright lies, U.S. information leaders carefully edited their broadcasts on race relations in the United States. In December 1954, a massive study of agency operating assumptions contained startling recommendations for announcing racial problems:

> It is unwise to focus attention on bad conditions unless this helps maintain credibility in a major way, or shows that the U.S. is attacking its social problems. . . . *A lynching should be reported without comment*, but the following week there should be a general report of U.S. progress in race relations.[28]

Privately, agency leaders considered the subordinate position of African Americans to be "America's major point of vulnerability, particularly in dealing with non-white peoples."

Rather than focusing on racial inequities, U.S. information experts stressed racial progress. In profiling soldiers fighting in Korea, VOA broadcasts to Indonesia proclaimed:

> A revolution is also taking place among the American troops in Korea. The American troops are not only having to defend world democracy; they are also building better democracy for their own people. The American troops include men of many different groups—light Americans and dark Americans, Americans with Polish, Irish, and Spanish names, American Indians, Mexicans, Puerto Ricans and Negroes. In Korea these different Americans are building a better equality and unity. In this way they are giving new strength to American democracy.[29]

But U.S. propagandists rarely offered such racially inclusive materials and instead focused on African Americans. They profiled prominent black citizens and historic figures.[30] In pamphlets like *The Negro Question Without Propaganda* and *Americans of Negro Descent: An Advancing Group*, the USIS emphasized recent political, economic, and social advances by the African American community. U.S. propagandists dispatched "Negro Notes" addressing racial issues to U.S. diplomats stationed abroad.[31] U.S. policymakers attempted to balance journalistic and cultural portrayals of racial violence with more positive materials on minorities in the United States.

But unlike their communist counterparts, U.S. leaders could not control all of the messages disseminated abroad. On March 6, 1953, Senator Bourke Hickenlooper (R-Iowa) complained to Eric Johnston, the president of the Motion Picture Association of America, about the negative impact of U.S. films on foreign audiences. Hickenlooper criticized commercial motion pictures that proved "damaging to the prestige of the United States" and that counteracted the efforts of American information experts. He cited the film *Devil's Doorway*, a sensationalized depiction of the exploitation of Native Americans, as an example. After the USIS center in Manila showed a film depicting "the humane treatment of the American Indian," a Filipino man announced, "How can you expect me to believe what I have just seen after seeing *Devil's Doorway* last evening at the Avenue Theater?" Hickenlooper also derided Johnston for allowing the international distribution of films like *No Way Out* and *Pinky* that addressed racial discrimination in the United States. Johnston, however, rejected the suggestion that U.S. film companies censor their exports.[32]

Facing such obstacles, U.S. information strategists carefully devised publications for improving international perceptions of race relations in the United States. In May 1953, the USIA released *What Are the Facts About Negroes in the United States?*, a booklet featuring exhaustive answers to fourteen common questions about slavery, racial violence, segregation, and the political and economic status of African Americans. The pamphlet claimed that the economic gap between whites and blacks was steadily closing. Although whites continued to have larger incomes, the text read, African Americans owned more than 12 million acres of farm land and held more than 1.5 million industrial jobs. Blacks owned banks, credit unions, and insurance companies. Nonetheless, the booklet recognized that "it would be stretching the facts" to assert that blacks possessed full civil rights. After admitting the existence of racial discrimination in housing and voting, the pamphlet argued that lynching and segregation were declining. Finally, in response to the query, "What do Negroes themselves think of American democracy?," the text quoted Walter White, secretary of the NAACP. Although the United States lacked "perfect democracy," White averred, American blacks lived under greater freedom than those living under totalitarian regimes "where critics of the government are shipped off to exile or stood up against a wall and shot." Racism, the booklet implied, was a less egregious social evil than communism.[33]

Hoping to persuade foreigners to accept this opinion, USIA officials conducted extensive tests on potential propaganda materials. In August 1954, Agency evaluators asked thirty-nine Indians and seventy-one Filipinos to rate two versions of *The Negro in American Life*. At the suggestion of the respondents, Agency writers replaced complicated words like fiat, ethos, perspicacity, and manumission with simpler terms. In the original text, one paragraph claimed that in the year 1900 most people viewed blacks as lazy, irresponsible, and humorous. The pamphlet then declared, "Today, there is scarcely a community where that concept has not been drastically modified." After the test group rejected such sweeping generalizations, USIA editors changed the sentence to "Since that time, this concept has been drastically modified in community after community." Following the survey, Agency researchers concluded that audiences responded more positively to the modified version of the pamphlet, "despite its softened assertions about progress toward solution of race relations problems."[34]

USIA leaders also tried to combat anti-American invective that castigated capitalism as well as racism. For example, in February 1950, Hungarian propagandists denouncing Voice of America's commemoration of Abraham Lincoln's birthday asserted:

> VOA permits itself to speak on the freedom of the Negroes. But world public opinion witnesses with increasing indignation the increasingly obvious racial discrimination in the U.S. Lincoln emancipated the Negroes but Wall Street tolerates and encourages the Ku Klux Klan, lynchings, and the indescribable misery of the Negroes. Lincoln opposed exploitation of slaves but Wall Street daily intensifies the bloody exploitation of U.S. people and other peoples kneeling under Yankee imperialism.[35]

In order to counter Soviet claims that the United States wished to oppress all peoples of color, the researchers suggested publicizing the fact that "the Negro minority in the U.S. has made greater progress than any other comparable minority in the world."[36]

As part of this strategy, U.S. information experts publicized positive portraits of American life by visitors to the United States. A January 1952 propaganda packet directed at foreign workers featured Antonio V. Prendiville, president of the United Mine Workers Organization of New Zealand, recounting his three-month tour. "Before I came here," he explained, "I had the impression—like many people abroad—that the American Negro was a serf, without privileges." Prendiville discovered, however, that his original views of the United States were "completely distorted." He continued, "I saw Negro students in large universities, I saw Negro and white workers side-by-side in industries, and I found Negroes taking not only an active but a leading part in the trade union movement." Prendiville returned to New Zealand convinced that "In America it is up to the individual—regardless of race—whether or not he makes the grade."[37]

The USIA adopted similar tactics in propaganda directed at developing nations. In February 1957, USIS centers in India and Southeast Asia distributed *An African Looks at the American Negro*. The booklet highlighted Isaka Okwirry, a Kenyan legislator who visited the United States during the fall of 1955. The cover featured a rare agency photograph of a black family. Okwirry lovingly smiles at his infant son cradled in his mother's arms. As a participant in the State Department's "foreign leader" program, Okwirry spent three months viewing American schools and farms. He proclaims America "a land of people who are hard-working, religious, and understanding." After praising the educational opportunities, loans, and land ownership available to U.S. blacks, Okwirry asserts, "I have seen that in America the Negro is a free man."[38]

Many foreigners did not share Okwirry's opinion. In July 1956, Agency researchers conducted an extensive survey of West European opinions of race relations in the United States. The study revealed strikingly negative opinions. British and Dutch very harshly assessed U.S. treatment of minorities. When asked to identify incidents that created unfavorable impressions, many Europeans listed the Autherine Lucy affair, the murder of Emmett Till, and an attack on singer Nat King Cole by an Alabama mob. Fewer than 10 percent of those surveyed praised U.S. attempts to mitigate racial discrimination.[39]

In 1957, U.S. prestige plummeted even further when vicious white crowds prevented school desegregation in Little Rock, Arkansas. Without question, the protests were a public relations disaster for U.S. information strategists. Arkansas Governor Orval Faubus's blatant disregard of federal authority and the jeering mobs gathered outside Central High School in Little Rock gained worldwide attention. U.S. policymakers struggled to maintain composure as the news traveled to points as far as Leopoldville, Seoul, and Quito. On September 11, one USIA official conceded, "Let's face it, this Little Rock story is a tough one for us—a majority of the world's peoples are colored. But we're playing straight, we're covering it fully, without apology, though we are trying to put the story in perspective by pointing out what has been accomplished so far."[40]

The *New York Times* assailed USIA leaders for conveying the impression that federal legal action would ensure immediate integration. The paper cited Agency dispatches that failed to clarify that integration might be delayed by months of legal proceedings. USIA officials tried to deflect attention from Little Rock by pointing to peaceful integration in other southern states. But this tactic failed dismally. A few hours before an explosion rocked an elementary school in Nashville, Tennessee, Voice of America broadcasts declared, "Nashville city schools opened with white and Negro first graders attending integrated classes . . . there was some peaceful picketing—but no disturbances."[41]

During the desegregation crises, the world communist movement exhibited a rare talent for letting events speak for themselves. Amidst the deafening chorus of negative global press coverage, the Soviets hardly needed to wage an aggressive propaganda campaign of their own. Radio Moscow, with roughly 160 commentaries in the third quarter of 1957, was somewhat more vocal than its Bloc colleagues, especially in broadcasts targeting Asia and the Middle East. But communist broadcasters usually limited their remarks to recitations of Western news accounts.[42]

In general, the noncommunist press heavily publicized the racial incidents and deplored their occurrence. Many people in Western Europe expressed genuine remorse at the further decline of America's reputation as the exemplar of democracy.[43] Latin American reporters were more critical and often cited their own tradition of racial integration. Near and Far Eastern writers, however, voiced tremendous disdain for U.S. treatment of minorities. Indian audiences consistently identified racial discrimination as the "one outstanding social weakness" of the United States.[44] Noting the damage Little Rock inflicted on American foreign policy, The *Indonesian Times* asserted:

Asians and Africans suffering from traumatic scars left by colonial memories react violently to such incidents, and suddenly all patient

good will garnered by the American Foreign Service and the United
States Information Service is dissipated in a matter of minutes.
Americans must ask themselves if Faubus is not a greater traitor to
their country than the small fry caught stealing atomic data for a
foreign power and whether the Governor should not be hauled
before the Un-American Activities Committee for alienating half
the world.

The *Manila Chronicle* urged the USIA to repair America's tattered prestige:

It has become the standard practice of the USIA to devote paragraphs in its releases to the careers and achievements of outstanding
Negroes. These paragraphs are clearly intended to give the lie to the
accusation that race prejudice prevails in the U.S., but the official
glorification of a Marion Anderson or a Richard Wright hardly
proves anything . . . What must be shown is what is being done to
save the millions of colored Jacks and Janes from the score or so of
Governor Faubuses.

The Seoul *Han-Kook Ilbo* declared U.S. segregation problems "the main cause
of suspicion and antagonism of colored people all over the world toward
American democracy and the American way of life."[45]

These reports greatly dismayed the Eisenhower administration. On September 24, Secretary of State John Foster Dulles and Attorney General Herbert Brownell discussed the president's decision to send federal troops to
enforce integration in Arkansas. Although both men approved Eisenhower's
reaction, Dulles feared that Little Rock was "ruining" American foreign policy and predicted that "The effect of this in Asia and Africa will be worse than
Hungary was for the Russians." The following afternoon, Brownell and
Dulles ordered USIA leaders to stress improving racial conditions in the
United States. Agency officials declared that the disruptive elements in Little
Rock were not representative of the community. USIS centers displayed pictures of interracial activities to counteract international media coverage of the
mob scenes at Central High School.[46]

In February 1958, USIA Director George Allen praised the agency's response to Little Rock in his semiannual report to Congress. The disturbances,
he argued, were merely "an episode in a period of social change." The fight for
integration displayed the vibrancy of American democracy. "The story of

freedom, in contrast to the story of life in a police state," he concluded, "appeals powerfully to people everywhere."[47]

Allen's remarks infuriated journalists in the American South. "What a mockery of the word freedom" retorted the *Shreveport Journal* on February 28, 1958. Launching a bitter attack on the USIA's response to segregation, the article continued:

> And what a terrible waste of the taxpayers' money to give people abroad an incorrect, interracialist's-eye-view of life in the United States. What do we have but a police state when our own President sends paratroopers armed with rifles and bayonets to force white boys and girls of Little Rock to accept racial integration in their high school?. . . . The United States Information Agency has not reported how it is answering THESE questions. . . . Isn't it about time we quit spending money to spread interracial propaganda overseas? Americans won't buy the Eisenhower administration's interracial program, so why should they pay to try to sell it to foreigners?[48]

It appeared anything that USIA said about American race relations alienated someone.

Not surprisingly, African Americans offered the harshest reviews of U.S. propaganda on racial issues. Civil rights organizations frequently implored American policymakers to present an accurate picture abroad of the problems facing minority citizens of the United States. In January 1946, Floyd Patterson, the president of the United Negro College Fund, urged Assistant Secretary of State for Public Affairs William B. Benton to include information about African Americans in U.S. propaganda materials. Patterson then suggested his organization "as one source of material and information on Negro life—better still, life in America." Two weeks later, Benton assured Patterson that all USIS centers would distribute publications that "depict the culture, institutions, and activities of all of the people of our nation, including Negro Americans." He did not, however, accept Patterson's offer of assistance.[49]

In early 1950, African Americans continued to complain of their exclusion from State Department advisory committees. On February 28, U.S. information leaders recommended that blacks receive "careful consideration" for consultant positions.[50] Nonetheless, the State Department continued to resist input from African Americans. In July 1950, the National Council of Negro Women charged Voice of America with repeatedly broadcasting a "dangerous distortion of the history and present status of race relations in the United States." The women's group derided VOA newscasts on the civil rights programs of the Truman administration as "an apology for the conservative Southern point of view." The radio broadcasts, the women claimed, misrepresented the work of the NAACP. The women recommended several changes in the U.S. information program including the establishment of a program on minority affairs in the United States, the appointment of an expert on race relations to the division, and the creation of an advisory committee comprised of religious and racial minorities. The State Department rejected all three suggestions.[51]

Despite these rebuffs, many civil rights leaders continued to support the international information program. Firm believers in the promise of American democracy, they urged Congress to provide additional funding for propaganda operations. On July 6, 1950, Walter White, executive secretary of NAACP, submitted a poignant letter in favor of expanding U.S. information activities. Citing racism as one of the strongest impediments to a democratic victory over communism, White asserted:

> Two-thirds of the earth's population is non-white. Increasingly, the white minority is being regarded with extreme skepticism by the non-white peoples of the world because that minority talks glibly of freedom but continues to practice racial discrimination and exploitation. Our own country is one of the greatest culprits on this issue. . . . As a result our most noble statements of principle are today not only ignored but even laughed at.[52]

Despite his disdain for American racism, White stressed his support for "the substantial advances we are making at home against bigotry."

But U.S. information leaders were not in the vanguard for racial equality in the United States. On October 3, 1946, State Department administrator Fitzhugh Granger wrote a memorandum on the employment of African Americans. Granger offered some acute observations. Although he believed that many black Americans possessed the qualifications required by the State Department, he doubted that foreign audiences, even predominately black ones, would respect African American cultural and information officers. "While it might be possible to assign Negroes as staff personnel to Haiti and possibly to Cuba and Brazil," Granger continued, "my feeling is that the risks involved far outweigh the benefits. . . . I believe it would be *definitely* unwise to attempt to send Negroes to *any* of the Latin American countries." Granger explained,

> Realistically, we must take into consideration the clannishness of social life within an embassy where the probable prejudices of the other American members of the staff themselves create very difficult problems, which would inevitably be talked about in public.
>
> Even in Latin America where race tolerance is a by-word and Negroes frequently dominate, I believe it is a reasonable statement to say that Latin American people look upon the United States as a white country, although recognizing the presence of millions of Negroes, and therefore would not readily accept a Negro as a responsible and official representative of this country.[53]

Throughout the 1950s, the State Department remained reticent to appoint blacks to important diplomatic and advisory positions.[54] U.S. propagandists espoused racial equality much more readily than they executed it.

Prominent African Americans excoriated the gap between democratic rhetoric and the reality of U.S. racism. Jazz singer Josephine Baker, actor and singer Paul Robeson, writer W. E. B. Du Bois, and others frequently informed foreign audiences about racial discrimination in the United States. In the wake of the Little Rock protests in 1957, Louis Armstrong told the State Department to "go to hell" when U.S. cultural attachés asked him to tour the Soviet Union. The federal government responded negatively to these comments. The State Department occasionally confiscated the passports of people drawing attention to America's racial problems. Congressional investigative bodies and the Federal Bureau of Investigation subjected civil rights advocates to close scrutiny. Opponents of racial equality frequently smeared their adversaries with accusations of communist bias.[55] In March 1953, Senator Joseph R. McCarthy invoked anticommunism while attempting to have the works of poet Langston Hughes and historian Herbert Aptheker, both ardent critics of U.S. race relations, removed from USIS information centers abroad.[56]

Although sensitive to black criticism of American race relations, U.S. information leaders carefully emphasized the achievements and opportunities attained by U.S. minorities. They used portraits of successful African Americans as indications of overall progress in U.S. race relations. An April 1953 USIA labor packet declared President Eisenhower's appointment of attorney J. Ernest Wilkins as assistant secretary of labor "a recognition of high professional and scholarly achievement by an American Negro and an affirmation of America's repudiation of race prejudice." USIA officials stressed Wilkins's supervision of international labor affairs and service as the American representative to the International Labor Organization. His achievements, the Agency proclaimed, "affirm [the] democratic principle of equal rights and opportunities for all citizens regardless of race or color."[57] In March 1956, a USIA youth publication included an article on folk singer Harry Belafonte. "This profile," Agency leaders told their public affairs officers, "was prepared to show again that race or color is [of] no importance to artist's progress in the United States if he has talent."[58]

At the same time, the USIA began sending black athletes and performers abroad in order to accentuate American culture and to counter Soviet propaganda on U.S. race relations. In 1955, despite the opera's inclusion of controversial characters including a pimp and a drug dealer, the Agency sponsored an extensive international tour of *Porgy and Bess* performed by an entirely black cast.[59] By 1960, USIA's impressive roster of "goodwill ambassadors" included basketball masters the Harlem Globetrotters, track star Jesse Owens, jazz artist Dizzie Gillespie, and dancer Katherine Dunham.[60]

Agency films spotlighted acclaimed African Americans. In 1957, after Althea Gibson won her first U.S. Open and Wimbledon tournaments, USIA commissioned a ten-minute film about the tennis star. The previous year, during a State Department-sponsored tour of the Far East, Gibson had proved herself a formidable competitor. Despite having encountered innumerable obstacles on account of her race, Gibson told foreign reporters who inquired about black life in the United States, "We have problems, but I think they can and will be solved." Those who paired talent and patriotic humility were the Agency's ideal international spokespeople.[61]

The USIA film *Althea Gibson: Tennis Champion* reflected these preferences. As in other U.S. propaganda materials depicting the lives of famous African Americans, any limitations Gibson faced in reaching her potential were attributed to factors other than racism. In her case, a lack of self-confidence and poverty were the culprits. Through hard work and perseverance, Gibson reached her full potential—and illustrated USIA's mantra that America's democratic promise was available to all.[62]

But none of these tactics erased the stain of racism from America's reputation. In December 1958, an internal study prepared by the Eisenhower administration's Civil Rights Commission lamented the limited impact of over a decade of American efforts to improve international perceptions of U.S. race relations. The "adverse" effect of racial discrimination on foreign public opinion continued to weaken "our moral position as the champion of freedom and democracy" and raised or reinforced doubts about "the sincerity and strength of our professions of concern for the welfare of others, particularly the non-white world."[63] Well into the 1960s, the international attention riveted on the U.S. civil rights movement overwhelmed even the most skillful propaganda prepared by the USIA and the State Department. No invocation of the heritage of democratic freedom and achievements of African Americans could outweigh the fact that racial inequalities persisted in the United States. In their struggle to defeat communism, U.S. information officials were forced to defend America's indefensible race relations.

Conclusion: The Costs and Limits
of Selling "America"

There are two kinds of propaganda: propaganda when you know you're lying and propaganda when you think you're telling the truth.
—Kevin Rafferty, documentary filmmaker

FROM THE INCEPTION of the postwar information program, U.S. officials wrestled with the contradictions inherent in a democracy engaging in propaganda. While communist propagandists were aided by a state-controlled press and a one-party political system, U.S. information strategists faced the continual and often hostile scrutiny of the mass media and Congress. Because the 1948 Smith-Mundt Act barred domestic dissemination of American propaganda materials, U.S. citizens knew little about what the information programs actually did. Accordingly, politicians and journalists eager to prove their credentials as unassailable patriots, culture warriors, or fiscal hawks could easily attack information activities. Caught in a maelstrom of budget vacillations, organizational inefficiency, and political infighting, U.S. propagandists did difficult, delicate work under trying and unpredictable circumstances.

But if some of the limits of the U.S. ideological offensive were externally imposed, others were by conscious design. Although the United States went to great lengths to prevent the spread of communism, information activities received an almost laughable percentage of the expenditures directed at national security. In 1960, following years of Eisenhower's ostensibly making propaganda a top priority in his foreign policy, only *1 percent* of the approximately $50 billion spent annually on guarding the United States went to information programs.[1] Whatever rhetorical energies U.S. policymakers directed at promoting propaganda, they never even came close to according it financial status equivalent to military or economic manifestations of American power.

Throughout the Cold War, U.S. information officials engaged in what could be described as dual containment. Unwilling to sell "America" in ways that triggered an exodus of Eastern Europe refugees or a third world war, American policymakers contained the potential ramifications of attacking communism as well as the expansion of communism. Ironically, the Soviet government assisted these efforts by spending enormous sums on jamming U.S. efforts to reach communist audiences.[2] If the Soviets had diverted these funds to producing some of the products their citizens found irresistible at the 1959 American National Exhibition, perhaps the "Soviet way of life" would have been more attractive—and more enduring.

But selling "the American way of life" entailed far more than a celebration of consumerism. Throughout the early Cold War, U.S. information strategists presented the United States as a nation that valued freedom, tolerance, and individuality. They emphasized the egalitarian nature of the U.S. political system and the vibrancy of American culture. They extolled the U.S. standard of living and capitalism. While muting coverage of racism and economic inequalities, they offered a markedly liberal vision of America that promised progress and prosperity for individuals and families. But did their appeals work? If they "sold" America successfully, what exactly, did foreigners buy?

The end of the Cold War offers us some clues. Although it is difficult to assess the role of U.S. propaganda in the collapse of communism, evidence of the international impact of democratic capitalism abounds in the former USSR and Eastern Europe. Since 1989, representative government, political pluralism, and self-determination have taken hold in these nations. To varying degrees, governments permit freedom of speech and freedom of the press. People openly practice their religions. American cultural exports and consumer goods are enormously popular. U.S. officials correctly believed that democratic capitalism would appeal to peoples oppressed by communist political oppression, economic regimentation, and police surveillance.

But the advent of democratic capitalism in the former Soviet states also illustrates the weaknesses of the U.S. ideological offensive. By soft-pedaling or omitting images of poverty, unemployment, and crime from their propaganda, U.S. officials created an idealized vision of democratic capitalism.

Many ex-communists now long for the days of guaranteed employment, fixed prices, and safe neighborhoods. While the collapse of communism has enriched savvy business people, it has also unleashed ethnic violence and xenophobia. The transition to a free market economy hardly represents the nirvana depicted by U.S. information experts.[3]

It is indisputable that the end of the Cold War had a significant impact on U.S. public diplomacy. From 1993 to 2001, the budget for the State Department's cultural and educational exchanges dropped 33 percent, from $349 million to $232 million. From 1995 to 2001, the number of participants in cultural exchanges dropped from 45,000 to 29,000. VOA and U.S. overseas libraries experienced similar cutbacks.[4] "The idea after the Cold War was that we didn't have to worry about influencing foreign publics," a Foreign Service officer who wished to remain anonymous told *U.S. News & World Report* in March 2003. "Everybody would simply start watching American films and buying our products."[5] But, as 9/11 demonstrated with terrifying clarity, the global popularity of U.S. goods and American culture has not created universal acceptance of U.S. foreign policies and the American way of life. Indeed, the U.S. war in Iraq, the demise of the Soviet Union, the rise of Internet technologies, and globalization have greatly increased international criticism of American power and culture.[6]

This political climate has triggered substantial increases in funding for U.S. international information activities. In 2005, the State Department spent $1.36 billion on its international information, cultural, and broadcasting activities, an almost 35 percent increase over 2002 expenditures.[7] But the figure is miniscule compared to $323 billion devoted to U.S. military expenditures in the first three years of the war on terrorism or the $222 billion that private U.S. companies spend annually on overseas advertising.[8] Furthermore, President George W. Bush and other officials have offered simplistic explanations of and strategies for combating anti-Americanism. Repeatedly claiming foreign distrust of the United States stems from hatred of American "freedoms" and "values," they call for America to do a better job of "selling" itself overseas. Like their predecessors in the Cold War, they combine advertising techniques and a nationalism that downplays America's ethnic and economic divisions.[9] So far, polling, focus groups, and fact-gathering missions have neither curbed antiAmericanism nor capitalized on the global appeal of American democracy.

Charlotte Beers, Bush's first appointee as undersecretary of state for public diplomacy and public affairs, experienced these realities. Confirmed shortly after 9/11, Beers was a successful advertising executive who had served as chairman of J. Walter Thompson (1997–2001) and Ogilvy & Mather (1992–1997), two of the world's largest advertising agencies. She earned acclaim for "branding" companies like IBM and American Express. A soft-spoken Texan, Beers began her career as the first woman product manager at Uncle Ben's Rice. In the 1970s, she entered the advertising business, becoming the first female senior vice-president in J. Walter Thompson's Chicago office.[10] In early 2001, although she had no foreign affairs experience, Beers jumped at the chance to lead the nation's international information efforts.

As Beers assumed office, several members of Congress were calling for drastic improvement in the State Department's public diplomacy programs. On October 10, Henry J. Hyde (R-Ill.), chairman of the House Committee on International Relations, convened hearings on "the role of public diplomacy in the anti-terrorism campaign." Decrying the "poisonous" image of the United States held by much of the world, Hyde and others claimed that budget cuts and the 1999 merger of the United States Information Agency and the Department of State had impaired America's public diplomacy activities and thereby jeopardized national security.[11] Critics across the political spectrum were debating the proper role of "soft power" in the post-9/11 world.[12]

In an October 2001 appearance before the House Committee on International Relations, Beers put forward her vision for U.S. public diplomacy. She asserted:

> If you think of the September 11 attack as a big building going down, you haven't gotten it. If you think of it as how many orphans were made that day and how many people are still weeping and mourning, you will remember. It is part of our goal to put those pictures in the communication process that is so active now in all forms of public diplomacy. We need to become better at communicating the intangibles, the behavior, the emotions that reside in lofty words like democracy. . . . This is a war about a way of life and fundamental beliefs and values. We did not expect to ever have to explain and defend concepts like freedom and tolerance. We have to prepare our people for an era of vigilance for nearly invisible enemies with goals that are quite unfamiliar: to destabilize, to make radical, to hate all that we hold dear.[13]

To achieve these objectives, Beers urged the State Department to make its campaigns more emotional and to improve its use of radio, television, and other media. As an example, she pointed to her revisions of the government's main Web site on 9/11 (usinfo.state.gov). In sections called "Response to Terrorism" and "Islam in the U.S.," Beers added poignant photographs of Muslim American candlelight vigils for victims and a map highlighting the eighty nations that incurred casualties in the attacks. She also announced plans to launch television commercials created in collaboration with the Ad Council. "It is almost as though we have to redefine what America is," she concluded, "This is the most sophisticated brand assignment I have ever had."[14]

Secretary of State Colin Powell echoed many of these assertions. Testifying before the Senate Foreign Relations Committee on October 25, Powell said that U.S. diplomats were fighting anti-Americanism by cooperating with foreign media outlets such as al-Jazeera television, Turkish Star TV, the *Hindu Daily* newspaper, and N-TV of Russia. He praised a new State Department booklet documenting Osama bin Laden's role in 9/11 and quoting Muslim leaders denouncing terrorism. The pamphlet was being translated into twelve languages for electronic distribution at all U.S. embassies. Rebuffing those who questioned Beers's qualifications for the State Department post, Powell declared, "She got me to buy Uncle Ben's Rice and so there is nothing wrong with getting somebody who knows how to sell something." "The point is, we have got to get creative people from the most creative media society on the face of the Earth to put their time, attention, and mind power to this, and I am determined to do that."[15]

Many American journalists commented on the challenges facing those attempting to sell the United States abroad. *AdAge* columnist Rance Crain wrote,

> We won the Cold War not because we convinced the world our
> cause was just, but because the Soviet Union ran out of money. The
> job of convincing people around the world that our way of life is
> best is made more difficult and complex now because of the perva-
> siveness of our culture. Our movies, music, fashion, consumer brand
> names such as McDonald's and Coca-Cola, embody what are
> widely seen as our crass and overly secular society.[16]

While applauding Beers's plans to place freedom at the core of U.S. information campaigns, Crain urged her "to show the world that our concept of freedom goes beyond the Golden Arches and the Pause that Refreshes,"[17] Margaret Carlson of *Time* magazine also described the difficulties of post-9/11 public diplomacy. "Beers has to rebrand Osama bin Laden as a mass murderer to millions of Muslims who have never seen a 767 or a skyscraper, much less one flying into the other. She has to do it in languages, like Pashto and Dari, that don't even have a word for terrorist. And all this without having control over Voice of America or Radio Free Europe." Acknowledging "this would be a tall order for anyone, much less someone with no diplomatic experience," Carlson cautioned "Uncle Sam is a harder sell these days than Uncle Ben ever was."[18]

Despite these obstacles, the Bush administration is expanding efforts to persuade foreign audiences to embrace the American way of life. Throughout 2002, Beers worked to better integrate public diplomacy into the formulation and implementation of U.S. foreign policy and to earn greater recognition for specialists in public diplomacy.[19] In March 2002, the U.S. International Broadcasting Bureau launched Radio Sawa ("together" in Arabic), a 24-hour, commercial-free radio network aimed at the 99 million Middle Easterners aged 15 to 34—nearly 60 percent of the region's population. Armed with a $30 million budget, Radio Sawa features a mix of Arabic and Western popular music and Arabic-language news updates. According to Norman J. Pattiz, Radio Sawa's creator and chairman of the largest U.S. radio network, Westwood One, Radio Sawa's mission is "to promote freedom and democracy through the dissemination of accurate, reliable, and credible news and information about America and the world to audiences overseas."[20] Pattiz was also instrumental in the development of Alhurra ("The Free One"), an Arabic-language satellite television station launched on February 14, 2004. Alhurra aims to present "accurate, balanced, and comprehensive news" to Middle Eastern viewers.[21]

While it is too soon to gauge the success of these initiatives, the early signs are not encouraging. During Ramadan 2002, Beers's office began its Shared Values Initiative with the release of five minidocumentaries featuring Muslim Americans describing their lives in the United States. The films sought to disprove widely held stereotypes of Americans as decadent, faithless, and anti-Islamic. But only Indonesia, Malaysia, Pakistan, and Kuwait allowed the videos to air.[22] Jolted by a chorus of outrage in the Muslim world, the U.S. government yanked the ads.[23] In March 2003, amid extensive coverage of the Bush administration's push for war with Iraq, Beers resigned as undersecretary of state for public diplomacy because of unspecified health problems. Her departure coincided with enormous anti-American protests held worldwide. While Powell praised Beers for bringing "incredible expertise from Madison Avenue to Foggy Bottom" and for reaching "younger, broader, and deeper audiences," others criticized her for not making a stronger case for U.S. policies on Iraq, the Middle East peace process, and the war on terrorism.[24]

In the months following the American invasion of Iraq, the debate on public diplomacy intensified. In December 2003, Margaret Tutwiler, a former State Department spokesperson and former U.S. ambassador to Morocco, succeeded Beers. She inherited a program beset by limited funding and inadequate personnel. Mark Helmke, a senior staffer at the Senate Foreign Relations Committee, called U.S. information efforts in Iraq "a complete and utter disaster" and castigated the lack of coordination among agencies running media operations there. Policy experts warned that American support for Israel and for autocratic regimes in the Middle East alienates younger Arabs. They claimed that Americans' lack of knowledge about Arabic culture and language exacerbates weaknesses in U.S. public diplomacy efforts.[25] In March 2004, a survey documenting attitudes toward the United States in nine countries found increasing discontent with America and its policies, especially those pertaining to the Iraq War. More Europeans reported their desire for foreign policy and security measures independent from those of the United States. Large majorities in Morocco and Jordan viewed as justified suicide attacks against Americans and other Westerners in Iraq.[26] A month later, Tutwiler resigned from the State Department to become executive vice-president for communications and government relations at the New York Stock Exchange.[27] The top public diplomacy post remained unfilled for almost a year before President Bush appointed Karen Hughes, a former television reporter and a long-time Bush advisor, as Tutwiler's successor. Upon accepting the nomination, Hughes declared her commitment "to stand for what President Bush has called the nonnegotiable demands of human dignity: the rule of law, limits on the power of the state, respect for women, private property, free speech, equal justice and religious tolerance."[28] When Hughes announced her resignation in October 2007, she could point to few successes in advancing such grandiose goals.[29]

Selling "America" will never work if we do not close the gap between how we define ourselves—and how we actually act at home and abroad. In June 2007, the Pew Global Attitudes survey revealed "broad and deepening dislike of American values and a global backlash against the spread of American ideas and customs." Respondents in forty-seven countries blasted U.S. policies for increasing the gap between the world's rich and poor and for harming the environment.[30] Those statistics represent a threat to national security every bit as grave as a terrorist attack.

No amount of money or radio programming or television or subtly (or forcibly) implanted news items can persuade foreigners to embrace "the American way of life" if we validate the worst stereotypes of our nation. When our proclamations of empathy for the burqa-clad women suffering under the Taliban give way to U.S. soldiers killing Afghani civilians and torturing Iraqi prisoners, who can blame foreigners for considering public diplomacy a joke? When our leaders conflate "freedom" with vacuous consumerism and blind patriotism, who would want to "buy" a nation embodying such superficiality and hypocrisy?

These contradictions, however, demonstrate why the struggle to define the United States must continue. The United States is a jingoistic, parochial, materialistic, and racist nation. But it is also a bastion of freedom, tolerance, economic opportunity, and innovation. This complexity has never eluded U.S. information experts. They have always defended a way of life that permits each citizen to define what he or she values most about America. Our differing opinions of those values exemplify the essence of our democratic heritage. Our collective challenge is to live our ideals, to be the nation we say we are.

NOTES

INTRODUCTION

Epigraphs: NSC–68, United States Objectives and Programs for National Security, April 14, 1950, http://www.fas.org/irp/offdocs/nsc-hst/nsc-68.htm; National Security Strategy of the United States of America, September 2002, http://www.whitehouse.gov/nsc/nssall.html.

1. The National Security Strategy remains the best explanation of the Bush Doctrine.

2. The nature of "American empire" is widely disputed. See, for example, Robert Kagan, "The Benevolent Empire," *Foreign Policy* (Summer 1998): 24–35; Andrew J. Bacevich, *American Empire: The Realities & Consequences of U.S. Diplomacy* (Cambridge, Mass.: Harvard University Press, 2002); Joseph S. Nye, Jr., *The Paradox of American Power: Why the World's Only Superpower Can't Go It Alone* (New York: Oxford University Press, 2002); Amy Kaplan, "Violent Belongings and the Question of Empire Today: Presidential Address to the American Studies Association, October 17, 2003," *American Quarterly* 56 (March 2004): 1–18; Niall Ferguson, *Colossus: The Rise and Fall of the American Empire* (New York: Penguin, 2005).

3. "President Bush Delivers Graduation Speech at West Point," June 1, 2002, http://www.whitehouse.gov/news/releases/2002/06/20020601-3.html.

4. These assertions have sparked intense debate. See, for example, Ellen Schrecker, ed., *Cold War Triumphalism: The Misuse of History After the Fall of Communism* (New York: New Press, 2004); Fareed Zakaria, *The Future of Freedom: Illberal Democracy at Home and Abroad* (New York: Norton, 2003); Michael Ignatieff, "Who Are Americans to Think That Freedom Is Theirs to Spread?," *New York Times Magazine*, June 26, 2005, 42–47; Eric Hobsbawm, "The Dangers of Exporting Democracy," *The Guardian*, January 22, 2005, http://www.guardian.co.uk/comment/story/0,3604,1396038,00.html; Peter Baker, "The Realities of Exporting Democracy," *Washington Post*, January 25, 2006, http://www.washingtonpost.com/wp-dyn/content/article/2006/01/24/AR2006012401901.html; Michael Mandelbaum, *The Ideas That Conquered the World: Peace, Democracy, and Free Markets in the Twenty-First Century* (New York: Public Affairs, 2002); Amy Chua, *World on Fire: How Exporting Free Market Democracy Breeds Ethnic Hatred and Global Instability* (New York: Doubleday, 2003).

5. "Dr. Rice Addresses War on Terror," August 19, 2004, http://www.whitehouse.gov/news/releases/2004/08/print/20040819-5.html.

6. The term "public diplomacy" originated in 1965 at the Fletcher School of Law and Diplomacy at Tufts University. It refers to government-sponsored communications that are designed to shape international public opinion and to minimize misunderstandings and misperceptions among nations. For several definitions, see "What Is Public Diplomacy?" http://www.publicdiplomacy.org/1.htm.

7. Arthur Goodfriend, *My America* (New York: Simon and Schuster, 1955), 6, Pamphlet Files, USIAA.

8. Goodfriend, *My America*, 18.

9. On the genesis of the postwar information program, see Frank Ninkovich, *The Diplomacy of Ideas: U.S. Foreign Policy and Cultural Relations, 1938–1950* (New York: Cambridge University Press, 1981); Walter F. Hixson, *Parting the Curtain: Propaganda, Culture, and the Cold War, 1945–1961* (New York: St. Martin's Press, 1997); Scott Lucas, *Freedom's War: The American Crusade Against the Soviet Union* (New York: New York University Press, 1999); Gregory Mitrovich, *Undermining the Kremlin: America's Strategy to Subvert the Soviet Bloc, 1947–1956* (Ithaca, N.Y.: Cornell University Press, 2000); Kenneth Osgood, *Total Cold War: Eisenhower's Secret Propaganda Battle at Home and Abroad* (Lawrence: University Press of Kansas, 2006).

10. See, for example, George M. Allen, *Presidents Who Have Known Me* (New York: Simon and Schuster, 1950); Edward W. Barrett, *Truth Is Our Weapon* (New York: Funk and Wagnalls, 1953); Charles Thayer, *Diplomat* (New York: Harper, 1959); Charles A. H. Thomson, *Overseas Information Service of the United States Government* (Washington, D.C.: Brookings Institution, 1948); Wilson P. Dizard, *The Strategy of Truth: The Story of the U.S. Information Service* (Washington, D.C.: Public Affairs Press, 1961).

11. Works representing this trend include Wilson P. Dizard, Jr., *Inventing Public Diplomacy: The Story of the U.S. Information Agency* (Boulder, Colo.: Lynne Rienner, 2004); Charles A. Thomson and Walter H. C. Laves, *Cultural Relations and U.S. Foreign Policy* (Bloomington: Indiana University Press, 1963); John W. Henderson, *The United States Information Agency* (New York: Praeger, 1969); Robert E. Elder, *The Information Machine: The United States Information Agency and American Foreign Policy* (Syracuse, N.Y.: Syracuse University Press, 1968); Thomas C. Sorenson, *The Word War: The Story of American Propaganda* (New York: Harper and Row, 1968); Allen C. Hansen, *USIA: Public Diplomacy in the Computer Age* (New York: Praeger Special Studies, 1984); Randolph Wieck, *Ignorance Abroad: American Educational and Cultural Foreign Policy and the Office of Assistant Secretary of State* (Westport, Conn.: Praeger, 1992); Fitzhugh Green, *American Propaganda Abroad* (New York: Hippocrene, 1988); Hans N. Tuch, *Communicating with the World: U.S. Public Diplomacy Overseas* (New York: St. Martin's Press, 1990).

12. Christina Klein, *Cold War Orientalism: Asia in the Middlebrow Imagination, 1945–1961* (Berkeley: University of California Press, 2003); Melani McAlister, *Epic Encounters: Culture, Media, and U.S. Interests in the Middle East Since 1945*, updated ed. (Berkeley: University of California Press, 2005). Several excellent examples are also found in Christian

G. Appy, ed., *Cold War Constructions: The Political Culture of United States Imperialism, 1945–1966* (Amherst: University of Massachusetts Press, 2000).

13. Seminal critiques of cultural imperialism include Ariel Dorfman and Armand Mattelart, *How to Read Donald Duck: Imperialist Ideology in the Disney Comic*, trans. David Kunzle (New York: International General, 1975); Herbert Schiller, *Communication and Cultural Domination* (White Plains, N.Y.: International Arts and Sciences Press, 1976); and Edward Said, *Orientalism* (New York: Pantheon, 1978). Important studies that emphasize multinational processes of cultural dissemination and appropriation include Richard Pells, *Not like U.S.: How Europeans Have Loved, Hated, and Transformed American Culture Since World War II* (New York: Basic Books, 1997); Rob Kroes, Robert Rydell, and Doeko F. J. Bosscher, eds., *Cultural Transmissions and Receptions: American Mass Culture in Europe* (Amsterdam: VU University Press, 1993); John Tomlinson, *Cultural Imperialism: A Critical Introduction* (Baltimore: Johns Hopkins University Press, 1991); Ralph Willet, *The Americanization of Germany, 1945–1949* (London: Routledge, 1989); Richard F. Kuisel, *Seducing the French: The Dilemma of Americanization* (Berkeley: University of California Press, 1993); Reinhold Wagnleitner, *The Coca-Colonization and the Cold War: The Cultural Mission of the United States in Austria After the Second World War* (Chapel Hill: University of North Carolina Press, 1994). For an insightful overview of pertinent historiography, see Jessica Gienow-Hecht, "Shame on *US*? Academics, Cultural Transfer, and the Cold War: A Critical Review," *Diplomatic History* (Summer 2000): 465–94.

14. Frank Costigliola, *Awkward Dominion: American Political, Economic, and Cultural Relations with Europe, 1919–1933* (Ithaca, N.Y.: Cornell University Press, 1984); Emily S. Rosenberg, *Spreading the American Dream: American Economic and Cultural Expansion, 1890–1945* (New York: Hill and Wang, 1982); Jessica Gienow-Hecht, *Transmission Impossible: American Journalism as Cultural Diplomacy in Postwar Germany, 1945–1955* (Baton Rouge: Louisiana State University Press, 1999); Gilbert M. Joseph, Catherine C. Legrand, and Ricardo D. Salvatore, eds. *Close Encounters of Empire: Writing the Cultural History of U.S.-Latin American Relations* (Durham, N.C.: Duke University Press, 1998); Christopher Endy, *Cold War Holidays: American Tourism in France* (Chapel Hill: University of North Carolina Press, 2004); Petra Goedde, *GIs and Germans: Gender, Culture, and Foreign Relations, 1945–1949* (New Haven, Conn.: Yale University Press, 2002).

15. Hixson, *Parting the Curtain*; Lucas *Freedom's War*; Mitrovich, *Undermining the Kremlin*; Osgood, *Total Cold War*; David F. Krugler, *The Voice of America and the Domestic Propaganda Battles, 1945–1953* (Columbia: University of Missouri Press, 2000).

16. Naima Prevots, *Dance for Export: Cultural Diplomacy and Cold War* (Middletown, Conn.: Wesleyan University Press, 1998); Michael J. Krenn, *Fall-Out Shelters for the Human Spirit: American Art and the Cold War* (Chapel Hill: University of North Carolina Press, 2005); Damion Lamar Thomas, "'The Good Negroes': African-American Athletes and the Cultural Cold War, 1945–1968" (Ph.D. dissertation, University of California at Los Angeles, 2002); David Caute, *The Dancer Defects: The Struggle for Cultural Supremacy During the Cold War* (New York: Oxford University Press, 2003); Yale Richmond, *Cultural Exchange & the Cold War: Raising the Iron Curtain* (University Park: Pennsylvania State

University Press, 2003); Penny Von Eschen, *Satchmo Blows Up the World: Jazz Ambassadors Play the Cold War* (Cambridge, Mass.: Harvard University Press, 2004).

17. A good example is Krugler, *Voice of America*. While he provides a marvelous explication of how competing views of statism and internationalism influenced the "domestic propaganda battles," Krugler does not connect disputes over the content of America's information campaigns to long-standing quarrels over the defining characteristics of "the American way of life" and domestic political culture. Other scholars either completely ignore or inadequately address the content of U.S. propaganda. Gregory Mitrovich's analysis of U.S. attempts to use propaganda activities to rollback communism treats information as a tool of foreign policy, not as a concerted effort to define American national identity for foreign audiences. See *Undermining the Kremlin*. Walter Hixson's *Parting the Curtain* devotes only portions of a single chapter to the ways that policymakers defined race, capitalism, and American culture; see chapter 5, "'People's Capitalism': USIA, Race Relations, and Cultural Infiltration," 121–50. Kenneth Osgood takes a similar approach; see *Total Cold War*, chapter 8, "Facts About the United States: The USIA Presents Everyday Life in America," 253–87. Scholars have also closely examined the difficulties American propagandists faced in explaining and defending segregation in the early Cold War era. These works, however, do not address other important elements of the international promotion of American political culture. See, for example, Mary Dudziak, *Cold War Civil Rights: Race and the Image of American Democracy* (Princeton, N.J.: Princeton University Press, 2002).

18. "USIA Basic Guidance and Planning," Paper 2, September 17, 1958, Subject Files—Policy, USIAA.

19. The definition of propaganda is found in Clayton D. Laurie, *The Propaganda Warriors: America's Crusade Against Nazi Germany* (Lawrence: University Press of Kansas, 1996), 6. For a helpful historical overview, see Richard Alan Nelson, "Propaganda," in *Handbook of Popular Culture*, ed. M. Thomas Inge, 2nd ed. (New York: Greenwood Press, 1989), 1011–1123.

20. Examples of the literature on covert propaganda include Lucas, *Freedom's War*; Rhodri Jeffreys-Jones, *The CIA and American Democracy* (New Haven, Conn.: Yale University Press, 1987); Sig Mickelson, *America's Other Voice: The Story of Radio Free Europe and Radio Liberty* (New York: Praeger, 1983); Frances Stonor Saunders, *The Cultural Cold War: The CIA and the World of Arts and Letters* (New York: New Press, 2000).

21. Ninkovich, *The Diplomacy of Ideas*; Hixson, *Parting the Curtain*; Lucas, *Freedom's War*; Mitrovich, *Undermining the Kremlin*; Osgood, *Total Cold War*.

CHAPTER ONE. THE TRUMAN YEARS

1. Odd Arne Westad, *The Global Cold War: Third World Interventions and the Making of Our Times* (New York: Cambridge University Press, 2005); Melvyn P. Leffler, *A Preponderance of Power: National Security, the Truman Administration, and the Cold War* (Stanford, Calif.: Stanford University Press, 1992); Tony Smith, *America's Mission: The United*

States and the Worldwide Struggle for Democracy in the Twentieth Century (Princeton, N.J.: Princeton University Press, 1994).

2. Michael J. Hogan, *A Cross of Iron: Harry S. Truman and the Origins of the National Security State* (Cambridge: Cambridge University Press, 1998); Aaron Friedberg, *In the Shadow of the Garrison State: America's Anti-Statism and Its Cold War Grand Strategy* (Princeton, N.J.: Princeton University Press, 2000).

3. For the history of U.S. propaganda during World War II, see Clayton D. Laurie, *The Propaganda Warriors* (Lawrence: University Press of Kansas, 1996); Frank Ninkovich, *The Diplomacy of Ideas: U.S. Foreign Policy and Cultural Relations, 1938–1950* (Cambridge: Cambridge University Press, 1981); Holly Cowan Schulman, *The Voice of America: Propaganda and Democracy, 1941–1945* (Madison: University of Wisconsin Press, 1990); Allen M. Winkler, *Politics of Propaganda: The Office of War Information, 1942–1945* (New Haven, Conn.: Yale University Press, 1978). For an examination of racism in propaganda, see John Dower, *War Without Mercy: Race and Power in the Pacific War* (New York: Pantheon, 1986). On the uses of gendered imagery, see Leila J. Rupp, *Mobilizing Women for War: German and American Propaganda, 1939–1945* (Princeton, N.J.: Princeton University Press, 1978); Sonya Michel, "American Women and the Discourse of the Democratic Family in World War II," in Margaret Randolph Higonnet et al., eds., *Behind the Lines: Gender and the Two World Wars* (New Haven: Yale University Press, 1987), 154–67; Maureen Honey, *Creating Rosie the Riveter: Class, Gender, and Propaganda During World War II* (Amherst: University of Massachusetts Press, 1984).

4. The American response to propaganda in the aftermath of World War I is instructive. See Brett Gary, *Nervous Liberals: Propaganda Anxieties from World War I to the Cold War* (New York: Columbia University Press, 1999); David M. Kennedy, *Over Here: The First World War and American Society* (New York: Oxford University Press, 1980), 45–92; Stephen Vaughn, *Holding Fast the Inner Lines: Democracy, Nationalism, and the Committee on Public Information* (Chapel Hill: University of North Carolina Press, 1980).

5. Statement by the President, "Termination of OWI and Disposition of Certain Functions of OIAA," August 31, 1945, Department of State, *Bulletin* 13 (September 2, 1945): 306–7.

6. Secretary of State James F. Byrnes appointed Benton in September 1945. Benton later served as a U.S. senator from Connecticut noted for championing information programs and proposing the expulsion of Joseph McCarthy. See Sydney Hyman, *The Lives of William Benton* (Chicago: University of Chicago Press, 1969).

7. Edward W. Barrett, *Truth Is Our Weapon* (New York: Funk and Wagnall, 1953), 53; John W. Henderson, *The United States Information Agency* (New York: Praeger, 1969), 38.

8. The bill, H.R. 4368, was offered as an amendment to the 1938 legislation establishing cultural and educational exchange programs in Latin America, the Philippines, and Liberia. For more on these programs, see Ninkovich, *Diplomacy of Ideas*, 28–34.

9. For Benton's statements before Congress, see U.S. House Committee on Foreign Affairs, *Interchange of Knowledge and Skills Between the People of the United States and Peoples of Other Countries*, Hearings before the Committee on Foreign Affairs, House of

Representatives, 79th Cong., 1st and 2nd sess., October 16, 17, 18, 19, 23, 24, 1945; May 14, 1946. Benton gave similar testimony to the House Appropriations Committee. See Department of State, *Bulletin* 13 (October 21, 1945): 589–95.

10. Harriman to Secretary of State, September 13, 1945, *FRUS, 1945*, 5: 880–81; Harriman to Secretary of State, November 19, 1945, *FRUS, 1945*, 5: 919–20.

11. On the estimated readership of *Amerika*, see Smith to Benton, April 18, 1946, RG 59, Lot 811.917, NA2.

12. Brooks Atkinson, "Moscow 'Eats Up' Portrayal of U.S.," *New York Times*, October 28, 1945.

13. Kennan to Secretary of State, January 30, 1946, *FRUS, 1946*, 6: 686–87.

14. The Office of Information and Cultural Affairs was the successor to the Interim International Information Administration that disbanded on December 31, 1945. William T. Stone was appointed the division's first director. See Charles Thompson, *Overseas Information Programs of the United States* (Washington, D.C.: Brookings Institution, 1948), 206. Henderson served as a Foreign Service officer in Ireland and the Soviet Union for more than twenty years before being transferred to the State Department post. He eventually became one of the chief architects of the policies announced in the Truman Doctrine speech. See H. W. Brands, *Inside the Cold War: Loy Henderson and the Rise of the American Empire, 1918–1960* (New York: Oxford University Press, 1991).

15. "Our International Information Policy," Department of State, *Bulletin* 13 (December 16, 1945): 948.

16. Ibid., 950.

17. Ibid. Given the tumultuous state of American labor relations in the immediate postwar period, Fisher's question was certainly appropriate. See Nelson Lichtenstein, *Labor's War at Home: The CIO in World War II* (New York: Cambridge University Press, 1982). On U.S. race relations in the aftermath of World War II, see Manning Marable, *Race, Reform, and Rebellion: The Second Reconstruction in Black America, 1945–1990*, 2nd ed. (Jackson: University Press of Mississippi, 1991).

18. Ninkovich, *Diplomacy of Ideas*, 40.

19. Alan Brinkley, *The End of Reform: New Deal Liberalism in Recession and War* (New York: Knopf, 1995); Winkler, *Politics of Propaganda*; Schulman, *Voice of America*; Ninkovich, *Diplomacy of Ideas*.

20. Ninkovich, *Diplomacy of Ideas*, 121–22.

21. "State Department Hit on News Plan," *New York Times*, February 15, 1946.

22. Hyman, *Lives of William Benton*, 350–51.

23. *New York Times*, January-April 1946; Robert L. Messer, *The End of An Alliance: James F. Byrnes, Roosevelt, Truman, and the Origins of the Cold War* (Chapel Hill: University of North Carolina Press, 1982), 156–80; Hyman, *Lives of William Benton*, 349.

24. Harriman to the Secretary of State (Byrnes), January 20, 1946, *FRUS, 1946*, 6: 676–78

25. Ibid.

26. Kennan to Byrnes, February 12, 1946, *FRUS, 1946*, 6: 694–709.

27. Ibid. Kennan's telegram received wide support in U.S. policymaking circles and articulated the emerging containment policy. See John Lewis Gaddis, *Strategies of Containment: A Critical Appraisal of American National Security Policy* (New York: Oxford University Press, 1982). For a provocative interpretation of Kennan's rhetoric, see Frank Costigliola, "'Unceasing Pressure for Penetration': Gender, Pathology, and Emotion in George Kennan's Formulation of the Cold War," *Journal of American History* 83 (March 1997): 1309–39.

28. Leffler, *Preponderance of Power*, 100–110; Fraser J. Harbutt, *The Iron Curtain: Churchill, America, and the Origins of the Cold War* (New York: Oxford University Press, 1986); Stephen L. MacFarland, "A Peripheral View of the Origins of the Cold War: The Crises in Iran, 1941–47," *Diplomatic History* 4 (Fall 1980): 333–51.

29. Statement of Assistant Secretary William Benton, February 28, 1946, U.S. House Committee on Appropriations, Hearings on the Department of State Appropriation Bill for 1947, 79th Cong., 2nd sess., 431. Benton's testimony on information and cultural programs was preceded by similar comments by Secretary of State James F. Byrnes. See Statement of Hon. James F. Byrnes, February 19, 1946, ibid., 9–13.

30. Ibid., 432.

31. On the ALA's delicate relationship with the State Department, see Gary E. Kraske, *Missionaries of the Book: The American Library Profession and the Origins of United States Cultural Diplomacy* (Westport, Conn. Greenwood Press, 1985).

32. U.S. House Committee on Appropriations, Hearings on the Department of State Appropriation Bill for 1947, 79th Cong., 2nd sess., 465–66. Later that day, Rabaut asked John Begg, acting chief of the International Motion Picture Division, for a list of the State Department's film holdings. Ibid., 479–91.

33. "Understanding Among Peoples," Department of State, *Bulletin* 14 (March 17, 1946): 409–10.

34. Ibid., 410–11.

35. $5.4 million of these funds were to sustain existing scientific and cultural exchange programs established in 1938. See Thompson, *Overseas Information Service of the United States Government*, 206–7, 234–35n. On July 31, Congress responded more positively and unanimously passed the Fulbright Act. Introduced in September 1945 by Senator J. William Fulbright (D-Ark.), the legislation, an amendment to the 1944 Surplus Property Act, channeled revenues from the sale of surplus American war matériel toward the establishment of educational exchange programs. The bill mandated the creation of a Board of Foreign Scholarships (BFS), appointed by the president, to administer binational exchanges in the fields of science, education, and culture. The BFS was designed to ensure that the Fulbright Program would remain nonpartisan. Emanating from a long tradition of private philanthropic efforts, the Fulbright scholarships encountered little of the resistance haunting Benton. Prior to World War II, Congress had supported successful educational exchanges with China, Belgium, and Latin America. Fulbright's ingenious financing scheme made his program comparatively inexpensive and independent of annual congressional review. In 1948, only forty-seven Americans and thirty-six foreigners received Fulbright grants, but the program grew rapidly. By the time of Fulbright's death in February

1995, almost 250,000 people had participated in educational exchanges sponsored by the Fulbright Foundation. See Raymond Wieck, *Ignorance Abroad: American Educational and Cultural Foreign Policy and the Office of Assistant Secretary of State* (Westport, Conn.: Praeger, 1992), 14–15; Hyman, *Lives of William Benton*, 334–35; Randall B. Woods, *Fulbright: A Biography* (New York: Cambridge University Press, 1995); Ninkovich, *Diplomacy of Ideas*, 1–34, 140–44; Frank Eugene Brown, *J. William Fulbright: Advice and Dissent* (Iowa City: University of Iowa Press, 1985), 29; R. W. Apple, Jr., "J. William Fulbright, Senate Giant, Is Dead at 89," *New York Times*, February 10, 1995.

36. Office of International Information and Cultural Affairs, Regional Issues Guide for Czechoslovakia, November 25, 1946, Papers of Charles Hulten, Program Planning Board Files, box 8, HSTL.

37. See James R. Boylan, *The New Deal Coalition and the Election of 1946* (New York: Garland, 1981); Hyman, *Lives of William Benton*, 365–66.

38. For background on art exchanges sponsored by the State Department, see Frank Ninkovich, "The Currents of Cultural Diplomacy: Art and the State Department, 1938–1947," *Diplomatic History* 1 (Summer 1977): 215–38.

39. J. Leroy Davidson to Alice Curran, September 10, 1946, RG 59, Lots 587 and 52–48, Records of the Assistant Secretary of State for Public Affairs, 1945–1950, box 7, Subject Files, 1945–1950, NA2; Hyman, *Lives of William Benton*, 378–89

40. Hyman, *Lives of William Benton*, 378.

41. For an engaging overview of the complicated relationships among the art community, Congress, and U.S. information specialists, see Michael L. Krenn, *Fall-Out Shelters for the Human Spirit: American Art and the Cold War* (Chapel Hill: University of North Carolina Press, 2005).

42. Buseby quoted in Frances K. Pohl, *Ben Shahn: New Deal Artist in a Cold War Climate, 1947–1954* (Austin: University of Texas Press, 1989), 35.

43. "Your Money Bought These Pictures," *Look* 11 (February 18, 1947): 80–81; Lewis transcript found in RG 59, Lots 587 and 52–48, Records of the Assistant Secretary of State for Public Affairs, 1945–1950, box 7, Subject Files, 1945–1950, NA2.

44. The collection was paid for with money appropriated the previous year by the OWI and OIAA, not the OIC. See Benton to Colonel McKee and Benton to Howland Sargeant, February 10, 1947, ibid.

45. Benton to Sargeant, February 10, 1947, ibid.

46. See Memorandum on Art Program, February 1947, ibid.

47. House Committee on Appropriations, Hearings before the Subcommittee on Appropriations, House of Representatives, 80th Cong., 1st sess., March 20, 1947, 412–17; Hyman, *Lives of William Benton*, 378–81.

48. George Marshall replaced James Byrnes as secretary of state in January 1947. For Marshall's remarks, see Anthony Leviero, "Marshall Plea to House Fails to Save Cultural Program," *New York Times*, May 6, 1947. On the protests of the arts community, see "Recall of Art Tour Protested by Truman," *New York Times*, May 2, 1948; "U.S. Will Call Experts in Art Show Dilemma," *New York Times*, May 18, 1947; Pohl, *Ben Shahn*, 37.

49. Jane De Hart Mathews, "Art and Politics in Cold War America," *American Historical Review* 81 (October 1976): 762–87.

50. Mathews, "Art and Politics in Cold War America."

51. Ben Shahn's *Hunger* and Yasuo Kuniyoshi's *Circus Girl Resting* ranked among the most controversial paintings in the exhibit. See Serge Guilbaut, *How New York Stole the Idea of Modern Art: Abstract Expressionism, Freedom, and the Cold War* (Chicago: University of Chicago Press, 1983); Mathews, "Art and Politics in Cold War America"; Pohl, *Ben Shahn*; William Graebner, *The Age of Doubt: American Thought and Culture in the 1940s* (Prospect Heights, Ill.: Waveland Press, 1991), 132–38.

52. Benton to Byrnes, January 14, 1947, RG 59, Lots 587 and 52–48, Records of the Assistant Secretary of State for Public Affairs, 1945–1950, box 4, Office Symbol Files, 1945–50, NA2.

53. For an examination of the changing political environment of 1946–48, see Susan M. Hartmann, *Truman and the 80th Congress* (Columbia: University of Missouri Press, 1971).

54. Confidential Memo to Acheson, January 27, 1947, RG 59, Lots 587 and 52–48, Records of the Assistant Secretary of State for Public Affairs, 1945–1950, box 4, Office Symbol Files, 1945–1950, NA2.

55. Benton to Marshall, January 31, 1947, ibid. In contrast to the warm personal relationship he shared with Byrnes, Benton found Marshall aloof and uncommunicative. See Hyman, *Lives of William Benton*, 372–33.

56. Stereotyped Concepts about the United States Presented in Selected Foreign Countries, February 5, 1947, Papers of Charles Hulten, Department of State Information Programs, box 4, folder on 1947 Stereotypes of the United States, HSTL.

57. Leffler, *Preponderance of Power*, 141–81.

58. Objectives for USSR and Russia, December 1946, RG 59, Lot 52D389, Records Relating to International Information Activities, 1938–1953, box 42, NA2.

59. On Thayer's early career and tenure at the National War College, see Thomas George Corti, "Diplomat in the Caviar: Charles Wheeler Thayer, 1910–1969" (Ph.D. dissertation, Saint Louis University, 1988), 1–387.

60. George F. Kennan told Benton that Nabokov was "an extraordinary man with a fifth sense, with remarkable intuition and understanding of Russian psychology." See Benton to Stone, November 5, 1946, RG 59, Lot 52–202 and 587, Records of Assistant Secretary of State William Benton, box 15, Memoranda, 1945–1947, NA2. On personnel interviewed for the Russian desk, see Nabokov to Allen, November 7, 1946, Papers of Charles S. Thayer, box 5, Alphabetical Correspondence Files, HSTL. See also Corti, "Diplomat in the Caviar," 390–95; Charles W. Thayer, *Diplomat* (New York: Harper & Brothers, 1959), 186–88.

61. Basic Guide for Russian Language Broadcasts, February 6, 1947, Papers of Charles W. Thayer, box 5, Alphabetical Correspondence Files, HSTL.

62. After VOA executives received letters from a colony of expatriate Cossacks in Peru thanking them for the Russian broadcasts, radio engineers discovered and then rewired an antennae in Munich mistakenly directed toward South America. Although the

reception difficulties ceased, Joseph McCarthy would eventually use the incident as evidence of "an engineer's plot" to sabotage VOA. See Thayer, *Diplomat*, 187–91; "U.S. Gets News to Russians as Official Broadcasts Begin," *New York Times*, February 18, 1947; "U.S. to Liven Broadcasts to Russia with Jazz Tunes and More News," *New York Times*, February 27, 1947; Smith to Benton, February 18, 1947, *FRUS, 1947*, 4: 533–34. Two months later, a confidential review of American media coverage of the OIC concluded that stories on the VOA broadcasts to Russia were mostly favorable despite initial reports about transmission difficulties in the Soviet Union and tepid audience response. See Press and Radio Opinion of the Information and Cultural Affairs Program, April 4, 1947, RG 59, Lot 52–202, Records of the Assistant Secretary of State for Public Affairs, 1947–1950, Office Symbol Files, 1947–1949, box 2, Official Subject Files, NA2; "Reception in USSR of Voice of America," Department of State, *Bulletin* 16 (April 6, 1947): 624.

63. Joseph Jones, *The Fifteen Weeks: An Inside Account of the Genesis of the Marshall Plan* (New York: Harcourt Brace Jovanovich, 1955).

64. For the text of Truman's speech, see *New York Times*, March 13, 1947.

65. Congress approved Greek and Turkish aid on May 8, 1947. For more on the Truman Doctrine speech, see Richard M. Freeland, *The Truman Doctrine and the Origins of McCarthyism* (New York: Knopf, 1975); Leffler, *Preponderance of Power*, 141–46.

66. The amount represented an increase of $11,174,182. The specific figures for Greece and Turkey were $125,000 and $190,000 respectively. See Benton to Henry Luce, March 13, 1947, RG 59, Lots 587 and 52–48, Records of the Assistant Secretary of State for Public Affairs, 1945–1950, Office Files of William Benton, box 12, Correspondence, 1945–1948, NA2.

67. House Committee on Appropriations, Hearings before the Subcommittee on Appropriations, 80th Cong., 1st sess., 1947, 369–407. On conservative visions of national security and the state, see Hogan, *Cross of Iron*.

68. House Committee on Appropriations, Hearings before the Subcommittee on Appropriations, 80th Cong., 1st sess., 1947, 408–12.

69. Graebner, *Age of Doubt*, 142; Alan M. Wald, *The New York Intellectuals: The Rise and Decline of the Anti-Stalinist Left from the 1930s to the 1980s* (Chapel Hill: University of North Carolina Press, 1987), 223–27, 273.

70. Taber's allusion to Wallace referred to a review of the book, *The Wallaces of Iowa*, broadcasted once by the VOA in German. Benton denied that that the bulletin board notice was officially sanctioned. See Anthony Leviero, "Marshall Plea to House Fails to Save Cultural Program," *New York Times*, May 6, 1947. Taber's attempt to link the OIC and Wallace was quite significant. To many leftists and liberals, Wallace, Truman's secretary of commerce, was the legitimate heir to the New Deal legacy and a voice of reason in a cacophony of anticommunism. In a September 1946 speech at a labor rally held at Madison Square Garden, Wallace warned that American military expansion would antagonize the Soviets and jeopardize world peace. Unwilling to let a subordinate publicly undermine his foreign policies, Truman fired Wallace. Throughout the spring of 1947, Wallace toured Europe and America denouncing the Truman Doctrine and U.S. plans to aid Greece and Turkey. See Norman D. Markowitz, *The Rise and Fall of the People's Century: Henry A. Wallace*

and American Liberalism, 1941–1948 (New York: Free Press, 1973), 124–245; J. Samuel Walker, *Henry A. Wallace and American Foreign Policy* (Westport, Conn.: Greenwood Press, 1976): 170–75. Many Democratic liberals distanced themselves from Wallace's views. See Steven M. Gillon, *Politics and Vision: The ADA and American Liberalism, 1947–1985* (New York: Oxford University Press, 1987), 1–30; Mary Sperling McAuliffe, *Crisis on the Left: Cold War Politics and American Liberals, 1947–1954* (Amherst: University of Massachusetts Press, 1978), 1–29.

71. Benton to Marshall, May 7, 1947, RG 59, Lots 587 and 52–48, Records of the Assistant Secretary of State for Public Affairs, 1945–1950, box 4, Office Symbol Files, 1945–1950, NA2.

72. David F. Krugler, "'If Peace Is to Prevail': Karl E. Mundt and America's International Information and Education Programs, 1943–1953," *South Dakota History* 31 (Spring 2001): 53–56. See also R. Alton Lee, "'New Dealers, Fair Dealers, Misdealers, and Hiss Dealers': Karl Mundt and the Internal Security Act of 1950," *South Dakota History* 10 (Fall 1980): 277–90.

73. Krugler, "'If Peace Is to Prevail'," 57–60.

74. House Committee on Foreign Affairs, Hearings on the United States Information and Educational Exchange Act of 1947, 80th Cong., 1st sess., 1947; "Broadcasts Gain in House Survey," *New York Times*, May 16, 1947; Samuel A. Tower, "Marshall Insists 'Voice' Must Go On," *New York Times*, May 17, 1947; "Broadcasts Vital, Benton Declares," *New York Times*, May 19, 1947; Krugler, "'If Peace Is to Prevail'," 63–66.

75. Many critics of "Advancing American Art" claimed that *Circus Girl Resting*, a portrait of a Parisian acrobat, was "obscene." See, for example, *Congressional Record*, 80th Cong., 1st sess., 1947, pt. 4: 5283–86; "Broadcasts Gain in House Survey," *New York Times*, May 16, 1947.

76. See House Committee on Foreign Affairs, Hearings on the United States Information and Educational Exchange Act of 1947, 80th Cong., 1st sess., 1947, 185–91; "Taber Expresses Partial Approval of U.S. Broadcasts," *New York Times*, May 18, 1947.

77. Samuel A. Tower, "House Group Votes to Keep U.S. Radio," *New York Times*, May 21, 1947. A week later, the House Rules Committee, in a 7-to-5 vote, sent the Mundt bill to the floor. See "Rules Body Pushes Voice of America," *New York Times*, May 29, 1947.

78. Cox and Adolph Sabath (D-N.Y.) mentioned several businessmen, media executives, educators, veterans groups, and religious and labor leaders who supported the legislation. See *Congressional Record*, 80th Cong., 1st sess., 1947, pt. 5: 6539–45.

79. Ibid., pt. 5: 6547.

80. Ibid., pt. 5: 6559.

81. On the Marshall Plan and its origins, see Michael J. Hogan, *The Marshall Plan: America, Britain, and the Reconstruction of Western Europe, 1947–1952* (New York: Cambridge University Press, 1987); Jones, *The Fifteen Weeks*. The text of Marshall's address is found in *New York Times*, June 6, 1947. On Soviet actions in Eastern Europe, see Norman Naimark and Leonid Gibianskii, eds. *The Establishment of Communist Regimes in Eastern Europe, 1944–1949* (Boulder, Colo.: Westview Press, 1997).

82. C. P. Trussell, "Broadcasts Bill Again Kept Alive," *New York Times*, June 11, 1947.

83. The statistic came from a report released on May 17, 1947 by the Radio Advisory Committee, an independent group of broadcasting executives and educators appointed by Benton to assess the Voice of America. Emphasizing the increasing size of the listening audience, the committee recommended expansion of short-wave facilities abroad. When publicizing these findings, Benton mentioned another study done by the American Society of Newspaper Editors (ASNE) that praised VOA's Russian language broadcasts. See "Radio Advisory Committee Urges Strengthening of Voice of America," Department of State, *Bulletin* 16 (May 25, 1947): 1038–41.

84. Prior to the vote, debate on the legislation consumed much of June 10 and 13, see *Congressional Record*, 80th Cong., 1st sess., 1947, pt. 5: 6740–54, pt. 6: 6962–99, pt. 6: 7609–17. About sixty of the ninety Republicans who opposed the bill represented traditionally isolationist states in the Midwest. See ibid., pt. 5: 6563–65. Scholars offer different assessments of the impact of these congressional European trips in creating advocates of the information program. For example, Edward W. Barrett, who served as assistant secretary of state for public affairs in 1950–52, claims that these tours, "more than any other factor," increased support for the information program. See Barrett, *Truth Is Our Weapon*, 61. Historian Frank Ninkovich dismisses Barrett's argument as "a minor myth," and contends that "a heightening fear of Communism" produced support for propaganda activities. See Ninkovich, *The Diplomacy of Ideas*, 130–31. Placed in the context of international affairs and domestic politics, these interpretations hardly appear mutually exclusive.

85. "Voice of America Finally Approved," *New York Times*, July 4, 1947.

86. After the House passed the Mundt bill on June 24, Arthur Vandenberg, the chairman of the Senate Foreign Relations Committee, appointed Smith and Carl Hatch (R-N.M.) to investigate Voice of America and the State Department's budget request for the OIC. See *Congressional Record*, 80th Cong., 1st sess., 1947, pt. 6: 7886.

87. Department of State, *Bulletin* 17 (July 13, 1947): 105–6.

88. The ten were dismissed summarily and denied the right to appeal their discharges to the Civil Service Commission. Marshall declared the fired employees could appeal to him if they so desired, but insisted, "We are not engaged in a witch hunt . . . . I mean to see that the rights of the personnel as well as the interests of the Government are secured." See Bertram D. Hulen, "State Department Outs Ten as 'Risks' to U.S. Security," *New York Times*, June 28, 1947; "Marshall Reveals Aides He Ousted Were Linked With Foreign Nations," July 3, 1947. Seven of the employees did appeal and were subsequently allowed to "resign without prejudice." See "7 'Bad Risks' Allowed to Resign in Shift by State Department," *New York Times*, November 18, 1947.

89. The Senate directed the investigatory committee to report its findings on February 1, 1948. See C. J. Trussell, "Senate Unit Asks Inquiry on 'Voice,'" *New York Times*, July 17, 1947.

90. Hyman, *Lives of William Benton*, 385.

91. The reorganization reduced the domestic staff from 1,013 to 649 and the number of foreign nationals employed overseas dropped from 1,500 to 767. The cuts necessitated

closing OIE offices in Australia, Canada, New Zealand, South Africa, Afghanistan, Portugal, El Salvador, Honduras, Nicaragua, and the Dominican Republic. Simultaneous Voice of America broadcasts were cut from 55 hours to 33 hours a day worldwide through the implementation of a "block programming" system that concentrated on peak nighttime listening times. See Department of State, *Bulletin* 17 (August 10, 1947): 304–6.

92. Hyman, *Lives of William Benton*, 386–87; Bertram D. Hulen, "Benton Quits Post as Marshall Aide," *New York Times*, September 25, 1947.

93. On Soviet reaction to the Truman Doctrine and the European Recovery Plan, see Vojtech Mastny, *The Cold War and Soviet Insecurity: The Stalin Years* (New York: Oxford University Press, 1996), 27–29.

94. Sydney Gruson, "New Information Bureau Will Seek to Unify Strategy of Reds," *New York Times*, October 6, 1947; "Comintern Stirs U.N. Worry, Helps Marshall's Program," *New York Times*, October 7, 1947. On Cominform and its relationship to Soviet foreign policy, see Vladislav Zubok and Constantine Pleshakov, *Inside the Kremlin's Cold War: From Stalin to Khrushchev* (Cambridge, Mass.: Harvard University Press, 1996), 110–37.

95. Smith to Marshall, November 15, 1947, *FRUS, 1947*, 4: 619–22.

96. Ibid.

97. U.S. Information with Regard to Anti-American Propaganda, December 1, 1947, RG 59, Lot 53D47, Records Relating to International Information Activities, 1938–1953, box 3, Files of William T. Stone, NA2. The State Department sent these guidelines to American embassies worldwide. See dispatch by Acting Secretary of State Robert Lovett, December 8, 1947, *FRUS, 1947*, 4: 630–33. The National Security Council also called for a stronger, more coordinated response to Soviet propaganda. See Report by the National Security Council, December 9, 1947, RG 59, Lot 53D47, Records Relating to International Information Activities, 1938–1953, box 7, Files of William T. Stone, NA2.

98. Committee on Foreign Affairs, *The United States Information Service in Europe*, 80th Cong., 2nd sess., 1947, Committee Print, 1–23. The need for additional funds and salary increases was especially acute. USIS officers from clerks to ambassadors frequently spent their own money in order to subsidize information activities. Furthermore, serving in countries with unstable currencies often resulted in inadequate wages. See, for example, Smith to Marshall, December 30, 1947, *FRUS, 1947*, 4: 648–49. Karl Mundt began publicizing the committee's recommendations. See, for example, "We Are Losing the War of Words in Europe," *New York Times Magazine*, November 9, 1947, 11, 61–64.

99. Public Law 402, 80th Cong., 2nd sess. (January 27, 1948), United States Information and Educational Exchange Act of 1948. For debate on the final draft of the legislation, see *Congressional Record*, 80th Cong., 2nd sess., 1948, pt. 1: 243–72.

100. Negotiations on ERP and Germany were held at the London meeting of the Council of Foreign Ministers. See Leffler, *Preponderance of Power*, 198–99. On the Smith-Mundt Act, see William S. White. "Stronger 'Voice of America' Is Backed to Counter Soviets," *New York Times*, January 17, 1948; "Truman Signs Bill Broadening 'Voice,'" *New York Times*, January 28, 1948. On the Allen appointment, see Bertram D. Hulen, "Information Post Slated for Allen," *New York Times*, January 9, 1948.

101. *Congressional Record*, 80th Cong., 2nd sess., 1948, pt. 2: 2165–68.

102. *Congressional Record*, 80th Cong., 2nd sess., 1948, pt. 2: 2165–68; Robert W. Pirsein, *Voice of America: An History of the International Broadcasting Activities of the United States Government, 1940–1962* (New York: Arno Press, 1979), 145–66.

103. *Congressional Record*, 80th Cong., 2nd sess., 1948, pt. 5: 6462–73; "'Voice' Broadcasts Infuriate Senate; Descriptions of States Held 'Lies,'" *New York Times*, May 27, 1948.

104. *Congressional Record*, 80th Cong., 2nd. sess., 1948, pt. 5: 6552–65; "Truman and Congress Rush 'Voice' Broadcast Inquires," *New York Times*, May 28, 1948; "NBC Takes Blame on 'Voice' Scripts," *New York Times*, May 29, 1948; "New Plan Tightens Controls of 'Voice,'" *New York* Times, June 6, 1948; "U.S. Will Expand 'Voice of America,'" *New York Times*, June 10, 1948; "Sources of 'Voice' Blamed for Slurs," *New York Times*, June 16, 1948.

105. "State Department to Take Over 'Voice' Broadcasts After Sept. 30," *New York Times*, July 2, 1948; U.S. Congress, *Voice of America Joint Report of a Subcommittee of the Committee on Foreign Relations and the Investigations Subcommittee of the Committee on Expenditures in the Executive Departments*, 81st Cong., 1st sess., December 31, 1948; David Krugler, *Voice of America and the Domestic Propaganda Battles, 1945–1953* (Columbia: University of Missouri Press, 2000), 80–84; Corti, "Diplomat in the Caviar," 406–10.

106. On Soviet jamming, see "'Curtain of Static' Bars Broadcasts to Moscow," *New York Times*, February 26, 1948. On the Smith-Molotov exchange, see Sargeant to Berkow, May 17, 1948, RG 59, Lots 587 and 52–48, Records of the Assistant Secretary of State, 1945–1950, box 3; NA2; "Text of Marshall's Statement and His Interview with Press," *New York Times*, May 16, 1948; J. Samuel Walker, "'No More Cold War': American Foreign Policy and the 1948 Soviet Peace Offensive," *Diplomatic History* 5 (Winter 1981): 75–91.

107. "Marshall Warns of Cynical Peace," *New York Times*, May 29, 1948.

108. United States Information Policy with Regard to Anti-American Propaganda, July 20, 1948, RG 59, Lot 53D47, Records Relating to International Information Activities, 1938–1953, box 3; William T. Stone Files, NA2.

109. Ibid.

110. Department of State, *Bulletin* 19, 474 (August 1, 1948): 145–47. By August, VOA reached almost all of Europe, the Far East, and Latin America with more than twenty-six hours of daily simultaneous broadcasts in twenty-two languages. VOA operatives, still receiving complaints about poor reception, sought drastic improvement of radio transmitter facilities. See "'Voice of America' Being Beamed to Every Vital Part of the World," *New York Times*, August 12, 1948.

111. "Kasenkina Case Is Major News on 'Voice' Broadcasts to Russia," *New York Times*, August 14, 1948.

112. Kohler to the Secretary of State, April 26, 1949, *FRUS, 1949*, 5: 609.

113. "Kohler Named Chief of Voice of America," *New York Times*, April 23, 1949; Kohler to Secretary of State, May 17, 1949, *FRUS, 1949* 5: 613–15.

114. Kirk to Acheson, September 29, 1949, *FRUS, 1949*, 5: 658–59; Leffler, *Preponderance of Power*, 323–41.

115. Acheson succeeded Marshall as secretary of state in January 1949. On the changing character of congressional politics and foreign policy, see Susan M. Hartmann, *Truman and the 80th Congress*, 159–85; David R. Kepley, *The Collapse of the Middle Way: Senate Republicans and the Bipartisan Foreign Policy, 1948–1952* (New York: Greenwood Press, 1988), 1–84; James T. Patterson, *Mr. Republican: A Biography of Robert A. Taft* (Boston: Houghton Mifflin, 1972), 442–44; Arthur H. Vandenberg, Jr., *The Private Papers of Senator Vandenberg* (Boston: Houghton-Mifflin, 1952), 463–557.

116. On November 29, 1949, George V. Allen resigned as assistant secretary of state for public affairs to accept an appointment as U.S. ambassador to Yugoslavia. See "Barrett Is Named as Aide to Acheson," *New York Times*, January 1, 1950.

117. "Voice's Progress Slow, Board Finds," *New York Times*, January 5, 1950.

118. Effectiveness of the Voice of America, January 6, 1950, RG59, Lot 53D48, International Information Director's Office, 1948–1952, box 114, NA2; Frenkley to Puhan, Effectiveness of VOA Russian Broadcasts, January 26, 1950, ibid.

119. Ibid.

120. House Appropriations Committee, Hearings on Department of State Appropriations for 1951, 81st Cong., 2nd sess., pt. 2, 1053–55.

121. See Cody to Sargeant, January 16, 1950, RG59, Lot 53D47, Records of William T. Stone, box 2, NA2; Devine to Stone, February 1, 1950, ibid. On political instability in Southeast Asia, see Gary R. Hess, *The United States' Emergence as a Southeast Asian Power, 1945–1950* (New York: Columbia University Press, 1987).

122. USIS refers only to the international facilities of the American information program. USIE (United States Information and Educational Exchange Program) encompassed both the domestic and foreign dimensions of the U.S. propaganda apparatus. When the United States Information Agency (USIA) was created in 1953, the acronym USIA replaced USIE. The Czech government tentatively agreed to allow distribution of *Amerika* in March 1949. But, after VOA began airing broadcasts hostile to the regime, the Czech Foreign Ministry withdrew its permission. By early February 1950, Department of State leaders had concluded any attempt to reopen negotiations on *Amerika* would be fruitless. See Briggs to Acheson, February 8, 1950, *FRUS, 1950*, 4: 528–31; Acheson to the Embassy in Czechoslovakia, February 10, 1950, *FRUS, 1950*, 4: 531–33; Acheson to the Embassy in Czechoslovakia, February 21, 1950, *FRUS, 1950*, 4: 533–35.

123. For a detailed account of these events, see Krugler, *VOA and the Domestic Propaganda Battles*, 96–102.

124. Examples of the voluminous historiography on McCarthy include Robert Griffith, *The Politics of Fear: Joseph R. McCarthy and the Senate* (Lexington: University of Kentucky Press, 1970); David M. Oshinsky, *A Conspiracy So Immense: The World of Joe McCarthy* (New York: Free Press, 1983); Alan D. Harper, *The Politics of Loyalty: The White House and the Communist Issue, 1946–1952* (Westport, Conn.: Greenwood Press, 1969); David Caute, *The Great Fear: The Anti-Communist Purge Under Truman and Eisenhower* (New York: Simon and Schuster, 1979).

125. For McCarthy's accusations, see *Congressional Record*, 81st Cong., 2nd sess. 96, pt. 2, February 20, 1950: 1952–81.

126. "Truman Brands McCarthy Charges as False; Won't Yield Loyalty Files Even to Subpoena," *New York Times*, February 24, 1950; "Senate Inquiry Set on Acheson Staff," *New York Times*, February 26, 1950. On July 17, the Tydings Committee dismissed McCarthy's charges of communist infiltration of the State Department. See William S. White, "Red Charges by McCarthy Ruled False," *New York Times*, July 18, 1950.

127. Truman to Acheson, March 1, 1950, *FRUS, 1950*, 4: 271; Barrett to Acheson, March 2, 1950, *FRUS, 1950*, 4: 272; Barrett to Webb, March 6, 1950, *FRUS, 1950*, 4: 274–75; Barrett to Acheson, March 9, 1950, *FRUS, 1950*, 4: 275–76.

128. U.S. Views on Capturing the Initiative in Psychological Field, *FRUS, 1950*, 4: 296–302.

129. Appointed by his former advertising partner and the governor of Connecticut Chester Bowles, Benton succeeded Raymond Baldwin, a liberal Republican who retired after enduring months of criticism from McCarthy and Robert Taft. See Hyman, *Lives of William Benton*, 406–7.

130. Senators Ralph E. Flanders (R-Vt.), J. William Fulbright (D-Ark.), Frank P. Graham (D-N.C.), Robert C. Hendrickson, (R-N.J.), Herbert H. Lehman (D-N.Y.), Brien McMahon (D-Ct.), Wayne Morse (R-Ore.), Karl E. Mundt (R-S.D.), Margaret Chase Smith (R-Me.), John W. Sparkman (D-Ala.), and Charles W. Tobey (R-N.H.) cosponsored the resolution. See *Congressional Record*, 81st Cong., 2nd sess. 96, 1950, pt. 3, 3763–69.

131. In response to the Korean War, Truman approved NSC-68 on September 30, 1950. See NSC 68, April 14, 1950, *FRUS, 1950*, 1: 234–92; Ernest R. May, ed. *American Cold War Strategy: Interpreting NSC-68* (New York: Bedford Books, 1993).

132. For an analysis on the language of NSC-68 and its relation to the U.S. propaganda offensive, see Emily S. Rosenberg's comments in May, ed., *American Cold War Strategy*, 160–64.

133. "Truman Proclaims World-Wide Fight to Crush Red Lies," *New York Times*, April 21, 1950.

134. "Red China Bans 'Voice,'" *New York Times*, April 16, 1950; "5,000 in Prague Jam U.S. Library," *New York Times*, April 21, 1950; Editorial Note, *FRUS, 1950*, 4: 550–51. On *Amerika*, see Kirk to Acheson, April 25, 1950, *FRUS, 1950*, 4: 1163–64.

135. The term "state-private network" is from Scott Lucas, *Freedom's War: The American Crusade Against the Soviet Union* (New York: New York University Press, 1999).

136. Michael Nelson, *War of the Black Heavens: The Battles of Western Broadcasting in the Cold War* (Syracuse, N.Y.: Syracuse University Press, 1997), 46–49; Frances Stonor Saunders, *The Cultural Cold War: The CIA and the World of Arts and Letters* (New York: The New Press, 1999), 12–13, 51; Lucas, *Freedom's War*, 164.

137. Lucas, *Freedom's War*, 96–97; Saunders, *Cultural Cold War*, 63–72.

138. Rough Notes on European Trip, June 6, 1950, RG59, Lot 52D432, box 5, Office Files of Edward Barrett, 1950–51, NA2.

139. For more on U.S. policy toward the satellite nations, see Lay to NSC, May 26, 1950, *FRUS, 1950*, 4: 31–32.

140. Maureen Namecek, "Speaking of America: The Voice of America, Its Mission and Message, 1942–1982" (Ph.D. dissertation, University of Maryland, 1984), 106–9; Raymond Swing, *Good Evening: A Professional Memoir* (New York: Harcourt, Brace, & World, 1964), 266–67; Pirsein, *The Voice of America*, 155–56; Barrett, *Truth Is Our Weapon*, 209–10; Edwin M. J. Kretzmann, "McCarthyism and the Voice of America," *Foreign Service Journal* 44 (February 1967): 26–27.

141. Michael L. Hoffman, "I.R.O. Warns West on Snub to Iron Curtain Refugees," *New York Times*, May 29, 1950.

142. Sig Mickelson, *America's Other Voice: The Story of Radio Free Europe and Radio Liberty* (New York: Praeger, 1983), 30–33; Krugler, *Voice of America and the Domestic Propaganda Battles*, 155–56; Nelson, *War of the Black Heavens*, 39.

143. Walter F. Hixson, *Parting the Curtain: Propaganda, Culture, and the Cold War, 1945–1961* (New York: St. Martin's Press, 1997), 59–60; Lucas, *Freedom's War*, 99–101.

144. On the U.S. decision to commit troops to Korea, see "Resolution Adopted by the United Nations Security Council," June 27, 1950, *FRUS, 1950*, 7: 211. For examples of Soviet propaganda, see *New York Times*, July 2, 16, 1950.

145. For Benton's testimony, see *Expanded International Information and Education Program*, Hearings before the Senate Foreign Relations Committee, 81st Cong., 2nd sess., July 5–7, 1950, 4–13.

146. *Expanded International Information and Education Program*, 160–61.

147. See Hearings on the Supplemental Appropriation Bill for 1951: Hearings before the Subcommittee of the House Committee on Appropriations, 81st Cong., 2nd sess., on Supplemental Appropriation Bill for 1951, Department of State (Washington, D.C.: Government Printing Office, 1950); Editorial Note, *FRUS, 1950*, 4: 316–17; *Congressional Record*, 81st Cong., 2nd sess., August 26, 1950: 13532–49.

148. The term USIE encompassed both the domestic and international operations of the U.S information program. In 1953, the worldwide program was renamed the United States Information Agency (USIA). Kenneth Osgood, *Total Cold War: Eisenhower's Secret Propaganda Battle at Home and Abroad* (Lawrence: University Press of Kansas, 2006), 43.

149. IMP's Part in The Campaign of Truth, USIA Subject Files, Motion Pictures folder #1, USIAA.

150. These assumptions also informed U.S. development and modernization theory of the era. See David C. Engerman et al., eds. *Staging Growth: Modernization, Development, and the Global Cold War* (Amherst: University of Massachusetts Press, 2003).

151. On the war's relation to NSC-68, see Gaddis, *Strategies of Containment*, 89–126.

152. Country Paper for USSR, October 1950, RG59, Lot 53D47, William T. Stone Files, 1938–1953, box 19, NA2.

153. Ibid. In late 1950, Truman also appointed a group of diplomatic, military, communications, and intelligence officials to consider ways to compel or induce the Soviets to

stop jamming VOA broadcasts. See Soviet Jamming of Voice of America, December 4, 1950, *FRUS, 1950*, 4: 333–36.

154. Barbour to Acheson, December 12, 1950, *FRUS, 1950*, 4: 1273–74.

155. Barrett to Public Affairs Officers Overseas, December 19, 1950, RG59, Lot 52D389, box 53, NA2.

156. An Analysis of the Principal Psychological Vulnerabilities in the USSR and of the Principal Assets Available to the U.S. for Their Exploitation, undated, RG59, Lot 52D432, Bureau of Public Affairs, box 5, Office Files of Edward Barrett, 1950–51, NA2.

157. After the creation of the PSB, the existing Interdepartmental Foreign Information Organization was redesignated the Psychological Operations Coordinating Committee (OCC). See Presidential Directive, April 4, 1951, *FRUS, 1951*, 4: 58–60.

158. Osgood, *Total Cold War*, 43–45.

159. Previously, USIE officers received instructions from the assistant secretary of state for public affairs, the USIE general manager, and regional bureau directors. This situation held no one person responsible for USIE affairs and made integrating information activities into larger foreign policy objectives unnecessarily difficult. See "New Office to Run Voice of America Established by State Department," *New York Times*, January 19, 1952; State Department Announcement, January 16, 1950, *FRUS, 1952–1954*, 2: 1591–95; Strengthening U.S. International Information Program, January 30, 1952, *FRUS, 1952–1954*, 2: 1595–1616.

160. Notes Regarding Indigenous Operations, February 4, 1952, RG 59, Lot 52D432, box 5, Office Files of Edward Barrett, 1950–51, NA2.

161. "Propaganda Steps by U.S. Criticized," *New York Times*, June 1, 1952; *The Objectives of the United States Information Program*, 82nd Cong., 2nd sess., June 1952, doc. 143.

162. Betty Milton Gaskill, "Russia's New Hate-America Campaign," *Saturday Evening Post*, August 9, 1952; JCS to Clark, June 5, 1952, *FRUS, 1952–1954*, 15: 308–10; Barrett, *Truth Is Our Weapon*, 175–78.

163. Kennan to Acheson, June 27, 1952, *FRUS, 1952–1954*, 8: 1016–17. See also Kennan to Matthews, June 6, 1952, *FRUS, 1952–1954*, 8: 987–1000.

164. Acheson to All Diplomatic Offices, June 17, 1952, *FRUS, 1952–1954*, 2: 1626–27.

165. Press Release, July 15, 1952, *Amerika* files, USIAA; "Amerika 'Bankrupt,' Soviet Public Told," *New York Times*, July 31, 1952.

166. "Key Words in American and Free World Propaganda," RG 306, Records of the USIA, Office of Research Reports and Related Studies, 1948–1953, box 23, NA2.

CHAPTER TWO. THE EISENHOWER YEARS

1. On the foreign policy of the Eisenhower administration, see Kenneth Osgood, *Total Cold War: Eisenhower's Secret Propaganda Battle at Home and Abroad* (Lawrence: University Press of Kansas, 2006); Saki Dockrill, *Eisenhower's New Look National Security Policy, 1953–1960* (New York: St. Martin's Press, 1996); Stephen E. Ambrose, *Eisenhower*, vol. 2, *President* (New York: Simon and Schuster, 1983); Frederick W. Marks, *Power and Peace: The*

Diplomacy of John Foster Dulles (Westport, Conn.: Praeger, 1993); Charles C. Alexander, *Holding the Line: The Eisenhower Era, 1952–1961* (Bloomington: Indiana University Press, 1975); H. W. Brands, *Cold Warriors: Eisenhower's Generation and American Foreign Policy* (New York: Columbia University Press, 1988); Robert A. Divine, *Eisenhower and the Cold War* (New York: Oxford University Press, 1981); Richard A. Melanson and David Mayers, eds., *Reevaluating Eisenhower: American Foreign Policy in the 1950s* (Urbana: University of Illinois Press, 1988).

2. Robert Griffith, "Dwight D. Eisenhower and the Corporate Commonwealth," *American Historical Review* 87 (February 1982): 87–122; Thomas Frank, *The Conquest of Cool: Business Culture, Counterculture, and the Rise of Hip Consumerism* (Chicago: University of Chicago Press, 1997).

3. Excerpt from Eisenhower's Foreign Policy Speech, San Francisco, October 8, 1952, Subject Files, USIAA. See also Shawn J. Parry-Giles, "The Eisenhower Administration's Conceptualization of the USIA: The Development of Overt and Covert Propaganda Strategies," *Presidential Studies Quarterly* 24 (Spring 1994): 263–64.

4. Brands, *Cold Warriors*, 117–19.

5. C. D. Jackson served on the committee along with NSC chairman Robert Cutler; Roger M. Keyes, deputy secretary of defense; Gordon Gray, president of the University of North Carolina and former director of the PSB; and businessmen Backlie McKee Henry, John C. Hughes, and Sigmund Larmon. See Editorial Note, *FRUS, 1952–1954*, 2: 393; Ambrose, *Eisenhower*, 2: 42–43; Brands, *Cold Warriors*, 120–21. At the same time, two other groups began studying the information program including McCarthy's Senate Committee on Permanent Investigations and the President's Advisory Committee on Government Reorganization (Rockefeller Committee). See Parry-Giles, "Eisenhower Administration's Conceptualization," 263, 274.

6. For a detailed narrative of McCarthy's allegations, see Robert W. Pirsein, *The Voice of America: An History of the International Broadcasting Activities of the United States Government, 1940–1962* (New York: Arno, 1979), 236–93.

7. Senate Committee on Government Operations, Hearings on the State Department Information Program—Voice of America, 83d Cong., 1st sess., pt. 1, February 16–17, 1953, 1–11 (hereafter VOA Hearings).

8. For more on Eisenhower's delicate relationship with the conservative wing of the Republican Party, see Gary W. Reichard, *The Reaffirmation of Republicanism: Eisenhower and the Eighty-Third Congress* (Knoxville: University of Tennessee Press, 1975), 1–27; David W. Reinhard, *The Republican Right Since 1945* (Lexington: University Press of Kentucky, 1983), 79–95; Jeff Broadwater, *Eisenhower and the Anti-Communist Crusade* (Chapel Hill: University of North Carolina Press, 1992): 26–62; David R. Kepley, *The Collapse of the Middle Way: Senate Republicans and Bipartisan Foreign Policy, 1948–1952* (New York: Greenwood Press, 1988), 133–50.

9. "Deliberate Waste Charged to 'Voice,'" *New York Times*, February 17, 1953; "Voice's $65,000 Vehicle Called Nice Looking, But," *New York Times*, February 18, 1953; "Voice of America Held Inefficient," *New York Times*, February 18, 1953; C. P. Trussell, "Dr. Compton

Quits as Head of 'Voice,'" *New York Times*, February 19, 1953. On the Baker project cancellation, see C. P. Trussell, "New 'Voice' Likely to Replace Agency," *New York Times*, March 21, 1953. On the C. D. Jackson memo, see David M. Oshinsky, *A Conspiracy So Immense: The World of Joe McCarthy* (New York: Free Press, 1983), 270–71.

10. Memorandum of Telephone Conversation, February 19, 1953, *FRUS, 1952–1954*, 2: 1436–37.

11. Assistant Administrator for Policy and Plans Bradley Connor wrote the controversial author policy on February 3, 1953. For its text and Fast's testimony, see VOA Hearings, pt. 2, February 18, 1953, 98–112.

12. Connors to Scott, February 20, 1953, *FRUS, 1952–1954*, 2: 1673; Scott to Connors, February 27, 1953, ibid., 2: 1674–75; C. P. Trussell, "Voice Must Drop Works of Leftists," *New York Times*, February 20, 1953; C. P Trussell, "State Department Voids Curb in McCarthy's Study of 'Voice,'" *New York Times*, February 21, 1953.

13. C. P. Trussell, "Broadcast Chief of 'Voice' Removed," *New York Times*, February 25, 1953; C. P. Trussell, "Morton Restored to 'Voice' Position," *New York Times*, February 26, 1953.

14. Edwin J. Kretzmann, "McCarthy and the Voice of America," *Foreign Service Journal* 44 (February 1967): 44.

15. Pirsein, *Voice of America*, 273–75; David F. Krugler, *The Voice of America and the Domestic Propaganda Battles, 1945–1953* (Columbia: University of Missouri Press, 2000), 186–87.

16. "3 Voice Officials Deny Red Leanings," *New York Times*, February 21, 1953.

17. Telegrams on Information Bulletin No. 272, Subject File on McCarthyism, USIAA.

18. My interpretation of Eisenhower's foreign policy challenges revisionist accounts that suggest that Eisenhower hoped to ease Cold War tensions and improve U.S.-Soviet relations. See, for example, Divine, *Eisenhower and the Cold War*; Robert R. Bowie and Richard H. Immerman, *Waging Peace: How Eisenhower Shaped an Enduring Cold War Strategy* (New York: Oxford University Press, 1998).

19. "The Scope and Nature of Communist Propaganda," February 23, 1953, RG 306, Office of Research, Miscellaneous Reports and Studies, 1949–1953, box 2, NA2.

20. C. P. Trussell, "Educator Is Asked to Head the 'Voice,'" *New York Times*, February 24, 1953. The United States Advisory Commission on Information and Senator Karl E. Mundt (R-S.D.) made similar recommendations. See Charles E. Egan, "Propaganda Post in Cabinet Urged," *New York Times*, February 22, 1953; "Mundt Sees One Unit for U.S. Information," *New York Times*, February 23, 1953.

21. James Reston, "Own Rule Puzzles Information Unit," *New York Times*, March 3, 1953.

22. VOA Hearings, pt. 5, March 3, 1953, 331–87; C. P. Trussell, "Voice Aide Sees McCarthy Aiming at 'My Public Neck,'" *New York Times*, March 4, 1953; Oshinsky, *Conspiracy So Immense*, 274–76.

23. Gerald F. P. Dooher served as chief of the VOA Near East, South Asia, and Africa Division. Dr. Sidney Glazer created and led the VOA Hebrew language service. See VOA Hearings, pt. 6, March 4, 1953, 397–467. A month after his valiant fight against McCarthy,

a disgusted Reed Harris resigned from the federal government. See "Reed Harris Quits as 'Voice' Official," *New York Times*, April 15, 1953.

24. On the Malenkov coalition, see Vladislav Zubok and Constantine Pleshakov, *Inside the Kremlin's Cold War: From Stalin to Khrushchev* (Cambridge, Mass.: Harvard University Press, 1996), 138–73; James G. Richter, *Khrushchev's Double Bind: International Pressures and Domestic Coalition Politics* (Baltimore: Johns Hopkins University Press, 1994), 30–52. On the Eisenhower administration's response to Stalin's death, see W. W. Rostow, *Europe After Stalin: Eisenhower's Three Decisions of March 11, 1953* (Austin: University of Texas Press, 1982); Osgood, *Total Cold War*, 55–63.

25. Jackson to Cutler, March 4, 1953, Records of C. D. Jackson, box 2, Folder on Robert Cutler, DDEL.

26. NSC Meeting, March 4, 1953, *FRUS, 1952–1954*, 8: 1091–95; Dulles to Diplomatic Posts, March 5 and 6, 1953, *FRUS, 1952–1954*, 2: 1681–85.

27. For Eisenhower's remarks, see "Stalin Dies After 29-Year Rule," *New York Times*, March 6, 1953. For extensive excerpts of these broadcasts, see U.S. Senate, Committee on Foreign Relations, Subcommittee on Overseas Information Programs of the United States, *Voice of America Broadcasts on the Death of Stalin*, 83rd Cong., 1st sess., 1953, Committee Print; "'Voice' Forecasts Battle for Power," *New York Times*, March 7, 1953. See also Possible Consequences of the Death of Stalin and of the Elevation of Malenkov to Leadership in the USSR, March 12, 1953, *FRUS, 1952–1954*, 8: 1125–34.

28. Dulles to Certain Diplomatic Posts, March 17, 1953, *FRUS, 1952–1954*, 2: 1686–87; Walter H. Waggoner, "New Ruling Permits 'Voice' to Use Communist Writings," *New York Times*, March 19, 1953.

29. Martin Merson, *The Private Diary of a Public Servant* (New York: Macmillan, 1955), 46–57.

30. U.S. Senate, Hearings before the Permanent Subcommittee on Investigations of the Committee on Government Operations, *State Department Information Programs-Information Centers*, 83rd Cong., 1st sess., 1953. For Utley's testimony, see ibid., 129–38.

31. For library mission statement, see ibid., pt. 1, 1.

32. Dulles to Embassy in France, April 2, 1953, *FRUS, 1952–1954*, 1: 1438–39.

33. Merson, *Private Diary of a Public Servant*, 68, 72–74.

34. The tour included stops in Paris, Berlin, Munich, Frankfort, Vienna, Bonn, Belgrade, Athens, Rome, and London. See Nicolas von Hoffman, *Citizen Cohn: The Life and Times of Roy Cohn* (New York: Doubleday, 1988), 145–55; Ambrose, *Eisenhower*, 2: 81; Oshinsky, *Conspiracy So Immense*, 279; Reinhold Wagnleitner, *The Coca-Colonization and the Cold War: The Cultural Mission of the United States in Austria After the Second World War* (Chapel Hill: University of North Carolina Press, 1994), 136–39; German Press Comments on Cohn and Schine, April 21, 1953, *FRUS, 1952–1954*, 1: 1457.

35. Reorganization Plan No. 8 contained several of the recommendations of the Hickenlooper Committee. See Department of State, *Bulletin* 28 (June 15, 1953); Reorganization Plan No. 8, RG 306, Records of U.S. Advisory Commission on Information, box 1, NA2; Editorial Note, *FRUS, 1952–1954*, 2: 1709–11.

36. Broadwater, *Eisenhower and the Anti-Communist Crusade*, 75; Jackson to Eisenhower, July 3, 1953, Papers of C. D. Jackson, box 50, Alphabetical File, DDEL; Anthony Leviero, "Streibert Named Information Chief," *New York Times*, July 31, 1953.

37. See Report of President's Committee on International Information Activities, June 30, 1953, *FRUS, 1952–1954*, 2: 1795–96.

38. Ibid., 2: 1840.

39. Abbott Washburn to William H. Jackson, June 16, 1953, White House Central Files, Confidential Files, box 50, folder on President's Committee on International Information Activities, DDEL.

40. Streibert's budget fell from $96 million to $75 million. See Harold B Hinton, "Streibert Charts Information Goal," *New York Times*, August 7, 1953.

41. See John W. Henderson, *The United States Information Agency* (New York: Praeger, 1969), 54–55; Memo on USIA-NSC Relationships, June 29, 1953, RG 306, Office of Research and Intelligence, 1953–1959, General Records, box 2, File on Administration Relationship-National Security Council, NA2.

42. Interview #1 with Henry Loomis conducted by Cliff Groce, March 1987, GUFAC.

43. Ibid.

44. Ambrose, *Eisenhower*, 2: 81–83; Broadwater, *Eisenhower and the Anti-Communist Crusade*, 74–75.

45. Johnson to Dulles, June 22, 1953, Subject File on McCarthyism, USIAA.

46. "State Department Denounces Book Burnings as 'Wicked Act'," *New York Times*, July 9, 1953. For an incomplete list of those included, see ibid., July 16, 1953.

47. Valur Inigmundarsen, "The Eisenhower Administration, the Adenauer Government, and the Political Uses of the East German Uprising in 1953," *Diplomatic History* 20 (Summer 1996): 381–409. For insightful analysis and valuable primary sources, see Christian F. Ostermann, ed., *Uprising in East Germany, 1953* (Budapest: Central European University Press, 2001).

48. On the peace negotiations, see Rosemary Foot, *A Substitute for Victory: The Politics of Peacemaking at the Korean Armistice Talks* (Ithaca, N.Y.: Cornell University Press, 1990).

49. Gregory Mitrovich, *Undermining the Kremlin: America's Strategy to Subvert the Soviet Bloc, 1947–1956* (Ithaca: Cornell University Press, 2000), 134–48; Scott Lucas, *Freedom's War: The American Crusade Against the Soviet Union* (New York: New York University Press, 1999), 178–80; Bowie and Immerman, *Waging Peace*, 123–46; NSC 162, Review of Basic National Security Policy, September 30, 1953, *FRUS, 1952–1954*, 2: 493.

50. The revised mission statement read: "The purpose of the United States Information Agency shall be to submit evidence to peoples of other nations by means of communications techniques that the objectives and policies of the United States are in harmony with and will advance the legitimate aspirations of other peoples of the world." See NSC Meeting, October 22, 1953, *FRUS, 1952–1954*, 2: 1750–52.

51. "Eisenhower Gives Pledge to Agency," *New York Times*, November 11, 1953.

52. NSC 174, United States Policy toward the Soviet Satellites in Eastern Europe, December 23, 1953, *FRUS, 1952–1954*, 8: 110–27.

53. Washburn to Certain Diplomatic Posts, December 8, 1953, *FRUS, 1952–1954*, 2: 1758–60. Scholars differ widely in their appraisals of "Atoms for Peace." Some have characterized the initiative as a genuine, albeit inadequate, attempt to improve U.S.-Soviet relations and to lessen the dangers posed by atomic weapons. See, for example, Bowie and Immerman, *Waging Peace*, 222–41 and Ambrose, *Eisenhower*, 2: 147–51. This interpretation is complicated when one considers the primacy of propaganda considerations in determining the content and audience for the "Atoms for Peace" campaign. In offering disarmament proposals, Eisenhower aimed to convince American and other noncommunist audiences of the peaceful intentions of the United States. But, because he presented ideas that the Soviets would undoubtedly reject, his commitment to opening substantive arms talks is questionable. For this perspective, consult Osgood, *Total Cold War*, 153–80; Walter L. Hixson, *Parting the Curtain: Propaganda, Culture, and the Cold War, 1945–1961* (New York: St. Martin's, 1997), 94–95; Martin J. Medhurst, "Eisenhower's 'Atoms for Peace' Speech: A Case Study in the Strategic Use of Language," *Communication Monographs* 54 (July 1987): 204–20.

54. Summary of USIA'S Exploitation Since December 10 of President Eisenhower's Speech, December 17, 1953, White House Central Files, Confidential Files, 1953–61, box 13, Candor and United Nations Speech 12/8/53 (26), DDEL; Progress Report of the Working Group of the OCB, April 30, 1954, *FRUS, 1952–1954*, 2: 1403–10.

55. Lucas, *Freedom's War*, 210.

56. In conjunction with the Smith-Mundt legislation in 1948, President Harry S. Truman created the United States Advisory Commission on Information. Comprised of private citizens appointed by the president, the commission released annual oversight reports evaluating the U.S. information program.

57. Ninth Annual Report of the United States Advisory Commission on Information, January 1954, Subject Files, USIAA.

58. Ibid.

59. "Information Unit Ousted 31 as Risks," *New York Times*, February 22, 1953.

60. Streibert to Smith, March 1, 1954, *FRUS, 1952–1954*, 2: 1761–73.

61. See, for example, "The New Voice of America," *U.S. News and World Report*, March 26, 1954, 58–64.

62. The Board of the Foreign Service formerly held the authority. See "Agency Gets More Authority," *New York Times*, March 28, 1954.

63. On Castle's testimony, see "U.S. Urged to End Film Propaganda," *New York Times*, May 15, 1954. The House of Representatives trimmed the agency's original request of $89 million. See *New York Times*, July 3, 1954.

64. On the movement to censure McCarthy, see Robert Griffith, *The Politics of Fear: Joseph McCarthy and the Senate* (Rochelle Park, N.J.: Hayden, 1970), 270–317.

65. These themes are addressed at length later in this study.

66. David Caute, *The Dancer Defects: The Struggle for Cultural Diplomacy During the Cold War* (New York: Oxford University Press, 2003); J. D. Parks, *Culture, Conflict, and Coexistence: American-Soviet Cultural Relations, 1917–1958* (Jefferson, N.C.: McFarland, 1983).

67. "U.S. to Fight Reds on Cultural Line," *New York Times*, July 5, 1954.

68. For more on the appeal of American popular culture and consumerism among foreign audiences, see Ralph Willett, *The Americanization of Germany, 1945–1949* (London: Routledge, 1989); Richard Kuisel, *Seducing the French: The Dilemma of Americanization* (Berkeley: University of California Press, 1993); Richard Pells, "American Culture Abroad: The European Experience Since 1945," in Rob Kroes, Robert W. Rydell, and D. F. J. Bosscher, eds., *Cultural Transmissions and Receptions: American Mass Culture in Europe* (Amsterdam: VU University Press, 1993), 67–83; Wagnleitner, *Coca-Colonization of the Cold War;* Jessica C. E. Gienow-Hecht, *Transmission Impossible: American Journalism as Cultural Diplomacy in Postwar Germany, 1945–1955* (Baton Rouge: Louisiana State University Press, 1999). On the USIA jazz programs, see Penny von Eschen, *Satchmo Blows Up the World: Jazz Ambassadors Play the Cold War* (Cambridge, Mass.: Harvard University Press, 2004).

69. Streibert to USIS Posts, July 6, 1954, *FRUS, 1952–1954*, 2: 1773–75.

70. Lodge to Dulles, July 23, 1954, *FRUS, 1952–1954*, 2: 1775.

71. Eisenhower to Dulles, August 18, 1954, *FRUS, 1952–1954*, 2: 1790–91.

72. "Propaganda Unit Seeks Specialists," *New York Times*, October 31, 1954; Dana Adams Schmidt, "U.S. Aides Use Day to Recruit Staff," *New York Times*, November 2, 1954.

73. Ambrose, *Eisenhower*, 2: 217–22.

74. On the power struggle in the USSR, see Richter, *Khrushchev's Double Bind*, 30–68.

75. Diary Entry by Hagerty, March 22, 1955, *FRUS, 1955–1957*, 9: 521–22. On May 31, the Senate appropriated $85.5 million for information activities—cutting Eisenhower's request by only $3 million. See "Senate Restores Propaganda Fund," *New York Times*, June 1, 1955.

76. Parks, *Culture, Conflict, and Coexistence*, 134–39.

77. NSC 5508/1, March 26, 1955, *FRUS, 1955–1957*, 24: 200–206. The NSC also discussed loosening restrictions on the importation of communist periodicals such as *Pravda* and *Izvestia*. See Ibid., 24: 208–10.

78. Charles E. Bohlen, *Witness to History, 1929–1969* (New York: W.W. Norton, 1969), 373–77; Zubok and Pleshakov, *Inside the Kremlin's Cold War*, 182–88; Richter, *Khrushchev's Double Bind*, 68–71.

79. Ambrose, *Eisenhower*, 2: 260–67; Bohlen, *Witness to History*, 383–87. For a detailed account of the Open Skies proposal, see Osgood, *Total Cold War*, 190–98.

80. "Meeting of Heads of Government at Geneva," Department of State, *Bulletin* 33 (August 1, 1955): 171–77.

81. "A New Spirit of Cooperation in the Search for Peace," Department of State, *Bulletin* 33 (August 8, 1955): 215–19; Dwight D. Eisenhower, *The White House Years*, 2 vols., (New York: Doubleday, 1963), 1: 503–31.

82. Washburn to All USIS Posts, August 24, 1955, *FRUS, 1955–1957*, 9: 526–28.

83. On September 1, the NSC approved the wait-and-see policy. See Report by the Operating Control Board to the National Security Council, August 31, 1955, *FRUS, 1952–1954*, 9: 548–56.

84. Ibid. See also Streibert to the President, September 4, 1955, *FRUS, 1955–1957*, 9: 556–58.

85. Memorandum of Discussion at the 262d Meeting of the National Security Council, October 20, 1955, *FRUS, 1955–1957,* 9: 560–61; Development of East-West Contacts, Proposals by the Governments of France, The United Kingdom, and The United States of America, October 31, 1955, White House Office, NSC Staff, 1948–1961, OCB Central Files, box 18, DDEL.

86. On the Geneva proceedings, see "Opening of Geneva Meeting of Foreign Ministers," Department of State, *Bulletin* 33 (November 7, 1955): 727–29; "Four Foreign Ministers Discuss East-West Contacts and European Security," ibid., 33 (November 14, 1955): 773–85; "Report on the Foreign Ministers Conference," ibid., 33 (November 28, 1955): 867–87; Parks, *Culture, Conflict, and Coexistence,* 146–55.

87. Legislators attending the meeting included: Senators Alexander Wiley (R-Wis.), Walter George (D-Ga.), Richard B. Russell (D-Ga.), Carl Hayden (D-Ariz.), Harry W. Byrd (D-Va.), Speaker of the House Sam Rayburn (D-Tex.), and Representatives John Tabor (R-N.Y.), Clarence Cannon (D-Mo.), James P. Richards (D-S.C.), Robert B. Chiperfield (R-Ill.), John W. McCormack (D-Mass.), Daniel Reed (R-N.Y.), Carl Vinson (D-Ga.), Carl Albert (D-Okla.), and Jere Cooper (D-Tenn.). See Memorandum of a Meeting Between the President and Legislative Leaders, December 13, 1955, *FRUS, 1955–1957,* 9: 562–64. For the president's formal budget request, see *New York Times,* January 17, 1956. On June 20, Congress allotted $113 million for the USIA—$12 million less than Eisenhower requested, but a $28 million increase over fiscal 1956. See *New York Times,* June 21, 1956; U.S. Senate, Committee on Appropriations, *Departments of State, Justice, the Judiciary, and Related Agencies Appropriations,* 1957 *Hearings Before the Subcommittee of the Committee on Appropriations,* United States Senate, 84th Cong., 2nd sess., May 14, 1956.

88. Policy Information Statement for the USIA, February 8, 1956, *FRUS, 1955–1957,* 14: 56–58.

89. Zubok and Pleshakov, *Inside the Kremlin's Cold War,* 182–88; Richter, *Khrushchev's Double Bind,* 77–81.

90. For U.S. attempts to confirm rumors of the "secret speech," see Bohlen, *Witness to History,* 393–98.

91. Meeting of the NSC, March 22, 1956, *FRUS, 1955–1957,* 24: 72–75.

92. Editorial Note, *FRUS, 1955–1957,* 9: 582.

93. State Department Paper on East-West Exchanges, June 6, 1956, *FRUS, 1955–1957,* 24: 220–23.

94. House Committee on Foreign Affairs, *Strengthening International Relations through Cultural and Athletic Exchanges and Participation in International Fairs and Festivals,* 84th Cong., 2nd sess., 1956, Committee Print.

95. See, for example, Hoover to American Embassy, Prague, June 21, 1956, RG 59, box 2069, Decimal File 501/6–2166, NA2.

96. Dispatch from Embassy in Czechoslovakia, June 25, 1956, *FRUS, 1955–1957,* 25: 176–80.

97. Ibid.

98. Press Release, September 4, 1956, Subject Files, USIAA.

99. For an overview of the "People-to-People" program, see Osgood, *Total Cold War*, 214–52. See also *People to People: A Program of International Friendship*, Records of C. D. Jackson, 1931–1967, Alphabetical Subseries, General File, box 82, People-to-People (2), DDEL; McCardle to Murphy, undated, *FRUS, 1955–1957*, 9: 583–85.

100. In 1952, USIA halted publication of *Amerika* as a protest against Soviet censorship. The 1956 agreement permitted the distribution of 50,000 copies of *Amerika* in the Soviet Union in exchange for Soviet circulation of 50,000 copies of their *USSR* magazine in the United States. See "Soviets in Accord on U.S. Magazine," *New York Times*, October 22, 1956.

101. Flanagan to USIA, July 13, 1956, RG 306, Office of Research, Country Project Correspondence, 1952–1963, India, box 10, NA2.

102. *New York Times*, October 17–21, 1956; Meeting of the Policy Planning Staff, October 23, 1956, *FRUS, 1955–1957*, 25: 259–60; Special Intelligence Estimate, October 30, 1956, ibid., 25: 330–31. See also Mark Kramer, "New Evidence on Soviet Decision-Making and the 1956 Polish and Hungarian Crises," *Cold War International History Project Bulletin* 8/9 (Winter 1996/97): 358–62; Robert F. Byrnes, *U.S. Policy Toward Eastern Europe and the Soviet Union* (Boulder, Colo.: Westview Press, 1989), 19.

103. *New York Times*, October 21–29, 1956; Kramer, "New Evidence on Soviet Decision-Making," 362–68.

104. Editorial Note, *FRUS, 1955–1957*, 25: 342–43; Bohlen to Dulles, October 31, 1956, ibid., 25: 348–49; Barnes to Department of State, October 31, 1956, ibid., 25: 349–50. See also Charles Gati, *Hungary and the Soviet Bloc* (Durham, N.C.: Duke University Press, 1986), 138–48.

105. In October, a team of Soviets had arrived in the United States to observe the 1956 presidential campaign. See D'Alessandro to Button, October 25, 1956, *FRUS, 1955–57*, 25: 276–77.

106. See "President Backs Poles' Struggle," *New York Times*, October 21, 1956. On the U.S. refusal to intervene militarily, see "Dulles Is Hopeful, Sees Poles Beginning Return to Liberty—Bars U.S. Force," *New York Times*, October 22, 1956.

107. Notes on the Special Committee on Soviet and Related Problems, October 26, 1956, *FRUS, 1955–1957*, 25: 300–303; Embassy in Austria to Department of State, October 28, 1956, ibid., 25: 319. On October 29, *Pravda* claimed British and American imperialists had instigated the Hungarian insurgency. See Dulles to All Diplomatic Missions, October 30, 1956, ibid., 25: 344–45; Page to Department of State, October 30, 1956, ibid., 25: 342–43; Sig Mickelson, *America's Other Voice: The Story of Radio Free Europe and Radio Liberty* (New York: Praeger, 1983), 96–97. On October 29, Dulles vehemently dismissed the Soviet accusation that the United States was aiding the Hungarian rebels. See Dana Adams Schmidt, "Dulles Calls Charge of Soviet 'Tommyrot,'" *New York Times*, October 29, 1956.

108. Legation in Hungary to Department of State, October 23, 1956, *FRUS, 1955–1957*, 25: 260–65; Special Intelligence Estimate, October 30, 1956, ibid., 25: 331–35; Editorial Note, ibid., 25: 342–43; Dulles to All Diplomatic Missions, October 30, 1956, ibid., 25: 344–45; *New York Times*, November 1–2, 1956; Gati, *Hungary and the Soviet Bloc*, 148–52.

109. See Diane B. Kunz, *The Economic Diplomacy of the Suez Crisis* (Chapel Hill: University of North Carolina Press, 1991); Cole C. Kingseed, *Eisenhower and the Suez Crisis of 1956* (Baton Rouge: Louisiana State University Press, 1995); W. Scott Lucas, *Divided We Stand: Britain, the U.S. and the Suez Crisis* (London: Hodder & Stoughton, 1991).

110. *New York Times*, November 3–6, 1956; Andrew Felkay, *Hungary and the USSR, 1956–1988* (New York: Greenwood Press, 1989): 59–90; Kramer, "New Evidence on Soviet Decision-Making," 376.

111. In May 1958, the NSC adopted NSC 5811/1, a revised Eastern European policy that acknowledged the Soviets' renewed control over the satellite nations. See National Security Council Report 5811/1, May 24, 1958, *FRUS, 1958–1960*, 10: 18–31; Mitrovich, *Undermining the Kremlin*, 176; Lucas, *Freedom's War*, 266–74.

112. "Radio Free Europe Said to Stir Revolt," *New York Times*, November 13, 1956; Memorandum of Discussion at the 303d Meeting of the NSC, November 8, 1956, *FRUS, 1955–1957*, 9: 585–86; Memorandum of Telephone Conversations with the President, November 9, 1956, ibid, 25: 424–25; Notes on the 46th Meeting of the Special Committee on Soviet and Related Problems, November 13, 1956, ibid.: 436–40.

113. Washburn to Eisenhower, November 19, 1956, *FRUS, 1955–1957*, 25: 470–71.

114. Wailes to Department of State, November 19, 1956, ibid., 25: 472–73.

115. Dulles to Eisenhower, November 20, 1956, ibid., 25: 473–75. Historians support Dulles's claims. See, for example, Rhodri Jeffreys-Jones, *The CIA and American Democracy* (New Haven: Yale University Press, 1989), 94; Mickelson, *America's Other Voice*, 98–103.

116. Russell Baker, "Eisenhower Acts; Plans Special Steps to Speed Machinery of Refugee Law," *New York Times*, November 9, 1956.

117. "More Hungarian Refugees Offered Asylum," Department of State, *Bulletin* 35 (December 10, 1956): 913.

118. See, for example, Editorial Note, *FRUS, 1955–1957*, 25: 556–57.

119. Department of State to Embassy in the Soviet Union, November 13, 1956, ibid., 24: 253–54. On interest in cultural relations among the satellites, see, for example, Thayer to Department of State, November 14, 1956, ibid., 25: 453–57.

120. The surveys were conducted in Great Britain, France, Belgium, West Germany, Austria, and Italy. See "The Current State of Soviet Prestige in Western Europe," January 8, 1957, RG 306, Office of Research, Public Opinion Barometer Reports, 1955–1962, box 5, Western Europe, NA2.

121. Burton Kaufman, *The Arab Middle East and the United States: Inter-Arab Rivalry and Superpower Diplomacy*, (London: Twayne Publishers, 1996), 25; Ambrose, *Eisenhower*, 2: 377–88.

122. Osgood Caruthers, "U.S. Propaganda a Success in Cairo, Embassy Declares," *New York Times*, January 25, 1957; James Reston, "Mideast Propaganda Drive Mapped by Administration," *New York Times*, January 26, 1957.

123. "U.S. Adds Africa Broadcasts," *New York Times*, February 17, 1957.

124. Washburn to Eisenhower, February 8, 1957 and Washburn to Adams, February 25, 1957, White House Central Files, box 912, International Broadcasting Service (VOA),

DDEL; W. H. Lawrence, "President Urges World Red Curb," *New York Times*, February 26, 1957; Ambrose, *Eisenhower*, 2: 387–88.

125. "U.S. Finds Unrest in Soviet Sphere," *New York Times*, February 11, 1957.

126. John D. Morris, "U.S.I.A. Funds Cut 26% as President Is Balked on Plea," *New York Times*, April 13, 1957

127. Wilson P. Dizard, Jr., *Inventing Public Diplomacy: The Story of the U.S. Information Agency* (Boulder, CO.: Lynne Rienner, 2004): 76.

128. John D. Morris, "House Approves U.S.I.A. Fund Cut," *New York Times*, April 17, 1957; John D. Morris, "President Scores Cut of 37 Million in U.S.I.A. Budget," *New York Times*, April 18, 1957; James Reston, "Problem for the U.S.I.A.," *New York Times*, April 23, 1957.

129. Interview with Burnett Anderson by Jack O'Brien, January 5, 1990, GUFAC.

130. Interview with Edgar T. Martin conducted by Cliff Groce, March 24, 1988, GUFAC.

131. Interview with Robert Lochner conducted by G. Lewis Schmidt, October 17, 1991, GUFAC; Interview #1 with Henry Loomis conducted by Cliff Groce, March 1987, GUFAC.

132. "U.S.I.A. Head Asks Wider Drive to Expose Lies of Communism," *New York Times*, May 1, 1957; "Johnson Assails U.S. News Unit As the Most Wasteful of Agencies," *New York Times*, May 9, 1957.

133. Dulles vetoed the suggestion of placing USIA under the jurisdiction of the State Department. See Editorial Note, *FRUS, 1955–1957*, 9: 589. Fourteen liberal Republicans and Senator Richard L. Neuberger (D-Ore.) opposed the cuts. Thirty-eight Democrats and twenty-three Republicans supported the reduced budget. See W. H. Lawrence, "Eisenhower Calls Big Budget Slash Needless Gamble," *New York Times*, May 15, 1957; William S. White, "Senate Approves 102 Million Slash," *New York Times*, May 16, 1957. Eisenhower signed the USIA budget bill on June 11. See "U.S.I.A. Bill Signed," *New York Times*, June 12, 1957.

134. NSC 5720, Status of United States Programs for National Security as of June 30, 1957, September 11, 1957, *FRUS, 1955–1957*, 9: 594–95.

135. Eisenhower and Dulles initiated the changes at VOA. See Dulles to Larsen, June 27, 1957, ibid., 9: 590–91; Larsen to Dulles, July 23, 1957, ibid., 9: 592–93; Dulles to Eisenhower, August 9, 1957, ibid., 9: 593.

136. *New York Times*, June 1 and 6, 1957.

137. *New York Times*, June 7, 1957; Memo for Staats, June 11, 1957 and Memo on the Khrushchev Television Interview, June 18, 1957, White House Office Files, NSC, 1948–61, box 1, USSR #2 (6) July 1956-June 1957, DDEL; "Pravda is Noncommittal," *New York Times*, June 17, 1957; Morris Kaplan, "Nixon Bids Soviet Ease Travel Curb," *New York Times*, June 28, 1957.

138. Senator Pat McCarran (D-Nev.) sponsored the immigration restriction in 1952. Congress overrode President Truman's veto of the legislation. See Parks, *Culture, Conflict and Coexistence*, 128, 140–43, 168.

139. Ambrose, *Eisenhower*, 2: 411–19.

140. The Little Rock controversy will be addressed further in Chapter 6. See Telephone Conversation between Dulles and Brownell, September 24, 1957, *FRUS, 1955–1957*, 9: 612–3; For several examples of foreign reaction to the crisis, see RG 306, Records of USIA Research and Intelligence, 1955–1959, General Records, box 6, Little Rock, NA2.

141. Press Release, February 27, 1958, Subject Files, USIAA; Herter to all Diplomatic Posts, October 10, 1957, *FRUS, 1955–1957*, 24: 167–68; Ambrose, *Eisenhower*, 2: 456.

142. Jay Walz, "Envoy to Succeed Larson at U.S.I.A.," *New York Times*, October 17, 1957.

143. "U.S.I.A. to Have Role in Policy Discussions," *New York Times*, November 22, 1957.

144. Dana Adams Schmidt, "U.S. and Soviet Outline Plans for Cultural Exchanges," *New York Times*, October 29, 1957.

145. Ibid.

146. For a cursory explanation of the meetings, see Editorial Note, *FRUS, 1955–1957*, 24: 267–68.

147. Washburn to Adams, November 13, 1957, Records of Arthur Larson and Malcolm Moos, box 2, USIA, DDEL.

148. Interview with Alan Fisher conducted by G. Lewis Schmidt, July 27 and 28, 1988, GUFAC.

149. Interview with G. Lewis Schmidt conducted by Allen Hansen, February 8, 1988, GUFAC.

150. Interview with Albert E. Hemsing conducted by Robert Amerson, April 18, 1989, GUFAC.

151. Interview with Robert Lochner conducted by G. Lewis Schmidt, October 17, 1991, GUFAC.

152. Ibid.

153. James Reston, "U.S., Soviet Widen Exchange in Arts and Other Fields," *New York Times*, January 28, 1958. More a propaganda ploy than a serious offer, Eisenhower dropped the student exchange proposal after the State Department objected. See Ambrose, *Eisenhower*, 2: 445–46.

154. Policy Information Statement, January 29, 1959, *FRUS, 1958–1960*, 10: 2–6.

155. Statement of Mr. Allen before the Senate Committee on Foreign Relations, February 26, 1958, Subject Files, Agency History, 1958, USIAA.

156. On Khrushchev's political ascension and nuclear diplomacy, see Zubok and Pleshakov, *Inside the Kremlin's Cold War*, 188–94; Ambrose, *Eisenhower*, 2: 447–52.

157. Dana Adams Schmidt, "Propaganda Chief Rebukes Americans for Gloomy Views," *New York Times*, April 7, 1958.

158. Foster Haley, "U.S. Library Burned in Lebanon in Riot against Pro-Western Regime" and Jack Raymond, "Anti-Nixon Riots Stir U.S. Reviews of Ties to Latinos," *New York Times*, May 11, 1958; Tad Szulc, "U.S. Flies Troops to Caribbean as Mobs Attack Nixon

in Caracas," *New York Times*, May 14, 1958; Kaufman, *The Arab Middle East and the United States*, 27–28; Ambrose, *Eisenhower*, 2: 469–75.

159. Soviet Propaganda and World Opinion since the Twentieth Party Congress, July 14, 1958 and Attitudes Toward America in Recent Surveys, July 18, 1958, RG 306, Office of Research, Special Reports, 1953–1963, box 15; NA2.

160. For the August 20 floor debate, see House Committee on Foreign Affairs, *Review of United States Information Agency Operations*, Hearings before the Subcommittee on State Department Organization and Foreign Operations, 85th Cong., 2nd sess., September 22 and October 6, 1958, 1–24. See also "'Voice Chief Concedes Soviet 'Out-Guns' U.S. on Propaganda," *New York Times*, September 23, 1958.

161. House Committee on Foreign Affairs, *Review of United States Information Agency Operations*, 25–43.

162. Allen to Larmon, September 15, 1958, RG 306, Office of the Director, Director's Chronological Files, 1953–1964, box 2, microfilm reel 27, NA2.

163. "U.S. to Emphasize Its Culture Abroad," *New York Times*, September 22, 1958; Pirsein, *Voice of America*, 379–85.

164. "'Voice Is Reaching More People behind Iron Curtain, Chief Says" *New York Times*, March 30, 1959. VOA researchers extrapolated the audience estimates from surveys of Hungarian émigrés, refugees from the USSR, and Soviet tourists interviewed at the 1958 Brussels Fair. See VOA Audience Estimate, Radio #4 Subject File, USIAA.

165. "Nixon and Khrushchev Argue in Public as U.S. Exhibit Opens, Accuse Each Other of Threats," *New York Times*, July 25, 1959.

166. For detailed descriptions of the Exhibition, see material contained in USIA Subject Files on Moscow Fair, USIAA. On Soviet interaction with the fair guides, see Max Frankel, "U.S Guides Star at Moscow Fair," *New York Times*, August 15, 1959; Osgood Caruthers, "Russians Denounce Guides at U.S. Fair," *New York Times*, August 16, 1959.

167. On the agreement, see Press Release, November 10, 1958, Office of the U.S. Exhibition in Moscow, USIA Subject Files on Moscow Fair, USIAA.

168. Facts about the American National Exhibition in Moscow, August 18, 1959, ibid.

169. In October 1958, the Department of State identified the "primary theme" of the U.S. Exhibit as follows: "freedom of choice and expression and unimpeded flow of diverse goods and ideas as source of American cultural and economic achievement." Department of State memo, October 29, 1958, RG 306, Records Relating to the American National Exhibition in Moscow, box 7, NA2.

170. The exhibition was jointly administered by the State Department, the Department of Commerce, and the United States Information Agency in cooperation with private American industrial firms. See Facts about the American National Exhibition in Moscow, January 1959, USIA Subject Files on Moscow Fair, USIAA.

171. See Excerpts of a Roundtable Discussion on Plans for Moscow Exhibition Held with Newspaper Correspondents, January 8, 1959, ibid.

172. Sixty Russian-Speaking Guides Sought for Moscow Exhibition, February 18, 1959, ibid.

173. The four-man jury included painting instructor Francis C. Watkins, museum director Lloyd Goodrich, professor Henry Radford, and sculptor Theodore Roszak. See "U.S. Art Jury Is Named," *New York Times*, February 25, 1959.

174. Cooking Display in Moscow to Feature American Dishes, May 13, 1959, USIA Subject Files on Moscow Fair, USIAA.

175. U.S. To Show American Health, Medicine, at Moscow Exhibition, June 1, 1959, ibid.

176. See, for example, U.S. Moscow Exhibition Gets $5,000 Shipment from Sears, January 26, 1959, ibid; 39 New Contributors to Moscow Exhibition, April 10, 1959, ibid; 66 Sponsors Announced for Fashion Display in U.S.-Moscow Exhibition, June 19, 1959, ibid.

177. The floors were quickly paved with asphalt. For an account of the construction problems, see "How They Work in Russia," *U.S. News and World Report* (August 10, 1959): 47–49.

178. "Racial Mixing Assailed in Fashion Show for Moscow," *New York Times*, July 15, 1959.

179. "Soviet Ridicules Typical U.S. Home," *New York Times*, April 10, 1959; "U.S. Can See $5,000 Décor Due in Soviet," *New York Times*, May 23, 1959.

180. "Moscow to See Modern U.S. Art," *New York Times*, May 31, 1959; "Walter Says U.S.I.A. Chose Red Artists," *New York Times*, June 4, 1959.

181. "President Favors Art Liked by U.S.," *New York Times*, July 2, 1959; "President Hailed in Dispute on Art," *New York Times*, July 3, 1959.

182. "U.S. Exhibit Adds Traditional Art," *New York Times*, July 8, 1959.

183. "Russians Screen Books at Exhibit," *New York Times*, July 25, 1959. The books targeted for removal included Irving Levine's *Main Street USSR*, Sir Bernard Pare's *A History of Russia*, Dean Acheson's *Power and Diplomacy*, and Adlai Stevenson's *Friends and Enemies*. See Washburn to Moscow, July 27, 1959, RG 306, Records Relating to the American National Exhibition in Moscow, box 7, NA2.

184. Memorandum of Conversation, July 24, 1959, *FRUS*, X: 336–45; "Premier Taunts American Visitor," July 26, 1959.

185. Comparative Summary of Soviet Coverage of the Vice President's Visit, September 8, 1959, RG 306, Office of Research, Special Reports, 1953–63, box 17, NA2.

186. Osgood Caruthers, "U.S. Closes Bookmobile at Fair After Many Volumes Disappear," *New York Times*, August 19, 1959; Osgood Caruthers, "Bookmobile Reopens in Moscow," *New York Times*, August 28, 1959; "Russian Capitalists," *New York Times*, September 2, 1959.

187. File on Photo Coverage, August 3, 1959, RG 306, Records Relating to American Exhibition, Moscow, 1957–59, box 2, NA2.

188. "'Brain' Counts Russian Queries; U.S. Cigarettes Price Tops List," *New York Times*, August 5, 1959; Some Thoughts on the American Dream, USIA Subject Files on Moscow Fair, USIAA; I.B.M. Reports, August 29, 1959, RG 306, Records Relating to the American National Moscow Exhibition, 1957–59, box 2, NA2.

189. Summary of Soviet Press, August 1, 1959, RG 306, Records Relating to the American National Moscow Exhibition, 1957–59, box 2, NA2.

190. "Khrushchev Coming to U.S. Next Month," *New York Times*, August 4, 1959.

191. Report on American National Exhibition in Moscow, September 28, 1959, RG 306, Office of Research, Production Division Research Reports, 1956–59, box 7, NA2.

192. Ibid. See also Report Prepared by the Department of State, August 1959, *FRUS, 1958–1960*, 10: 37–40.

193. Ibid.

194. For the complete texts of Khrushchev's speeches, see *Khrushchev in America* (New York: Crosscurrents Press, 1960). See also Report on Khrushchev Visit, undated, *FRUS, 1958–1960*, 10: 485–92. Khrushchev had espoused similar views throughout his premiership. See Richter, *Khrushchev's Double Bind*, 103–8; Zubok and Pleshakov, *Inside the Kremlin's Cold War*, 200–201.

195. For global reaction to Khrushchev's tour, see "Soviet and Bloc Coverage of Khrushchev's Visit: With a Summary of Free World Reaction," RG 306, Office of Research, Special Reports, 1953–1963, box 17, NA2.

196. Editorial Note, *FRUS, 1958–1960*, 10: 51–52.

CHAPTER THREE. DEFINING DEMOCRACY: IMAGES OF THE AMERICAN
POLITICAL SYSTEM

1. *Social Change and Democracy*, USIA Film Collection, RG 306, Motion Picture, Sound, and Video Records, Special Media Archives Services Division, NA2.

2. In focusing on the *specific* ways that U.S. policymakers promoted democracy during the Cold War, this chapter illuminates an understudied aspect of American political and diplomatic history. There is, however, a vast body of literature on *general* connections between domestic politics and American diplomacy. Important examples include Felix Gilbert, *To the Farewell Address: Ideas of Early American Foreign Policy* (Princeton, N.J.: Princeton University Press, 1970); Tony Smith, *America's Mission: The United States and the Worldwide Struggle for Democracy in the Twentieth Century* (Princeton, N.J.: Princeton University Press, 1994); Ralph B. Levering, *The Public and American Foreign Policy, 1918–1978* (New York: Morrow, 1978).

3. William B. Benton testifying before House Appropriations Committee, February 26, 1946, RG 59, Lots 587 and 52–48, Records of the Assistant Secretary of Public Affairs, Memoranda, 1945–1947, box 14, NA2.

4. Department of State, *Bulletin* 18 (April 18, 1948): 518.

5. On the broad definition of freedom, see, for example, Acting Secretary Robert Lovett to Certain American Diplomatic Officers, December 8, 1947, *FRUS, 1947*, 4: 630–32; Report Prepared by the National Security Council, March 2, 1955, *FRUS, 1955–1957*, 9: 504–7; U.S. Information Policy with Regard to Anti-American Propaganda, December 1, 1947, RG 59, Lot 53D47, Records Relating to International Information Activities, 1938–1953, box 3,

NA2; "Soviet-Communism," December 29, 1948, RG 59, Lot 87D236, Historical Studies Division, Research Project, 1945–1954, box 7, ibid.; USIA Basic Guidance Paper, October 22, 1957, File on Agency History, USIAA. On the presentation of America as a pluralistic nation, see USIA Planning Paper—Themes on American Life and Culture, July 14, 1959, USIA Subject Files, USIAA.

6. Iron Curtain Radio and Press Comment, February 1950, RG 306, Reports and Related Studies, 1948–1953, box 10, NA2.

7. See, for example, U.S. Ambassador in the Soviet Union (Smith) to Secretary of State, January 17, 1947, *FRUS, 1947*, 4: 521–22; Annual USIS Assessment Report, November 5, 1957, RG 306, Office of Research, Country Project Correspondence, 1952–1963, India, box 10, NA2.

8. *Herblock Looks at Communism*, USIA Pamphlet Files, USIAA.

9. *Glossary of Soviet Terms*, 1951–1952, USIA Pamphlet Files, USIAA.

10. *Little Moe—His Life Behind the Iron Curtain*, May 1954, USIA Pamphlet Files, USIAA

11. *A Picture Story of the United States*, rev. ed., 1961, USIA Pamphlet Files, USIAA.

12. Manning H. Williams to Oren M. Stephens, February 5, 1958, White House Office Files, Office of the Special Assistant for National Security Affairs, 1952–1961, Operations Coordinating Board series, box 5, folder on Special OCB Committees, DDEL.

13. *In Search of Lincoln*, USIA Film Collection, RG 306, Motion Picture, Sound, and Video Records, Special Media Archives Services Division, NA2.

14. USIS Madras to USIA Washington, June 1, 1959, RG 306, Records Concerning Exhibits in Foreign Countries, 1955–1967, box 14, file on India, NA2.

15. Peter Lisagor, "Cheap U.S. 'Bibles' of Democracy on Their Way to Asia," *Chicago News*, April 26, 1956.

16. Dana Adams Schmidt, "Classics of U.S. Big Hit in India," *New York Times*, September 22, 1957.

17. *America Today*, RG 306, Exhibits Division, Records Concerning Exhibits in Foreign Countries, India, box 14, 1955–67, NA2.

18. VOA Korea, "Giants of Democratic Thought #4—The Dark Ages," October 11, 1951, RG 306, Voice of America Daily Content Reports and Script Translations, 1950–1955, box 27, NA2.

19. *Social Change and Democracy*, USIA Film Collection, RG 306, Motion Picture, Sound, and Video Records, Special Media Archives Services Division, NA2.

20. See, for example, "Voice of America Is Not the Voice of the American People," August 2, 1949, Iron Curtain Radio Comment on VOA, RG 306, Reports and Related Studies, 1948–1953, box 8, NA2.

21. *New York Times*, October 6, 1947.

22. Ibid., January 23, 1948.

23. Russia the Reactionary, 1949, RG 59, Lot 53D47, Records Relating to International Information Activities, 1938–1953, William T. Stone Files, box 1, NA2.

24. See, for example, *The Free World Speaks*, USIA Pamphlet Files, USIAA.

25. Weekly Information Policy Guide, August 9, 1950, RG 59, Lot 53D47, Records Relating to International Information Activities, 1938–1953, William T. Stone files, box 4, NA2

26. Emergency Plan for Psychological Offensive, March 9, 1951, *FRUS, 1951*, 4: 1232–36.

27. *Who Is the Imperialist?*, 1952–1958, USIA Pamphlet Files, USIAA.

28. Report Prepared by the National Security Council, March 2, 1955, *FRUS, 1955–1957*, 9: 504–7.

29. Annual USIS Assessment Report, November 5, 1957, RG 306, Office of Research, Country Project Correspondence, 1952–1963, India, box 10, NA2; and Country Plan for India, September 9, 1958, RG 306, Dispatches, 1954–1966, box 1, NA2.

30. Annual USIS Assessment Report, November 5, 1957, RG 306, Office of Research, Country Project Correspondence, 1952–1963, box 10, NA2.

31. *Bitter Harvest: The October Revolution in Hungary and Its Aftermath*, USIA Pamphlets, USIAA.

32. Annual USIS Assessment Report, November 5, 1957, RG 306, Office of Research, Country Project Correspondence, 1952–1963, box 10, NA2.

33. For a thoughtful essay exploring this trend, see Andrew Preston, "Bridging the Gap between the Sacred and the Secular in the History of American Foreign Relations," *Diplomatic History* 30 (November 2006): 783–812.

34. For examples of the U.S. response to Soviet anti-Semitism, see Durbrow to the Secretary of State, December 2, 1947, *FRUS, 1947*, 4: 628–30; Kohler to Secretary of State, March 19, 1949, *FRUS, 1949*, 5: 597–99. The Mindszenty arrest is addressed in Chapin to Secretary of State, December 29, 1948, *FRUS, 1948*, 4: 393–95.

35. See, for example, Kirk to Secretary of State, June 21, 1950, *FRUS, 1950*, 4: 1208; VOA Polish Transcript, January 30, 1952, RG 306, Voice of America Daily Content Reports and Script Translations, 1950–1955, box 35, NA2.

36. NSC 5509—Status of United States Programs for National Security as of December 31, 1954, Part 6-The USIA Program, March 2, 1955, *FRUS, 1955–1957*, 9: 509.

37. Thayer to Allen, May 25, 1949, RG 59, Records of the Assistant Secretary of State for Public Affairs, 1947–1950, Lot 52–202, General Correspondence A–Z, 1948–1949, box 1, NA2.

38. VOA Czech Transcript, April 9, 1950, RG 306, Voice of America Daily Broadcast Content Reports and Script Translations, 1950–1955, box 1, NA2.

39. Pinkus to Hulten, April 17, 1950, RG 59, Records Related to International Information Activities, 1938–1953, Lot 53D48, box 110, NA2. For a multidenominational list of religious figures appearing on VOA, see VOA Policy on Religion, April 12, 1951, Ibid.

40. See, for example, Harris to Barrett, October 18, 1950, RG 59, Records Relating to International Information Activities, 1938–1953, Lot 53D48, box 63, NA2.

41. "More Stress on Religion," *New York Times*, April 22, 1951.

42. Utilization of Moral and Religious Factors in USIE Program, March 5, 1951, RG 59, Records Relating to International Information Activities, 1938–1953, Lot 52D365, box 63, NA2.

43. Allen to Dodd, April 20, 1959, RG 306, Office of the Director, Director's Chronological Files, 1953–1964, box 3, microfilm reel 20, NA2.

44. USIA Basic Guidance and Planning Paper on Themes on American Life and Culture, July 14, 1959, USIA Subject Files, USIAA.

45. USIA Basic Guidance and Planning Paper on Religious Information Policy, May 1, 1959, USIA Subject Files, USIAA.

46. Guarco to Grondahl, February 23, 1951, RG 59, Records Relating to International Information Activities, 1938–1953, Lot 52D365, box 110, NA2.

47. Reprint of Cedric Larson, "Religious Freedom as a Theme of the Voice of America," *Journalism Quarterly* (June 1952), USIA Pamphlet Files, USIAA.

48. *Red Star over Islam*, 1952, USIA Pamphlet Files, USIAA.

49. VOA World Handbook, Regional Objectives Near and Middle East and Northern Africa, February 24, 1953, RG 306, International Information Administration, 1952–1953, box 1, NA2.

50. The nations included: Indonesia, India, Jordan, Lebanon, Libya, Malaya, Morocco, Pakistan, Sudan, Saudi Arabia, Syria, Tunisia, and Turkey. See Operating Coordinating Board, Inventory of U.S. Government and Private Organization Activity Regarding Islamic Organizations as an Aspect of Overseas Operations, May 3, 1957, Operating Coordinating Board Central Files, White House Office of the NSC Staff, 1948–1961, box 2, folder on Religion #2 (4)—January–May 1957, DDEL.

51. Ibid.

52. *Buddhism Under the Soviet Yoke*, 1952, USIA Pamphlet Files, USIAA.

53. *An Asian Looks at Communism*, 1952, USIA Pamphlet Files, USIAA.

54. Zarins and his family fled Riga when the Soviets captured the city in 1944. In 2001, the Latvian Republic bestowed its highest civilian honor, the *Tris Zvaigznu Ordenis* (Three Star Order), on Reverend Zarins. Two years later, the nation gave the award to the minister's son, Christopher Zarins, MD, chief of the Stanford University Medical School Division of Vascular Surgery. See Rosanne Spector, "It's Not Every Day that Zarins Takes Home the 'Tris Zvaigznu Ordenis,'" *Stanford Report*, December 10, 2003, http: //news-service .stanford.edu/news/2003/december10/zarins.html.

55. VOA Latvian Service, July 4, 1954, RG 306, VOA Daily Content Reports and Script Translations, 1950–1955, box 74, NA2.

56. *Soviet Communism Threatens Education*, May 22, 1952, USIA Pamphlets, USIAA.

57. *It's a Great Life, Comrades*, 1956, USIA Pamphlets, USIAA.

58. Kennan to the Secretary of State, January 3, 1946, *FRUS, 1946*, 6: 673–74.

59. Ambassador in the Soviet Union to the Secretary of State, January 24, 1947, *FRUS, 1947*, 4: 521–22.

60. Commentary, "The Supreme Soviet Meets," VOA Persian Service, April 21, 1954, RG 306, VOA Daily Content Reports and Script Translations, 1950–1955, box 72, NA2.

61. "Truman Outpaced in Campaign, State Department's 'Voice' Says," *New York Times*, October 11, 1948.

62. International Information Administration Special Instruction PO-53–1, 1952 U.S. Presidential Campaign, July 8, 1952, Papers of Howland H. Sargeant, box 5, International Information Administration, 1951–52, HSTL.

63. Interview with Barry Zorthian conducted by Cliff Groce, October 20, 1988, GUFAC.

64. VOA Russia transcript, September 10, 1950, RG 306, Voice of America Daily Broadcast Content Reports and Script Translations, 1950–1955, box 6, NA2.

65. VOA Poland transcript, May 9, 1951, RG 306, VOA Daily Content Reports and Script Translations, 1950–1955, box 18, NA2.

66. *You Can't Win!*, 1953, USIA Pamphlets, USIAA.

67. *This Is the Story of Sergei*, 1953, USIA Pamphlets, USIAA.

68. See, for example, *Facts About Communism-Justice*, 1956, USIA Pamphlet Files, USIAA.

69. Voice of America Handling of McCarthy Story, August 3, 1950, RG 59, Lot 52D36, Records Relating to International Information Activities, 1938–1953, box 43, NA2.

70. Effects of the Internal Security Act of 1950 on U.S. Foreign Relations, November 13, 1950, RG 59, Records Relating to International Information Activities, 1938–1953, Lot 52D365, box 50, NA2; Dillon to Department of State, March 31, 1954, *FRUS, 1954*, 1: 1552–56. For the reaction among Austrians, see Reinhold Wagnleitner, *Coca-Colonization and the Cold War: The Cultural Mission of the United States in Austria After the Second World War* (Chapel Hill: University of North Carolina Press, 1994): 137–38.

71. "Methods Used in U.S. in Political Struggle," VOA Russian, May 17, 1954, RG 306, VOA Daily Content Reports and Script Translations, 19501–955, box 73, NA2.

72. *Communists in the Daylight*, USIA Pamphlet File, USIAA.

73. What Is Left of U.S. Democracy?" December 27, 1951, Iron Curtain Press and Radio Comment, RG 306, Reports and Related Studies, 1948–1953, box 10, NA2.

74. *Communism Is Losing*, May 22, 1952, USIA Pamphlets, USIAA.

75. Ibid.

76. VOA Russia Broadcast, March 3, 1953, RG 306, VOA Daily Broadcast Content Reports and Script Translations, 1950–55, box 65, NA2.

77. Marshall to Certain Diplomatic Missions, July 16, 1948, *FRUS, 1948*, 4: 425–26.

78. *They Escaped to Freedom*, USIA Pamphlet Files, USIAA.

79. *Dance to Freedom*, USIA Film Collection, RG 306, Motion Picture, Sound, and Video Records, Special Media Archives Services Division, NA2.

80. *In Quest of Freedom*, USIA Pamphlet Files, USIAA.

81. *By Their Fruits Ye Shall Know Them*, May 1952, USIA Pamphlet Files, USIAA.

82. World in Brief, November 1954, Women's Packet #20, RG 306, Feature Packets, Recurring Themes, box 19, NA2.

CHAPTER 4. SELLING CAPITALISM: IMAGES OF THE ECONOMY, LABOR, AND CONSUMERISM

1. W. W. Rostow, *The Stages of Economic Growth: A Non-Communist Manifesto* (New York: Cambridge University Press, 1960).

2. Michael Hunt, *Ideology and U.S. Foreign Policy* (New Haven, Conn.: Yale University Press, 1987), 42. See also Anders Stephanson, *Manifest Destiny: American Exceptionalism and the Empire of Right* (New York: Hill and Wang, 1995).

3. On modernization, see Michael Latham, *Modernization as Ideology: American Social Science and "Nation Building" in the Kennedy Era* (Chapel Hill: University of North Carolina Press, 2000). On advertising in the 1950s, see Thomas Frank, *The Conquest of Cool: Business Culture, Counterculture, and the Rise of Hip Consumerism* (Chicago: University of Chicago Press, 1997). On connections between the U.S. foreign policy establishment and private citizens, see Scott Lucas, *Freedom's War: The American Crusade Against the Soviet Union* (New York: New York University Press, 1999); Allen Needell, "'Truth Is Our Weapon': Project TROY, Political Warfare, and Government-Academic Relations in the National-Security State," *Diplomatic History* 17 (Summer 1993): 399–420; Christopher Simpson, ed., *Universities and Empire: Money and Politics in the Social Sciences During the Cold War* (New York: Free Press, 1998).

4. There is an enormous literature supporting these contentions. Examples include: Emily Rosenberg, *Spreading the American Dream: American Economic and Cultural Expansion, 1890–1945*; Frank Costigliola, *Awkward Dominion: American Political, Economic, and Cultural Relations with Europe, 1919–1933* (Ithaca, N.Y.: Cornell University Press, 1984); Mary Nolan, *Visions of Modernity: American Business and the Modernization of Germany* (New York: Oxford University Press, 1994).

5. In a vast body of work on labor-business-government relations in this era, see Dana Frank, *Buy American: The Untold Story of Economic Nationalism* (Boston: Beacon Press, 1999), 102–28; Robert H. Haddow, *Pavilions of Plenty: Exhibiting American Culture Abroad in the 1950s* (Washington, D.C.: Smithsonian Institution Press, 1997); Elizabeth A. Fones-Wolf, *Selling Free Enterprise: The Business Assault on Labor and Liberalism, 1945–60* (Urbana: University of Illinois Press, 1994); Alan Brinkley, *The End of Reform: New Deal Liberalism in Recession and War* (New York:. Knopf, 1995); Nelson Lichtenstein, "From Corporatism to Collective Bargaining: Organized Labor and the Eclipse of Social Democracy in the Postwar Era," in *The Rise and Fall of the New Deal Order, 1930–1980*, ed. Steve Fraser and Gary Gerstle (Princeton, N.J.: Princeton University Press, 1989), 85–112; Howell Harris, *The Right to Manage: Industrial Relations Policies of American Business in the* 1940s (Madison: University of Wisconsin Press, 1982).

6. Department of State, *Bulletin* 13 (September 23, 1945): 430.

7. See, for example, Benton's October 16, 1945 statement in *Interchange of Knowledge and Skills Between the People of the United States and Peoples of Other Countries*, Hearings before the Committee on Foreign Affairs, House of Representatives, 79th Cong., 1st and 2nd sess., October 16, 17, 18, 19, 23, 24, 1945; May 14, 1946, 7.

8. Harriman to Secretary of State, January 20, 1946, *FRUS, 1946*, 6: 676–78.

9. Smith to Secretary of State, November 15, 1947, *FRUS, 1947*, 6: 619–21.

10. Secretary of State to Certain American Diplomatic and Consular Officers," July 20, 1948, RG 59, Records Relating to International Information Activities, 1938–1953, Lot 53D47, William T. Stone files, box 3, NA2.

11. Labor Advisor, undated memo, and Background Material, June 8, 1951 and Meeting on Discussion of Functions of Proposed Labor Information Officers, September 19, 1950, RG 59 Records Relating to International Information Activities, 1938–1953, Lot 52D365, box 61, NA2.

12. U.S. Information Agency Basic Guidance and Planning Paper No. 11, "The American Economy," July 16, 1959, Subject Files, Policy, USIAA.

13. U.S. Information Agency Basic Guidance and Planning Paper No. 11, "The American Economy," July 16, 1959, Subject Files on Policy, USIAA.

14. For more on attempts to influence international labor, see Ray Godson, *American Labor and European Politics: The AFL as a Transnational Force* (New York: Crane, Russak, 1976); Anthony Carew, *Labour Under the Marshall Plan: The Politics of Productivity and the Marketing of Management Science* (Manchester: Manchester University Press, 1987); Michael J. Hogan, *The Marshall Plan: America, Britain and the Reconstruction of Western Europe, 1947–1952* (New York: Cambridge University Press, 1987).

15. See Feature Packets on Labor, RG 306, Feature Packets, Recurring Themes, boxes 7–14, NA2.

16. See, for example, The U.S. Labor and Social Scene as Viewed by the Labor Press in the USSR, RG 59, Records Relating to International Information Activities, 1938–1953, Lot 52D389, box 42, NA2. See also Draft Statement for Secretary of State George Marshall on the United States International Information and Cultural Relations Program for his Budget Presentation before the House Appropriations subcommittee, January 27, 1947, RG 59, Lots 587 and 52–48, Records of the Assistant Secretary of State, 1945–1950, box 4, Office Symbol Files, 1945–1950, NA2.

17. Part III, Notes on Target Areas, Chapter V: Europe in Project Troy Report to the Secretary of State, February 1, 1951, Volume I, RG 59, Lot 52–283, Records of Relating to Project Troy, 1950–1951, box 1, NA2.

18. Basic IIA Document on Media Coverage of U.S. Free Enterprise System, March 20, 1952, RG 306, Office of Research and Intelligence, 1955–1959, General Records, box 2, Policy and Procedures, 1952–53, NA2.

19. The Indian Image of the United States, A Preliminary View: Part II: The American Way of Life, RG 306, Office of Research, Production Division Research Reports, 1956–1959, box 5, NA2.

20. Frances Hubbell, Feature on "U.S. Business Standards," November 20, 1951, RG 306, Voice of America Daily Content Reports and Script Translations, 1950–1955, box 31, NA2; box 31, NA2; Information Policy on the American Economy, October 3, 1955, Subject Files on Exhibits and Fairs—People's Capitalism, USIAA; Western European Attitudes Related to the People's Capitalism Campaign, December 31, 1956, ibid; and Japanese Attitudes Related to the People's Capitalism Campaign, October 7, 1957, ibid. See also Themes on American Life and Culture, Basic Guidance and Planning Paper No. 10, July 14, 1959, Subject Files on Policy, USIAA.

21. *A Primer on the American Economy*, USIA Pamphlet Files, USIAA.

22. A Summary of USIA Operating Assumptions, Vol. 3, RG 306, Office of Research, Special Reports, 1953–1963, box 7, PA 3–4, NA2.

23. Basic Guidance and Planning Paper No. 11, "The American Economy," Subject Files on Policy, USIAA; Refutation of Soviet Contention that Socialism Is Higher System than Capitalism, RG 306, Requestor Only Reports, 1956–62, box 2, NA2.

24. See, for example, Notes from the Soviet Provincial Press, October 1956, RG 306, Office of Research, Production Division Research Reports, 1956–59, box 3, NA2. The USIS analyses, *Iron Curtain Radio Comment on Voice of America*, provide numerous examples. For these reports, see RG 306, Reports and Related Studies, 1948–1953, boxes 8 and 9, NA2. On the American military-industrial complex, see Nikita Khrushchev, Speech at Jubilee Session of Supreme Soviet of USSR, November 6, 1957, *Speeches and Interviews on World Problems*, Moscow, 1958, Selected Statements from Khrushchev's Speeches, Writings, and Interviews (1938–1959), RG 306, Office of Research, Special Reports, 1953–1963, box 16, NA2.

25. "An Analysis of the Principal Psychological Vulnerabilities in the USSR and of the Principal Assets Available to the US for Their Exploitation," undated, RG 59, Lot 52D432, Bureau of Public Affairs, box 5, Office Files of Assistant Secretary Edward W. Barrett, 1950–51, NA2.

26. *The Truth Crushes Commie Lies*, RG 59, Lot 52D365, Records Relating to International Information Activities, 1938–1953, box 61, NA2.

27. *It Happened to Us*, USIA Pamphlets, USIAA

28. See, for example, Labor Packet, June 1953, RG 306, Feature Packets, Recurring Themes, box 7, NA2; *The New Slavery*, USIA Pamphlets, USIAA; "The Policy of Tyranny in China," February 25, 1952, RG 306, Voice of America Daily Content Reports and Script Translations, 1950–1955, box 35, NA2.

29. *The Road to Serfdom* and *Slave Labor*, USIA Pamphlets, USIAA.

30. *Meet Some Americans at Work*, USIA Pamphlets, USIAA.

31. VOA Rumanian Broadcast, April 1, 1953, RG 306, VOA Daily Content Reports and Script Translations, 1950–1955, box 67, NA2.

32. Information Policy on the American Economy, October 3, 1955, USIA Subject Files on Exhibits and Fairs—People's Capitalism, USIAA.

33. *Thomas Brackett*, USIA Pamphlet Files, USIAA.

34. "Workers Win 10-Year Fight Against Forced Labor," Labor Packet, Jul 1957, RG 306, Feature Packets-Recurring Themes, box 14, NA2; *The All Union Family*, an AFL-CIO publication included in Labor Packet, February 1957, RG 306, Feature Packets-Recurring Themes, box 11, NA2; *If You Were a Soviet Worker*, USIA Pamphlet Files, USIAA.

35. *American Labor Unions: Their Role in the Free World*, USIA Pamphlets, USIAA.

36. USIA Basic Guidance and Planning Paper No. 3, October 20, 1958, Subject Files, Policy, USIAA.

37. See, for example, George Brown's "Why Should We Be Interested in International Affairs?" Labor Packet, May 1957, RG 306, Feature Packets-Recurring Themes, box 14, NA2. Labor leaders also provided congressional testimony in behalf of the USIA. See the

comments of Boris Shishkin, Director of Research, American Federation of Labor, Hearings before a Subcommittee of the Committee on Foreign Relations United States Senate, 83rd Cong., 1st sess., *Overseas Information Programs of the United States*, 1953, 731–743. The State Department also consulted union leaders. See Briefing for Labor Advisory Committee, December 19, 1950, RG 59, Lot 52D365, Records Relating to International Information Activities, 1938–1953, box 61, NA2.

38. "U.S. Labor Unions Promote Political Education for Women," Women's Packet, October 1954, RG 306, Feature Packets-Recurring Themes, box 19, NA2; "Visitor Finds Negroes Active in U.S. Labor Movement," January 2, 1952, *Air Bulletin*, RG 306, *Air Bulletin*, box 2, NA2; William Green, "Organized Labor and the Negro," January 16, 1952, *Air Bulletin*, ibid.

39. "An American Worker's Family," Labor Packet, December 1955, RG 306, Feature Packets-Recurring Themes, box 12, NA2; "Living and Working in a Free Enterprise System," Labor Packet, July 1957, RG 306, Feature Packets-Recurring Themes, box 14, NA2.

40. "Manual Workers Gaining Over White Collar Groups," Labor Packet-October 1956; "Revolution in Income Distribution in the United States," Labor Packet-November 1956; "The Growth of Profit Sharing in the United States," Labor Packet-January 1957; "Low Cost Vacations for American Wage Earners," Labor Packet-July 1956; "American Industry Supports Higher Education," Labor Packet-August 1956; "Fringe Benefits Increase Among American Workers," Labor Packet-December 1956; all found in RG 306, Feature Packets, Recurring Themes, box 14, NA2.

41. Albert Parry, "Soviet Drones," *Wall Street Journal*, July 29, 1954 included in Labor Packet-September 1954, RG 306, Feature Packets, Recurring Themes, box 9, NA2.

42. U.S. attacks on class inequalities in the USSR were common. See, for example, VOA Chinese Transcript, March 3, 1952, RG 306, Voice of America Daily Broadcast Content Reports and Daily Translations, 1950–1955, box 35, NA2.VOA Estonian Transcript, April 23, 1952, Ibid, box 40; VOA Russian Transcript, September 18, 1952, ibid., box 52.

43. "Hardships of Workers behind the Iron Curtain Disclosed," *Air Bulletin*, January 23, 1952, RG 306, Air Bulletin, box 2, NA2.

44. "Refugee Returns from Grave of Communist Labor Camps," Women's Packet-November 1954, RG 306, Feature Packets, Recurring Themes, box 19, NA2; Matthew Woll, "Slave Labor Behind the Iron Curtain," *Air Bulletin*, March 7, 1951, RG 306, *Air Bulletin* files, box 2, NA2.

45. A Study of USIA Operating Assumptions, Volume 3, RG 306, Office of Research, Special Reports, 1953–1963, box 7, TC 19–20, NA2.

46. See, for example, "Wilkins Appointment Highlights Progress of American Negro," Labor Packet-April 1953, RG 306, Feature Packets, Recurring Themes, box 8, NA2.

47. See David Sarnoff, "RCA's Policy of Nondiscrimination in Employment," Labor Packet-December 1955, RG 306, Feature Packets, Recurring Themes, box 12, NA2.

48. "Communicating with the Soviet People: Suggestions for American Tourists and Students," RG 306, Office of Research, Special Reports, 1953–1963, box 19, NA2.

49. VOA Hebrew Broadcast, May 25, 1951, RG 306, VOA Daily Content Reports and Script Translations, 1950–1955, box 18, NA2.

50. "Forced Labor Prohibited Under U.S. Laws," Labor Packet-June 1953, RG 306, Feature Packets, Recurring Subjects, box 7, Labor, NA2.

51. "East German Women Tell of Privations," Women's Packet-October 1953, RG 306, Feature Packets, Recurring Themes, box 17, NA2; "Women in East Germany," June 1953, ibid.

52. Rare Visitor to USSR Reports on Soviet Woman's Status, August 1953, RG 306, Women's Packet #6, RG 306, Feature Packets, Recurring Themes, box 17, NA2

53. An Analysis of the Principal Psychological Vulnerabilities in the USSR and of the Principal Assets Available to the US for Their Exploitation, undated, RG 59, Lot 52D432, Bureau of Public Affairs, box 5, Office Files of Assistant Secretary Edward W. Barrett, 1950–51, NA2.

54. USIA Policy guidelines asserted, "Since the wage earner role offers the greatest opportunity for distortion overseas, . . . information showing the important place of women in America's labor force should nor be presented in isolation from facts showing them first as women." See Basic Guidance and Planning Paper No. 12 on Women's Activities (Part II), August 13, 1959, Subject Files on Policy, USIAA. For more on "the right and wrong way of housework," see "Help for Housewives with Heart Disease," Women's Packet-April 1954, RG 306, Feature Packets, Recurring Themes, box 18, NA2. On Soviet characterizations of American women, see Unsigned letter to Alice K. Leopold, Assistant to the Secretary of Labor, March 2, 1960, RG 306, Requestor Only Reports, 1956–62, box 2, NA2.

55. "A Visit with Mrs. Foster," Women's Packet-April 1953, RG 306, Feature Packets, Recurring Themes, box 16, NA2.

56. From 1941 until 1954, communist nations entered 133 trade fairs, but the United States had not taken part in any. See U.S. Senate, Committee on Foreign Relations, *International Cultural Exchange and Trade Fair Participation Act of 1956*, Hearings before a Subcommittee of the Committee on Foreign Relations, 84th Cong., 2nd sess., February 21, 1956.

57. Third Quarterly Report on President's Emergency Fund for Participation in International Affairs, January 1, 1955—March 31, 1955, White House Office Files, NSC Staff. 1948–1961, OCB Central File Series, box 14, Cultural Activities #1 (6) April 1954–June 1955, DDEL.

58. House Committee on Foreign Affairs, *Strengthening International Relations Through Cultural and Athletic Exchanges and Participation in International Fairs and Festivals*, 84th Cong., 2nd sess., June 22, 1956, Committee Print.

59. Memorandum for the Operations Coordinating Board, March 8, 1955, White House Central Office Files, NSC Staff, 1948–61, OCB Central File Series, box 14, Cultural Activities #1 (4), April 1954–June 1955, DDEL.

60. For more on the development and content of U.S. trade exhibits, see Haddow, *Pavilions of Plenty*. The statistic on the expansion of U.S. trade fair participation is found on page 15.

61. USIA researchers surveyed approximately 6,000 audience members at trade fairs in Tokyo, Djakarta, Phnom Penh, Karachi, New Delhi, Berlin, Vienna, and Bogotá. See

"The Impact of the U.S. Trade Fair Program, An Analysis of Visitor Reaction in the Far East, South Asia, Europe and Latin American," April 25, 1956, RG 306, Office of Research, Program and Media Studies, 1956–1962, box 1, NA2.

62. The USIS pamphlet *Sinews of America* provides a cogent example. See USIA Pamphlet Files, USIAA.

63. Testimony from April 23, 1953, *Overseas Information Programs of the United States*, Hearings before a Subcommittee of the Committee on Foreign Relations United States Senate, 83rd Cong., 1st sess., pt. 2, 986–87.

64. *The Pursuit of Happiness*, USIA Film Collection, RG 306, Motion Picture, Sound, and Video Records, Special Media Archives Services Division, NA2.

65. See the testimony of John A. Nalley, May 12, 1953, *Overseas Information Programs of the United States*, Hearings before a Subcommittee of the Committee on Foreign Relations United States Senate, 83rd Cong., 1st sess., pt. 2, 1298–99.

66. USIS Tokyo to USIA Washington, December 14, 1954, RG 306, Office of Research, Country Project Correspondence, 1952–1963, box 13, NA2.

67. "Mail Order Catalogues A Hit Around the World," *New York Times*, October 5, 1955; *Christian Science Monitor*, April 13, 1956; Frank Sullivan, "Our Best Seller Abroad," *New York Times Magazine*, November 13, 1955.

68. Statement of Eric Johnston, March 6, 1953, *Overseas Information Programs of the United States*, Hearings before a Subcommittee of the Committee on Foreign Relations United States Senate, 83rd Cong., 1st sess., pt. 2, 237.

69. See, for example, Memorandum by W. K. Schwinn and A. A. Micocci, April 7, 1950, RG 59, Lot 53D48, International Information Director's Office, box 115, Subject Files, 1949–51, NA2. See also Emergency Plan for Psychological Offensive (USSR), April 11, 1952, RG 59, Lot 52D432, Bureau of Public Affairs, box 5, Office Files of Edward W. Barrett, 1950–51, NA2.

70. Labor Packets, August 1953 and March–April 1954, RG 306, Feature Packets, Recurring Themes, boxes 7, 10, USIAA.

71. See, for example, Notes from the Soviet Provincial Press, May and June 1956, RG 306, Production Division Research Reports, 1956–59, box 1, NA2.

72. Walter Hixson, *Parting the Curtain: Propaganda, Culture, and the Cold War, 1945–1961* (New York: St. Martin's Press, 1997), 133.

73. Loomis to Washburn, November 28, 1955, RG 306, Office of Research Multi Area (World) Project Files, 1953–63, box 1, NA2.

74. Washburn to McClellan, January 3, 1956, RG 306, Office of the Director, box 1, Director's Chronological Files, 1953–1964, Microfilm Reel 10.

75. Extract of Speech by Theodore S. Repplier, October 27, 1955, RG 306, Office of Research, box 1, Multi Area (World) Project Files, 1953–1963, NA2.

76. Excerpt from Speech by Honorable Sherman Adams, December 1, 1955, ibid.

77. "Eisenhower Visits Capitalism Show," *New York Times*, February 14, 1956. For the revised text of the "People's Capitalism" exhibit, see USIA Subject Files on Exhibits and Fairs, "People's Capitalism," USIAA.

78. See, for example, "Agency Comments on People's Capitalism Exhibit," March 6, 1956, RG 306, Office of Research Files, box 1, Multi Area (World) Project Files, 1953–1963, NA2; "Non-Agency Comments on People's Capitalism Exhibit," March 15, 1956, ibid.

79. "U.S. Exhibit Ready to Vie with Reds," *New York Times*, August 19, 1956; "Latins Will View Economy Exhibit," ibid., September 3, 1956.

80. Streibert to All USIS Posts, June 12, 1956, Subject Files on Exhibits and Fairs—People's Capitalism, USIAA.

81. Jean White, "'Derailed' Capitalism Exhibit Re-Emerges," *Washington Post*, September 2, 1958.

82. *People's Capitalism: The United States Economy in Evolution*, USIA Pamphlet Files, USIAA.

83. The nations surveyed were Great Britain, France, Italy, West Germany, and the Netherlands. See West European Attitudes Related to the People's Capitalism Campaign, December 31, 1956, RG 306, Office of Research, Program and Media Studies, 1956–1962, box 1, NA2.

84. Larson to USIS Posts, March 1, 1957, Subject Files on "Disinformation," USIAA.

85. Ibid.

86. A Brief Overview of Recent Survey Findings on the Economic Image of America Abroad, November 1958, RG 306, Office of Research, Program and Media Studies, 1956–62, box 1, NA2.

87. Communist Propaganda and the Brussels Fair, January 22, 1958, RG 306, Office of Research, box 5, Production Division Research Reports, 1956–59, NA2.

CHAPTER 5. "THE RED TARGET IS YOUR HOME": IMAGES OF GENDER
AND THE FAMILY

1. *Air Bulletin*, RG 306, Air Bulletins (General), box 1, NA2.

2. The classic text on these trends is Elaine Tyler May, *Homeward Bound: American Families in the Cold War Era* (New York: Basic Books, 1988). See also K. A. Cuordileone, "'Politics in an Age of Anxiety': Cold War Political Culture and the Crisis in American Masculinity, 1949–1960," *Journal of American History* 87 (September 2000): 515–45.

3. Many scholars examine the gendered language of international relations discourse as a means of assessing the cultural values of U.S. policymakers. See, for example, Frank Costigliola, "'Unceasing Pressure for Penetration:' Gender, Pathology, and Emotion in George Kennan's Formulation of the Cold War," *Journal of American History* 83 (March 1997): 1309–39; Kristin L. Hoganson, *Fighting for American Manhood: How Gender Politics Provoked the Spanish-American and Philippine-American Wars* (New Haven, Conn.: Yale University Press, 1998); Robert D. Dean, "Masculinity as Ideology: John F. Kennedy and the Domestic Politics of Foreign Policy," *Diplomatic History* 22 (Winter 1998): 29–62; Carol Cohn, "Sex and Death in the Rational World of Defense Intellectuals," *Signs: Journal of Women in Culture and Society* 12 (Summer 1987): 687–718; Andrew J. Rotter, "Gender

Relations, Foreign Relations: The United States and South Asia, 1947–1964," *Journal of American History* 81 (September 1994): 518–42; Emily S. Rosenberg, "'Foreign Affairs' After World War II," *Diplomatic History* 18 (Winter 1994): 59–70; Michelle Mart, "Tough Guys and American Cold War Policy: Images of Israel, 1948–1960," *Diplomatic History* 20 (Summer 1996): 357–80; Emily S. Rosenberg, *Financial Missionaries to the World: The Politics and Culture of Dollar Diplomacy,* 1900–1930 (Cambridge, Mass.: Harvard University Press, 1999). Others attempt to determine whether men and women working in the foreign policy establishment approach international relations questions differently. Examples include Edward Crapol, ed., *Women and American Women Policy,* 2nd ed. (Wilmington, Del.: Scholarly Resources, 1992) and Rhodri Jeffreys-Jones, *Changing Differences: Women and the Shaping of American Foreign Policy,* 1917–1994 (New Brunswick, N.J.: Rutgers University Press, 1995).

4. USIA remained male-dominated for decades. In March 2000, 1,100 women won a class-action lawsuit against USIA and Voice of America, the radio broadcasting arm of the agency. The women claimed that they were denied employment opportunities while working at the agency between 1974 and 1984. After a twenty-three-year legal battle, the USIA and Voice of America settled the suit for $508 million—the largest award for job discrimination in U.S. history. See *Washington Post,* March 23, 2000.

5. Department of State, *Bulletin* 13, 338 (December 16, 1945): 951.

6. Ambassador to the Soviet Union (Harriman) to Byrnes, January 20, 1946, *FRUS, 1946,* 6: 676–78.

7. *Russia the Reactionary,* 1949, RG 59, Lot 53D47, Records Relating to International Information Activities, 1938–1953, Files of William T. Stone, box 1, NA2.

8. *The Free World Speaks,* 1951–52, USIA Pamphlet Files, USIAA.

9. *Democracy Begins in the Home,* May 1953, Women's Packet, RG 306, Feature Packets—Recurring Themes, box 16, NA2.

10. See *Overseas Information Programs of the United States,* Hearings before a Subcommittee of the Committee on Foreign Relations, United States Senate, 83rd Cong., 1st sess., 1486.

11. *The Women in Communist Countries,* USIA Pamphlet Files, USIAA.

12. See, for example, March 1, 1960 report, RG 306, USIA Requestor Only reports, 1956–1962, box 2, NA2.

13. Valentin Zorin, "A Clumsy Trick of American Propaganda," November 15, 1951, Iron Curtain Press and Radio Comment on the Voice of America, RG 306, Reports and Related Studies, 1948–1953, box 9, NA2.

14. March 21, 1951, *Labor Air Bulletin,* RG 306, *Air Bulletin,* box 2, NA2.

15. October 1953, Women's Packet #7, RG 306, Feature Packets, Recurring Themes, box 17, NA2.

16. An Analysis of the Principal Psychological Vulnerabilities in the USSR and of the Principal Assets Available to the US for Their Exploitation, 1950, RG 59, Lot 52D432, Bureau of Public Affairs, Office Files of Edward W. Barrett, 1950–1951, box 5, NA2. For the Soviet response to these trends, see Susan E. Reid, "Cold War in the Kitchen: Gender and Consumption in the Khrushchev Thaw," *Slavic Review* 61, 2 (2002): 211–52.

17. "Women Workers in U.S. Protected by Many Safeguards," January 23, 1952, *Labor Air Bulletin*, RG 306, *Air Bulletin*, box 2, NA2.

18. Hulten to Gould, March 20, 1951, RG 59, Lot 52D432, Bureau of Public Affairs, Office Files of Edward W. Barrett, 1950–51, box 2, NA2.

19. August 1954, Women's Packet #17, RG 306, Feature Packets, Recurring Themes, box 18, NA2.

20. Media and Communication and the Free World as Seen by Hungarian Refugees, March 3, 1953, RG 306, Office of Research, Reports, and Related Studies, 1948–1953, box 31, NA2.

21. Secretary of State to Certain American Diplomatic and Consular Officers, July 20, 1948, United States Information Policy with Regard to Anti-American Propaganda, RG 59, Records Relating to International Information Activities, 1938–1953, Lot 53D47, William T. Stone Files, box 3, NA2.

22. Iron Curtain Radio Comment on VOA, Report #44, March 17, 1950, RG 306, Reports and Related Studies, 1948–1953, box 8, NA2.

23. November 8, 1956, Present and Potential Communist Use of Television as an International Propaganda Medium, RG 306, Production Division, Research Reports, 1956–59, box 1, NA2.

24. Psychological Offensive vis-à-vis the USSR—Objective, Tasks, and Themes," undated, RG 59, Lot 52D432, Bureau of Public Affairs, Office Files of Assistant Secretary of State Edward W. Barrett, 1950–51, box 5, NA2.

25. Andrew Burling, Political Commentary, "'Lukewarm Love' in Communist China," November 28, 1951, RG 306, VOA Daily Content Reports and Script Translations, 1950–1955, box 31, NA2.

26. Edward W. Jelenko, "Such Trash as Love," April 10, 1952, Operations Intelligence Summary #215, RG 306, VOA Daily Broadcast Content Reports and Script Translations, 1950–1955, box 48, NA2.

27. The Communist Marriage Law, Chinese Branch—Mandarin Service, February 16, 1953, RG 306, VOA Daily Broadcast Content Reports and Script Translations, 1950–1955, box 64, NA2.

28. Musical Requests for Red Dignitaries, VOA Polish Service, November 21, 1954, RG 306, VOA Daily Content Reports and Script Translations, 1950–1955, box 75, NA2.

29. VOA Persian transcript, "The American Family," April 1, 1952, RG 306, Voice of America Daily Broadcast Content Reports and Script Translations, 1950–1955, box 38, NA2.

30. VOA Chinese transcripts, March 2 and 4, 1951, RG 306, Voice of America Daily Broadcast Content Reports and Script Translations, 1950–1955, box 14, NA2.

31. VOA Russian transcript, June 15, 1952, RG 306, Voice of America Daily Broadcast Content Reports and Script Translations, 1950–1955, box 44, NA2.

32. "Visitor to USSR Reports on Soviet Woman's Status," August 1953, Women's Packet #6, RG 306, Feature Packets, Recurring Themes, box 17, NA2.

33. February 1955, Women's Packet #23, RG 306, Feature Packets, Recurring Themes, box 19, NA2.

34. *Communism and the Family*, USIA Pamphlet Files, USIAA.

35. *Korea My Home*, 1953, USIA Pamphlet, USIAA.

36. Poster for USIS film *This Is My Home*, USIA Pamphlet Files, USIAA.

37. *When the Communists Came! The True Story of a Communist Village*, 1949, RG 59, Lot 52D36, Records Relating to International Information Activities, 1938–1953, box 43, NA2.

38. *When the Communists Came*, USIA Film Collection, RG 306, Motion Picture, Sound, and Video Records, Special Media Archives Services Division, NA2.

39. On U.S. concerns about international communist activities directed at the young, see Acting Secretary of State (Webb) to Certain Diplomatic and Consular Offices, June 21, 1949, *FRUS*, 5: 836–38; "The East Berlin Student and Youth Festival," undated, RG 59, Records Relating to International Information Activities, Lot 53D47, William T. Stone Files, box 23, NA2.

40. Bowman to Micocci and Kohler, November 27, 1950, box 8, File on Youth, 1950–1951, USIA/Freedom of Information Act Request #306–65–0175.

41. VOA Russia transcript, October 18, 1951, RG 306, Voice of America Daily Content Reports and Scripts, 1950–1955, box 28, NA2.

42. Youth Packet #1, April 1953, RG 306, Feature Packets—Recurring Themes, box 1, NA2.

43. Youth Packet #19, October 1954, RG 306, Feature Packets—Recurring Themes, box 3, NA2.

44. *Building the Community Through Family Life*, USIA Pamphlets, USIAA.

45. Cecilia King, "Voice of America Chooses Jerseyans," December 23, 1951, *Newark Sunday News*.

46. "Of Women's Interest," No. 31, Chinese Section, July 14, 1952, RG 306, VOA Daily Broadcast Content Reports and Script Translations, 1950–1955, box 48, NA2.

47. S.C. Chen, "The American Way of Life," Chinese Section, July 18, 1952, RG 306, VOA Daily Broadcast Content Reports and Script Translations, 1950–1955, box 51, NA2.

48. "Many U.S. Husbands Help Wives with Grocery Shopping," July 1953, Women's Packet, RG 306, Feature Packets, Recurring Themes, box 17, NA2.

49. *Smalltown U.S.A.*, USIA Film Collection, RG 306, Motion Picture, Sound, and Video Records, Special Media Archives Services Division, NA2.

50. "A Visit with Mrs. Forster," April 1953, Women's Packet #1, RG 306, Feature Packets, Recurring Themes, box 16, NA2.

51. *Women and the Community*, USIA Film Collection, RG 306, Motion Picture, Sound, and Video Records, Special Media Archives Services Division, NA2.

52. Albert G. Pickerell to Edward Barrett, July 17, 1951, RG 59, Lot 52D365, Records Relating to International Information Activities, 1938–1953, box 60, NA2.

53. Ibid.

54. *The Soviet Woman Under Communism*, USIA Pamphlet Files, USIAA.

55. Ibid.

56. On the Soviet characterizations of American women, see Unsigned letter to Alice K. Leopold, Assistant to the Secretary of Labor, March 2, 1960, RG 306, Requestor Only Reports, 1956–62, box 2, NA2.

57. See Bill Danch cartoon from *Independent Woman*, Women's Packet—June 1954, RG 306, Feature Packets, Recurring Themes, box 18, NA2.

58. On these contrasts, see, for example, Robert L. Griswold, "The Flabby American, the Body, and the Cold War," in *A Shared Experience: Men, Women, and the History of Gender*, ed. Laura McCall and Donald Yacovone (New York: New York University Press, 1998), 321–48.

59. "Choosing the Central Characters," Common Denominator Series, April 20, 1951, RG 306, Office of Research, Reports and Related Studies, 1948–1953, box 35, NA2.

60. "Beauty Not Bad Propaganda," *New York Post*, February 9, 1951.

61. Cover Sheet for "Home Is What You Make It," May 1954, Women's Packet #13, RG 306, Feature Packets, Recurring Themes, box 18, NA2.

62. Cover sheet to Public Affairs Officers, "Young Dress Designers Win Top Prizes for Sewing Efforts," March 1956, Women's Packet #35, RG 306, Feature Packets, Recurring Themes, box 5, NA2.

63. Kirk to Acheson, September 8, 1950, *FRUS, 1950*, 4: 1245.

64. Working Group Discussion, September 21, 1950, RG 59, Lot 52–202, Records of Assistant Secretary of State for Public Affairs, 1947–1950, Policy Papers and Meetings, 1949–1950, Public Relations Working Group, 1950, box 5, NA2.

65. *Women in the United States*, August 1953, Women's Packet #1, RG 306, Feature Packets, Recurring Themes, box 1, NA2.

66. "Soviet Practices Refute Propaganda on Equality of the Sexes," October 1953, Women's Packet #7, RG 306, Feature Packets, Recurring Themes, box 17, NA2. Virtually every monthly edition of the Women's Packet included an article on American women's political activism. See ibid., boxes 13–21.

67. *American Working Women*, USIA Film Collection, RG 306, Motion Picture, Sound, and Video Records, Special Media Archives Services Division, NA2.

68. Radio Programs for Women, July 1–September 30, 1949, Information Service Division, RG 59, Lot 53D47, Records Relating to International Information Activities, 1938–1953, William T. Stone Files, box 4, NA2. American officials took similar actions in Japan. See Susan J. Pharr, "The Politics of Women's Rights," in *Democratizing Japan: The Allied Occupation*, ed. Robert E. Ward and Sakamoto Yoshikazu (Honolulu: University of Hawaii Press, 1987), 221–52.

69. Problems of Film Production in Underdeveloped Countries, January 1953, RG 306, Office of Research, Reports and Related Studies, 1948–1953, box 34, NA2.

70. USIA Basic Guidance and Planning Paper No. 6, March 31, 1959, USIA Subject Files, USIAA.

71. USIA Basic Guidance and Planning Paper No. 12, August 13, 1953, USIA Subject Files, USIAA.

72. Ibid.

73. Ibid.

74. On the tumult of the 1960s, see Maurice Isserman and Michael Kazin, *America Divided: The Civil War of the 1960s* (New York: Oxford University Press, 2000).

CHAPTER 6. "A LYNCHING SHOULD BE REPORTED WITHOUT COMMENT":
IMAGES OF RACE RELATIONS

1. Department of State to Embassy in Ghana, October 9, 1957, *FRUS, 1955–1957*, 18: 378–79. For more on African diplomats' battles with U.S. segregation, see Renee Romano, "No Diplomatic Immunity: African Diplomats, the State Department, and Civil Rights, 1961–1964," *Journal of American History* (September 2000): 546–79.

2. Embassy in Ghana to the Department of State, October 10, 1957, *FRUS, 1955–1957*, 18: 380–81.

3. Mary Dudziak, "Desegregation as a Cold War Imperative," *Stanford Law Review* 41 (November 1988): 61–120. Historians including Mary Dudziak, Thomas Borstelmann, Carol Anderson, Brenda Gayle Plummer, Penny Von Eschen, and Michael Krenn show clear linkages among U.S. diplomacy, civil rights activism, domestic politics, and American national identity. See Mary Dudziak, *Cold War Civil Rights: Race and the Image of American Democracy* (Princeton, N.J.: Princeton University Press, 2002); Thomas Borstelmann, *The Cold War and the Color Line: American Race Relations in the Global Arena* (Cambridge, Mass.: Harvard University Press, 2001); Carol Anderson, *Eyes off the Prize: The United Nations and the African American Struggle for Human Rights, 1944–1955* (New York: Cambridge University Press, 2003); Brenda Gayle Plummer, *Rising Wind: Black Americans and U.S. Foreign Affairs, 1935–1960* (Chapel Hill: University of North Carolina Press, 1996); Penny Von Eschen, *Race Against Empire: Black Americans and Anticolonialism, 1937–1957* (Ithaca, N.Y.: Cornell University Press, 1997); Michael Krenn, *Black Diplomacy: African Americans and the State Department, 1945–1969* (Armonk, N.Y.: M.E. Sharpe, 1999).

4. Intelligence Research Report, February 5, 1947, Lot 61 F271, Racial Issues, box 4, folder on Racial Issues & Propaganda, USIAA. FOIA Request #306 62A185.

5. "The White and the Black," *Vokrug Sveta*, No. 1, January 1947 quoted in 'Soviet State on the Racial Question in the US, April 30, 1951, Lot 61F 271, box 4, Racial Issues, folder on Racial Issues and Propaganda, USIAA. FOIA# 306 62A185.

6. *Sovetskove Gosundaratvo i Pravo*, No. 6, 1948, Moscow Radio, January 22, 1949, and Radio Khabarovsk, February 3, 1949 quoted in Soviet State on The Racial Question in the US, April 30, 1951, Lot 61F 271, box 4, Racial Issues, folder on Racial Issues and Propaganda, USIAA. FOIA# 306 62A185.

7. "Indians" in Soviet State on The Racial Question in the US, April 30, 1951, Lot 61F 271, box 4, Racial Issues, folder on Racial Issues and Propaganda, USIAA. FOIA# 306 62A185.

8. Foreign Attitudes and Communist or Other Propaganda on the Negro Question, April 24, 1952, Lot 61F 271, Racial Issues, box 4, folder on Racial Issues and Propaganda, USIAA. FOIA# 306 62A 185.

9. Division of International Press and Publications—OII, November 1948, Lot 61 f 271, box 4—Racial Issues, folder on Advancement of the Negro in the U.S., USIAA. FOIA #306 62A 185.

10. *The Negro in American Life*, Howland Sargeant Papers, box 4, file on Assistant Secretary of State for Public Affairs, 1952, HSTL.

11. Ibid.

12. Ibid.

13. Ibid.

14. Ibid.

15. Ibid.

16. Melinda M. Schwenk-Borrell, "Selling Democracy: The U.S. Information Agency's Visual Portrayal of American Race Relations, 1953–1976" (Ph.D. dissertation, University of Pennsylvania, 2004), 75–76.

17. Yugoslav Report from America, May 20, 1950, RG 306, VOA Daily Content Reports and Script Translations, 1950–1955, box 3, NA2.

18. Research on Racial Minorities in the U.S., June 23, 1953, Lot 61 F 271, box 4, Racial Issues, folder on Minorities in the U.S., USIAA. FOIA# 306 62A185.

19. The Minority Question in U.S. Propaganda, June 26, 1953, Minorities, box 8, USIAA. FOIA# 306651075.

20. Commentary, VOA Chinese Branch, May 18, 1954, RG 306, VOA Daily Content Reports and Script Translations, 1950–1955, box 73, NA2.

21. "Equal Education for All," June 1954, Youth Packet #15, RG 306, Feature Packets, Recurring Themes, box 2, NA2;

22. "U.S. Women's Groups Support Racial Integration in Schools," October 1954, Women's Packet #19, ibid., box 19, NA2

23. Schwenk-Borrell, "Selling Democracy," 78. On USIA's recognition of the inflammatory nature of photography on civil rights issues, see Research on Racial Minorities in the U.S., June 23, 1953, Lot 61 F 271, box 4, Racial Issues, folder on Minorities in the U.S., USIAA. FOIA# 306 62A185.

24. Basic Planning Paper on Minorities, No. 5, December 4, 1958, USIA Subject Files, USIAA

25. Schwenk-Borrell, "Selling Democracy," 209–39.

26. French Attitudes Toward the United States, September 11, 1953, RG 306, Office of Research, Special Reports, 1953–1963, box 2, NA2.

27. *Communicating with the Soviet People*, RG 306, Office of Research, Special Reports, 1953–1963, box 19, NA2.

28. *A Study of USIA Operating Assumptions*, vol. 3, TC19–20, December 1954, RG 306, Office of Research, Special Reports, 1953–1963, box 7, NA2.

29. "The American Soldier #2," VOA Indonesia Desk, undated, RG 306—VOA Daily Content Reports and Script Translations, 19501–955, box 13, NA2.

30. See, for example, "George Washington Carver," VOA Vietnamese Service, April 13, 1951, RG 306—VOA Daily Content Reports and Script Translations, 19501–955, box 15, NA2.

31. Hulten to Paynter, June 18, 1951, RG 59, Lot 52D432, Bureau of Public Affairs, Office Files of Assistant Secretary of State for Public Affairs Edward Barrett, 1950–1951, box 2, NA2.

32. Hickenlooper testimony found in U.S. Senate. Committee on Foreign Relations, *Overseas Information Programs of the United States,* Hearings before a Subcommittee on Foreign Relations, United States Senate, 82nd Cong., pt. II, March 6–May 13, 1953, 239.

33. *What Are the Facts About Negroes in the United States?*, USIA Pamphlet Files, USIAA.

34. Experiments in Pre-Testing Printed Materials, August 1954, RG 306, Office of Research, Special Reports, 1953–1963, box 6, NA2.

35. "VOA Speaks for Wall Street's America, Not Lincoln's," February 24, 1950, Iron Curtain Radio Comment on VOA, Report 41, RG 306, Reports and Related Studies, 1948–1953, box 8, NA2.

36. Weekly Information Policy Guide, August 9, 1950, RG 59, Lot 53D47, Records Relating to International Information Activities, 1938–1953, William T. Stone Files, box 4, NA2.

37. "Visitor Finds Negroes Active in U.S. Labor Movement," January 2, 1952, RG 306, Air Bulletin, box 2, NA2.

38. *An African Looks at the American Negro*, USIA Pamphlet Files, USIAA

39. The USIA based the survey on interviews with approximately 800 people in each of the following countries: Great Britain, West Germany, France, Italy, and the Netherlands. See Opinion about U.S. Treatment of Negroes, July 24, 1956, RG 306, Office of Research, Public Opinion Barometer Reports, 1955–1962, Western Europe, box 4, NA2.

40. *New York Times*, September 11, 1957.

41. Ibid.

42. *Communist Propaganda: A Fact Book, 1957–1958*, RG 306, Office of Research, Special Reports. 1953–1963, box 15, NA2.

43. In January 1958, the USIA concluded that Little Rock had "no major effect" on Western European views of U.S. race relations, which were already in "a very depressed state" as a result of the Autherine Lucy and Emmett Till incidents. See Post-Little Rock Opinion on the Treatment of Negroes in the U.S., January 1958, RG 306, Office of Research, Program and Media Studies, 1956–1962, box 1, NA2.

44. The Indian Image of the United States: A Preliminary View, April 17, 1958, RG 306, RG 306, Office of Research, Production Division Research Reports, 1956–1959, box 5, NA2.

45. The World Looks at Little Rock: An Interim Report, undated, RG 306, Office of Research, Special Reports, 1953–1963, box 14, NA2.

46. Memorandum of a Telephone Conversation between the Secretary of State and the Attorney General, September 24, 1957, *FRUS, 1955–1957*, 9: 612–13.

47. *New York Times*, February 28, 1958.

48. *Shreveport Journal*, February 28, 1958, found in USIAA clipping files, USIAA.

49. Patterson to Benton, Benton to Patterson, January 12, 24, 1946, RG 59, Lot 53D47, Records of the Assistant Secretary of State for Public Affairs, 1945–1950, Office Files of William B. Benton, Correspondence, 1945–1948, box 11, NA2.

50. The Flow of Information on American Foreign Policy to Negro Americans, February 28, 1950, RG 59, Lot 52–202, Records of Assistant Secretary of Public Affairs, Policy Papers and Meetings, 1949–1950, box 4, NA2.

51. *The Afro-American,* July 15, 1950, 14, USIA clipping files, USIAA.

52. For White's testimony, see *Expanded International Information and Education Program,* Hearings before the United Senate Foreign Relations Committee, 81st Cong., 2nd sess., July 5–7, 1950, 160–61. On June 30, 1951, Assistant Secretary of State Edward W. Barrett thanked White and the NAACP for helping the State Department to combat "anti-American propaganda based on real or reported racial problems in this country." See Barrett to White, June 30, 1951, RG 59, Lot 52D432, Bureau of Public Affairs, Office Files of Edward W. Barrett, 1950–1951, box 3, NA2.

53. Discards-FRCS, Lot 68A1414 (Benton Files), Box 1043, USIAA files, USIAA.

54. See. for example, Joseph V. Baker's letter to USIA Director George Allen deriding the absence of African-Americans on the agency's domestic advisory committees, Allen to Baker, October 10, 1958, Agency History, USIAA.

55. See, for example, Mary L. Dudziak, "Josephine Baker, Racial Protest, and the Cold War," *Journal of American History* 81 (September 1994): 543–70.

56. For the testimonials of Hughes and Aptheker, see U.S. Senate, Hearings before the Permanent Subcommittee on Investigations of the Committee on Government Operations, *State Department Information Programs-Information Centers,* 83rd Cong., 1st sess., 1953, 73–83, 374–83.

57. "Wilkins' Appointment Highlights Progress of American Negro," April 1953, Labor Packet, RG 306, Feature Packets, Recurring Subjects, box 8, NA2.

58. Cover Sheet for "Harry Belafonte, Folk Singer," March 1956, Youth Packet #35, RG 306, Feature Packets, Recurring Themes, box 5, NA2.

59. "Porgy and Bess," *New York Times,* October 1, 1955.

60. See Dudziak, "Josephine Baker, Racial Protest, and the Cold War;" Lisa E. Davenport, "Jazz, Race, and American Cultural Exchange: An International Study of U.S. Cultural Diplomacy, 1954–1968" (Ph.D. dissertation, Georgetown University, 2002); Penny Von Eschen, *Satchmo Blows up the World: Jazz Ambassadors Play the Cold War* (Cambridge, Mass.: Harvard University Press, 2004). On the international role of black athletes, see Damion Lamar Thomas, "'The Good Negroes': African-American Athletes and The Cultural Cold War, 1945–1968" (Ph.D. dissertation, University of California, Los Angeles, 2002).

61. Schwenk-Borrell, "Selling Democracy," 100–113.

62. Ibid., 14.

63. Treatment of Minorities in the United States—Impact on Our Foreign Relations, December 1958, Lot 61 F 271, box 4, Racial Issues, file on Minorities in the U.S., USIAA, FOIA# 306 62A185.

CONCLUSION: THE COSTS AND LIMITS OF SELLING "AMERICA"

Epigraph: Quoted in Robert Brent Toplin, *Michael Moore's Fahrenheit 9/11: How One Film Divided a Nation* (Lawrence: University Press of Kansas, 2006), 11.

1. Hixson, *Parting the Curtain*, 227

2. The communists jammed Voice of America (VOA), Radio Free Europe (RFE), and Radio Liberation (RL, a CIA-run network targeting the USSR and later renamed Radio Liberty) for much of the Cold War. Although the Soviets stopped jamming VOA in 1963, they reinstituted the practice following the suppression of the Prague Spring in 1968. Jamming ceased again in 1973 in deference to détente, but resumed following the 1980 Soviet invasion of Afghanistan. The Soviets blocked RFE and RL throughout the Cold War. See Walter Hixson, *Parting the Curtain: Propaganda: Culture, and the Cold War* (New York: St. Martin's, 1997), 229.

3. On the end of the Cold War, see Richard Ned Lebow, *We All Lost the Cold War* (Princeton, N.J.: Princeton University Press, 1994); John Lewis Gaddis, *The United States and the End of the Cold War* (New York: Oxford University Press, 1992); Michael J. Hogan, ed. *The End of the Cold War: Its Meanings and Implications* (Cambridge: Cambridge University Press, 1992).

4. Peter G. Peterson, "Public Diplomacy and the War on Terrorism," *Foreign Affairs* 81 (September/October 2002): 93.

5. Dan Gilgoff and Jay Tolson, "Losing Friends? The Departure of a Top U.S. Diplomat Renews Questions about How to Fight Anti-Americanism," *U.S. News & World Report* (March 17, 2003): 40.

6. For recent assessments of global attitudes toward the United States, see The Pew Global Attitudes Project, *Global Opinion: The Spread of Anti-Americanism*, January 24, 2005, http://pewresearch.org/assets/files/trends2005-global.pdf ; The Pew Global Attitudes Project, *Views of a Changing World 2003*, June 3, 2003, http://people-press.org/reports/display.php3?ReportID=185. See also Forum on Public Diplomacy, *American Quarterly* 57 (June 2005): 309–54.

7. State Department and Related Agencies, FY2005 Appropriations and FY2006 Request, *Congressional Research Service Report for Congress*, February 11, 2005; U.S. Advisory Commission on Public Diplomacy, *Building America's Public Diplomacy Through a Reformed Structure and Additional Resources*, 2002, http://www.state.gov/r/adcompd/rls/

8. Estimated costs of the war on terrorism include the wars in Afghanistan and Iraq and come from a January 2006 Congressional Budget Office report. Martin Wolk, "Cost of Iraq War Could Surpass $1 Trillion," March 17, 2006, MSNBC.com, http://msnbc.msn.com/id/11880954/; Peterson, "Public Diplomacy the War on Terrorism," 93.

9. Scholars have devoted much attention to the ways that private individuals and public officials of diverse backgrounds and political persuasions have defined, deployed, and disputed the civic values central to American national identity. See, for example, Gary Gerstle, *American Crucible: Race and Nation in the Twentieth Century* (Princeton, N.J.: Princeton University Press, 2001); Wendy Lynn Wall, "The Idea of America: Democracy

and the Dilemmas of Difference, 1935–1965" (Ph.D. dissertation, Stanford University, 1998); Philip Gleason, *Speaking of Diversity: Language and Ethnicity in Twentieth-Century America* (Baltimore: Johns Hopkins University Press, 1992).

10. Charlotte Beers biography, U.S. Department of State, http://www.state.gov/r/pa/ei/biog/5319.htm.

11. *The Role of Public Diplomacy in Support of the Anti-Terrorism Campaign*, Hearing before the Committee on International Relations House of Representatives, 107th Cong., 1st sess., October 10, 2001, Serial 107–47. See also *The Message Is America: Rethinking U.S. Public Diplomacy*, Hearing before the House Committee on International Relations House of Representatives, 107th Cong., 1st sess., November 14, 2001, Serial 107–54. In spring 1997, the U.S. Advisory Commission on Public Diplomacy endorsed a restructuring of the U.S. foreign affairs bureaucracy, an idea first proposed by President Bill Clinton and Senate Foreign Relations Committee Chairman Jesse Helms (R-N.C.). Supporters of the consolidation argued that moving the USIA into the State Department would place information and cultural activities "at the heart of U.S. foreign policy." Congress passed the Foreign Affairs Reform and Restructuring Act of 1998 authorizing the consolidation of USIA, the Arms Control and Disarmament Agency, and the Agency of International Development into the Department of State. On October 1, 1999, the USIA was abolished. A new Office of International Programs in the State Department assumed control of most overseas information programs. A new State Department Bureau of Educational and Cultural Affairs now administers most exchanges including the Fulbright program. An independent government body, the International Broadcasting Bureau took over USIA's broadcasting elements including the Voice of America, Radio and TV Martí, and the WORLDNET Television and Film Service. USIA's Foreign Press Centers moved into the State Department's Office of Public Affairs and the USIA Office of Research and Media Reaction became part of State's Bureau of Intelligence and Research. In 2000, the U.S. Advisory Commission on Public Diplomacy concluded that the USIA-State consolidation "has to date a mixed record." While some former USIA employees enjoyed new opportunities for professional advancement, many expressed frustration with the complex bureaucracy of the Department of State. The Commission claimed it was too early to assess the impact of the merger on U.S. foreign policy. See United States Advisory Commission on Public Diplomacy, *Consolidation of USIA into the State Department: An Assessment After One Year*, October 2000, http://www.state.gov/r/adcompd/rls/. Five years later, four former USIA directors were not so ambivalent. Blasting the decision to disband USIA, they called for "the creation of a U.S. Agency for Public Diplomacy, linked to the State Department but with an autonomous structure and budget." See Leonard H. Marks, Charles Z. Wick, Bruce Gelb, and Henry E. Catto, "America Needs a Voice Abroad," *Washington Post*, February 26, 2005, A19.

12. Joseph S. Nye first coined the term "soft power" in the late 1980s. Defined as "the ability to get what you want through attraction rather coercion or payments," Nye attributes soft power to "the attractiveness of a country's culture, political ideals, and polices." See Joseph S. Nye, *Soft Power: The Means to Success in World Politics* (New York: Public

Affairs, 2004), x. See also Robert Satloff, *The Battle of Ideas in the War on Terror: Essays on U.S. Public Diplomacy in the Middle East* (Washington, D.C.: Washington Institute for Near East Policy, 2004); Liam Kennedy and Scott Lucas, "Enduring Freedom: Public Diplomacy and U.S. Foreign Policy," *American Quarterly* 57 (June 2005): 309–34.

13. *The Role of Public Diplomacy*, 15.

14. Vanessa O'Connell, "Veteran Beers Helps U.S. Craft Its Message," *Wall Street Journal*, October 15, 2001, B12.

15. *The International Campaign Against Terrorism*, Hearing before the Committee on Foreign Relations United States Senate, 107th Cong., 1st sess., October 25, 2001, 11, 25.

16. Rance Crain, "Charlotte Beers and the Selling of America," *AdAge.com*, November 05, 2001, http://www.adage.com/news.cms?newsId=33340.

17. Ibid.

18. Margaret Carlson, "Can Charlotte Beers Sell Uncle Sam? *Time* Online Edition, Wednesday, November 14, 2001, http://www.time.com/time/columnist/carlson/article/0,9565,184536,00.html

19. *Building America's Public Diplomacy*, 3–5.

20. Abdalla Hassan, "U.S. Radio Broadcasts Vie for the Hearts and Minds of Arab Youth," *World Press Review Online*, September 26, 2002, http://www.worldpress.org/Mideast/739.cfm

21. *Alhurra* is operated by the Middle Eastern Television Network, Inc., a nonprofit corporation funded by the U.S. Congress through the Broadcasting Board of Governors, the entity that also coordinates Voice of America, Radio Sawa, Radio Farda, Radio Free Europe/Radio Liberty, Radio Free Asia, and Radio/TV Martí. On the launch of *Alhurra*, see http://www.bbg.gov/_bbg_news.cfm?articleID=103&mode=general.

22. Online Focus Under Secretary Charlotte Beers, January 2003, *NewsHour with Jim Lehrer* Transcript, *Online NewsHour*, http://www.pbs.org/newshour/media/public_diplomacy/beers_1–03.html.

23. For a positive appraisal of the Shared Values Initiative, see Alice Kendrick and Jami A. Fullerton, "Advertising as Public Diplomacy: Attitude Change among International Audiences," *Journal of Advertising Research* 44 (September/October 2004): 297–311. For a sharply dissenting view, see Lawrence Pintak, "Dangerous Delusions: Advertising Nonsense about Advertising America," August 27, 2004, Common Dreams News Center, http://www.commondreams.org/views04/0827–07.htm.

24. Steven R. Weisman, "Powell Aide Quits Position Promoting U.S.," *New York Times*, March 4, 2003, A12; Gilgoff and Tolson, "Losing Friends?"

25. Christopher Marquis, "Effort to Promote U.S. Falls Short, Critics Say," *New York Times*, December 29, 2003; Report of the Advisory Group on Public Diplomacy for the Arab and Muslim World, *Changing Minds, Winning Peace*, October 1, 2003, http://www.state.gov/documents/organization/24882.pdf.

26. The Pew Global Attitudes Project, *A Year of Iraq War Mistrust of America in Europe Ever Higher, Muslim Anger Persists*, March 16, 2004, Web site of The Pew Research Center for the People and the Press, http://people-press.org/reports/pdf/206.pdf.

27. Christopher Marquis, "Promoter of U.S. Image Quits for Wall St. Job," *New York Times*, April 30, 2004.

28. Peter Baker, "Karen Hughes to Work on the World's View of U.S.," *Washington Post*, March 12, 2005; U.S. Department of State Press Release on Announcement of Nominations of Karen P. Hughes as Under Secretary of State for Public Diplomacy and Public Affairs and Dina Powell as Assistant Secretary of State for Educational and Cultural Affairs, March 14, 2005, http://www.state.gov/secretary/rm/2005/43385.htm. Hughes officially took office in September 2005.

29. Brain Knowlton, "Hughes, Loyal Bush Advisor, Leaving State Department," *New York Times*, October 31, 2007.

30. Pew Global Attitudes Project, *Global Unease with Major World Powers*, June 27, 2007, http://pewglobal.org/reports/display.php?ReportID=256.

INDEX

ACKNOWLEDGMENTS

THE YEARS I have spent working on this project have coincided with stunning transformations in world history: the sudden, peaceful end of the Cold War, globalization, 9/11. Each has forced me to reevaluate the role of propaganda in U.S. foreign relations. Those who have labored in this field know firsthand how daunting the scope of documentation is. So, before the global paradigm shifts yet again or the U.S. government releases another avalanche of pertinent papers, let me express my tremendous gratitude and relief at the end of this endeavor.

Throughout my academic career, I have been blessed with the finest of mentors. At the University of Georgia, William M. Leary changed the course of my life. I entered my junior year resigned to becoming yet another lemming heading to law school. But Bill's Honors seminar in U.S. history inspired me to take another path. Over the next two years, he spent countless hours honing my writing, shepherding me to professional functions, helping me select graduate programs, and most important, being a wonderful friend. It saddens me greatly that he did not live to see this book's publication. The world is a lesser place without his humor, intelligence, and kindness. Thanks to Bill, I also had the great fortune of working with William Stueck. While the experience wasn't always pleasant (Stueck treatment, anyone?), he made me a much better historian—and helped me grow the thick skin one often needs to survive in academe. Though Bill has certainly mellowed over the years, his support of me and my career has not ebbed at all. His productivity, political commitment, and forthrightness remain a great inspiration.

At the University of Virginia, my good fortune continued. Mel Leffler was and is an extraordinary advisor—and an extraordinary man. His integrity, brilliance, and dedication—in all areas of his life—have provided a wonderful model for how to be a great professor while remaining a great human being. I could never adequately express how much his faith in me has mattered. Ann J. Lane and Nelson Lichtenstein's fusion of activism and innovative scholarship greatly animate me too. They are also both generous and supportive friends. Finally, I must acknowledge the many superb colleagues who made the UVa years special and who remain vibrant parts of my life. Thank you Charlene and James Lewis, Bill McAllister, and Jessica Gienow-Hecht.

This project would not have been possible without the aide of a small army of archivists and researchers. At the Truman Library, Liz Safly's lovely demeanor and Dennis Bilger's incomparable skills made each day in the research room a pleasure. At the USIA Archives, Martin Manning endured a yearlong siege on his collection and Leslie Jensen performed declassification miracles. At the National Archives at College Park, Cary Conn and David Pfeiffer provided insightful and good-natured assistance through my efforts to amass my own personal version of RG 306. Sameer Popat proved an insightful and speedy photo researcher. At the Eisenhower Library, David Haight and Bonita Mulanax's heroic declassification team made a cold winter in Abilene worthwhile.

My colleagues at Oklahoma State University are exceptionally supportive. Special thanks to Elizabeth Williams, Jeff Cooper, and Lesley Rimmel. The graduate students in my readings seminar on modern U.S. history, especially Tally Fugate and Brett Billings, provided valuable and insightful commentary on the manuscript. I am also grateful to Jami Fullerton and Stacy Takacs for sharing their fine work on post-9/11 public diplomacy and media.

I have lost count of the many remarkable scholars who have critiqued and shaped my work in cultural diplomacy. Frank Costigliola, Mike Willard, Helen Laville, Scott Lucas, John Jenks, Melinda Schwenk-Borrell, Walter Hixson, Jessica Geinow-Hecht, Richard Pells, Bob Dean, David Krugler, Michael Krenn, Susan Brewer, and Bob Beisner have all provided invaluable feedback and encouragement.

This work would not have been possible without the generosity of financial assistance of several entities. I am indebted to the Harry S. Truman Institute, the Oklahoma Humanities Council, the OSU College of Arts and Sciences, and the OSU Department of History for their research support. I am especially obliged to the Oregon State Center for the Humanities, where I spent the 2002–2003 academic year as a residential fellow. My time in beautiful Corvallis was not only extremely productive but also exceptionally fun thanks to David Robinson, Wendy Madar, Franny Nudleman, David Holton, and Janet Winston.

I feel quite lucky to have had the opportunity to work with Robert Lockhart and the University of Pennsylvania Press. Bob has been a patient, caring editor whose enthusiasm for this project has never flagged.

I must also thank those who make my life a rich place outside the study and the library. Victoria Allison is a never-ending source of thought-provoking conversation and boundless love. Felicia Lopez offers informed compassion, appropriate righteous indignation, and hearty laughs. While Tulsa is the last place in the world I ever expected to live, the remarkable network of friends I have here more than makes up for the place's shortcomings.

Finally, I struggle to find words to capture my gratitude to my parents and sister. I am the first person in four generations of Belmontes to attend college (and, as the family joke goes, the last to leave). I have received magnificent love and encouragement from Mom, Dad, and Susan. They have endured years of truncated and far-too-infrequent visits, flying pasta, and financial sacrifices so I could make my biggest dream come true. While I will leave it to them to determine the value of their investment, I consider it priceless.